An Investment in Humanity

Edward Rector
AND HIS
Historic Scholarship Program
FOR
DePauw University

Lewis Gulick

DePauw University
Greencastle, Indiana

ISBN 978-0-936631-14-1

Contents

Foreword

During the 30 years I have been associated with DePauw, the name "Rector" has seemed to be so deeply embedded in the University life and history that it is hard to imagine our school without it. Edward Rector first came on the DePauw scene in 1915, nearly a century ago. That what he did and stood for continues with such impact is a tribute to this remarkable man.

Rector's contribution to DePauw for a scholarship program was outstanding in several respects. It was, for its time, one of the largest gifts ever to a school of this size. The gift enabled the University to offer full four-year scholarships to more than one hundred students a year, a significant portion of DePauw's student body. Notwithstanding the demands of his important law practice, Rector personally devoted what time he could to aiding DePauw and in particular, the scholarship program and its youthful beneficiaries. He did so from the start of the program until his untimely death six years later. While he was open to program adjustments to meet changing conditions, Edward Rector stood fast on underlying principles for his scholarships which have proven valid to this day.

This combination of strengths made Rector's philanthropy unmatched in its way at any other comparable institution that I know of. DePauw was fortunate to have such a benefactor generous not only with this fortune, but also in the giving of himself and his keen intellect. His program has provided a college education for thousands of meritorious students to date and this emphasis continues into the new century.

As this book relates, the Rector Scholarship program encountered stresses as well as successes over the years. The

University learned from these experiences and made administrative and financial adjustments as time marched on. Overall, the history of the Rector program is intertwined with that of DePauw itself, and I believe the school has done a good job.

Rector surely would be pleased were he to return today to survey the proceeds from what he termed his "investments in humanity." Today Rector Scholarships continue to be the top merit award at DePauw. After weathering some difficult years, the Rector endowment remains substantial and is growing. Most important from Edward Rector's humanitarian standpoint is the multitude of Rector Scholars who have graduated and enriched society in all walks of life in the 20th century – and more will be doing so in the 21st.

I am pleased that further remembrance and recognition of this exceptional man and his program will come with DePauw's publication of this book.

Robert G. Bottoms
President, DePauw University
June 2008

Introduction

A half century or so after I had graduated from DePauw, I was attending an alumni reunion in the 1990's and was moved during a spare moment to stop by the University's well-stocked Roy O. West Library. I intended to browse through a book or two on Edward Rector and his scholarship program. I had been a Rector Scholar, but over the years had known little more about the program than that it had helped many young men – and later young women – obtain a college education. So just who was Rector, what did he provide to DePauw, and what have been the results of his efforts?

Surprise! I found no volume about him or his program on the shelves beyond a booklet written in his honor by a past DePauw president shortly after Rector's death in 1925. Nor was there an account of how his monumental scholarship program had fared thereafter.

However, I found the University Archives. There, original unpublished material about Rector was voluminous. The stacks carried collections on the man and his program in many files totaling more than a thousand papers. Related material was in other collections. Some pointed to sources elsewhere.

I took a few notes and resolved to come back. Which I did, time and again. The idea formed slowly but naturally: with the wealth of material, why not write an in-depth narrative, as a way of repaying a debt to the man to whom I owed my college education and the great benefits to my life which ensued therefrom?

So that's *how* this book came about – and *what* it is about. The first chapter is a scene-setter summarizing DePauw's early years for those unfamiliar with this small liberal arts University in Greencastle, Indiana. After that, it is a story of a great benefactor of the school, and of his scholarship program which has helped so many young men and women to become contributors to society.

One salient point cannot be overemphasized: Rector's scholarship donation in 1919 – at the time the largest in history to an Indiana school and one of the biggest ever to a small liberal arts college - was so large for an institution of DePauw's size that it shaped the character of the school from the time of its introduction and for many years to come. DePauw had fewer than 1,000 students, and lagging grades among its men, when Rector announced his endowment to bring in *one hundred each year* of the best and brightest high school male graduates with full four-year tuition scholarships based on academic excellence. The program reached its enrollment peak in the 1932-33 school year when a total of 700 Rector Scholars on campus comprised nearly half of the entire undergraduate student body and 70 percent of the men.

Thus for years its Rector scholarship program distinguished DePauw in the college world, and the history of the program has been intertwined with that of the University. This book is the first published by DePauw since its *Pictorial History* in 1987. I trust it will be of interest both to the many hundreds of current and future Rector Scholars and to those of the DePauw community wishing to know more about the school's history. Still others may wish to include it in their readings on topics ranging from philanthropies to scholarship administration and careers of scholarship graduates.

In pursuing the research trail I found the subject matter at times tending to divide into two subtopics: one was on the personnel side, dealing with admissions and administration of the scholars on campus; the other emphasized the financial side, the handling of the Rector endowment assets and spending. To help reader understanding, I have addressed the financial history in separate chapters (8 and 9), notwithstanding a chronological redundancy with administrative developments over the same period.

For me the research trail led to many expectable findings but also some which came as a surprise. Among those in the latter category were:

- An unfinished and unpublished autobiography by Rector himself. It does not tell of his DePauw experience but does provide a wealth of information about his early years. (See Chapter 2)

- Portions of a diary by George R. Grose, a former DePauw president, who knew Rector well. The diary notes, recently acquired by the DePauw Archives, provided some close-up personal observations about Rector. (See Chapter 3)

- Firsthand remembrances of Rector's wife, Lucy Rowland, turned up in a dubbing of an audiotape of a speech given by a friend a half century ago, and live newsreel glimpses of Lucy Rowland at the DePauw centennial in 1937 showed her still active on campus at age 82. (See Chapter 4)

- The extent of involvement in and dedication to the scholarship program by Henry B. Longden, a prominent figure in DePauw's administration for many years. (See Chapter 5)

- The extraordinary amount of Rector's *personal* engagement with his program and the scholars. (See Chapter 6)

- The existence of an unpublished master's thesis analyzing aspects of the scholarship program, written more than 60 years ago by Robert H. Farber, a Rector Scholar who himself subsequently became an administrator of the program. (See Chapter 7)

- The wide swings in both the administration and financing aspects of the program. (See Chapters 7-10)

- The similarities and yet the differences between Rector as a donor and Philip Holton, whose unexpectedly large scholarship gift came to DePauw at the end of the period covered by the book. (see Chapter 11)

- The broad range and high quality of contributions to society by Rector Scholar alumni, not only from the superstars but also generally from among the less famous rank-and-file. (See Chapter 12)

Finally there is the Epilogue, composed by a team of current undergraduate Rector Scholars who volunteered for research work on the book. They too wished to honor their benefactor. I commend it to readers for a 21st century view.

The Acknowledgments cite the Archives chief, Wesley W. Wilson, and his staff; the Office of the President, Robert G. Bottoms; DePauw historian *emeritus* John J. Baughman; Mike Lillich, former DePauw editor; and many others for invaluable assistance on this project.

Overall, my research has been free from any pressures to come to one conclusion or another. I conducted it at my own expense, and wherever the narrative might lead - without direction from the University. It follows that the content is entirely my responsibility.

One lingering question for me is whether I missed some negatives about Edward Rector. I have sought integrity of scholarship, let the chips fall where they may. Both ups and downs are recorded in the passages about DePauw's financing and administration of the program over many years and complicated times.

But as for Rector as a person, I failed to find evidence of flaws in character or performance. It would have been more helpful for me if he had finished and published his autobiography. But he was not self-centered enough to make that a priority before his death. His interests lay in helping others.

In the final analysis, what is there to reproach about a man who gave almost completely not only of his wealth but also of himself to others in the crowning years of his life?

– Lewis Gulick

Chapter 1

DEPAUW'S EARLY YEARS[1]

"DePauw is in all respects typical of the small American college," David E. Lilienthal recalled about his alma mater, DePauw University, in the years immediately after World War I. "... I suppose it would be difficult to find a group more typical of college men the country over than those making up the student body at the time of which I speak."[2]
— David E. Lilienthal, DePauw '21

This description of DePauw immediately after World War I by Lilienthal, who subsequently rose to fame as first head of the Tennessee Valley Authority, was not accompanied by a sheaf of statistics. Yet "typical" may be as good a term as any in picturing DePauw as a small liberal arts school in rural Indiana at the time.

DePauw was one of many institutions of higher education for young men and women that had sprung up in the Midwest and elsewhere in America's early years. It had sectarian beginnings, a small-town location, modest enrollment, an active student body, a high rate of achievement among graduates and periodic financial problems.

DePauw historian William Warren Sweet aptly describes the social climate spawning new learning institutions as America's frontiers spread westward in the 19th century. "The reason for the multiplication of colleges on advancing American frontiers is not far to seek," he wrote. "The westward moving population was made up largely of men and women young in years and poor in pocket, and the sending of their sons to older institutions farther east was out of the question; therefore education must be brought to the frontier as the only means of training frontier youth."[3]

The setting for what later became DePauw University reflects such frontier roots. Indiana gained admission to the Union as a state in 1816. Many who settled in the central part of the state had emigrated from southeastern states such as Kentucky, Virginia and the Carolinas. They wanted good education for their children but could not afford to send them to established schools back east.

Another powerful factor in the growth of colleges was the dynamism of religions in the frontier societies. Revived and enthusiastic Protestant denominations – Presbyterian, Congregational, Baptist and Methodist – were strong in the communities and strong advocates of schooling.

Presbyterians, while smaller in numbers than the other denominations, initially were most active in setting up new colleges in the new west. Presbyterianism had a tradition of trained ministry and of creating schools alongside churches. Indiana University began as a small college in Bloomington that was largely Presbyterian-run. Other well-known Indiana colleges founded by Presbyterians in that era included Hanover in 1827 and Wabash in 1832.

Presbyterians thus had the early lead in setting up new colleges in the young state. But by 1832, Methodists outnumbered Presbyterians in Indiana by 20,000 to 4,000 and they wanted an institution of their own. In 1834 the Methodists sought, but failed to achieve, a major increase in the role of Methodists at the state college in Bloomington. In 1836 the Indiana Conference of the Methodist Episcopal Church[4] called for establishment of "an institution of the first order ... upon an extensive plan of operation and equal to any College or University in the valley of the Mississippi," to serve "the interests of our people and the public throughout the state of Indiana and in a qualified sense throughout a much greater extent of the American union." While under "the Methodist Connexion of Indiana," the institution would "not be either Theological or Sectarian in character … but shall be conducted on the most liberal principles acceptable to all our Citizens, without distinction of name or sect."

Acquiring the location for grounds for a new university was no problem in the still sparsely settled state. The Methodist Conference had the luxury of choosing among competing towns. It appointed a committee to review bids for the new school.

Indianapolis, the state capital, made a modest bid while the town of Rockville, represented by General Tilghman A. Howard, a prominent Presbyterian layman, presented a strong case and offered the largest cash inducement, $20,000. After he learned of Howard and Rockville's bid, Dr. Tarvin Cowgill, who headed an enthusiastic contingent from Greencastle, solicited among friends and raised Greencastle's offer to $25,000.

Greencastle was chosen as the winner because of its high bid, a claimed healthfulness (Howard admitted to some chills and fever at Rockville) and enough distance from Indianapolis to reduce college student engagement in its big-town temptations. Greencastle's final cost totaled $30,000 for college site and building, a tremendous amount for what was then little more than a village of about 500 residents at a time when money was short, the economy poor, and a student could live for less than one dollar a week.[5]

SMALL-TOWN GREENCASTLE

Greencastle, about 45 miles west of Indianapolis in rolling wooded and farming terrain, was in land that Indiana had bought from the Miami Indians in 1818. After the state formed Putnam County there in 1821, Greencastle was named county seat in 1823. In 1837, a decade after its founding,

Greencastle was still rudimentary at best, consisting of no more than a scattering of log and frame structures housing their few hundred inhabitants along dirt roads. The dwellers were mostly immigrants from Kentucky, Tennessee, and North Carolina. The town centered around a square whose principal building was a one-story brick courthouse. There were three plain-looking churches: Baptist, Presbyterian and Methodist.[6]

Greencastle retained small-town rural characteristics well into the 20th century, compared with other population centers in Indiana. Though it experienced significant growth, by the beginning of the 21st century its population still hardly exceeded 10,000.

In Greencastle's early days, just getting there was no easy task because of the frontier transportation system, or lack thereof, for those wishing to visit or attend the new "university." For example the school's first president, Matthew Simpson, graphically described his arduous weeks of travels after leaving his professorship at Allegheny College in Meadville, Penn., in March 1839 to proceed to his new post in Indiana.

Greencastle was a rural town during the early years of Indiana Asbury.

Greencastle Square, looking west, ca. 1890.

Simpson first went by stagecoach, then by two riverboats, to reach Cincinnati. After that he proceeded overland, first by stagecoach and then by private carriage, over "execrably bad" roads including one place where the mud was so deep as to overturn the coach. He finally arrived in Greencastle in late April after a couple of stops for family visits along the way; but his personal belongings, which went by boat from Pennsylvania down the Ohio River and up the Wabash River to Terre Haute, were delayed by low water and did not show up in Greencastle until the fall.[7]

ENTER INDIANA ASBURY

The Methodists' charter for the new institution in Greencastle, approved by the state legislature in 1837, remained the basic charter of the University thereafter with few amendments. The school was "forever to be conducted on the most liberal principles, accessible to all religious denominations, and designed for the benefit of our State of Indiana." It was to be maintained "for the benefit of the youth of every class of citizens, and of every denomination, who shall be freely admitted to equal advantages and privileges of education."

The charter named the institution Indiana Asbury University, after Francis Asbury, a revered pioneer bishop for American Methodism in the latter part of the 18th century. A number of other Methodist institutions elsewhere also bear his name.

The Indiana Asbury Charter provided for 25 trustees, appointed by the Methodist Church, to direct the university. The trustees' first meeting, in March 1837, was in Greencastle's Methodist church. Because of rigors of travel in Indiana at the time, only one of the 16 trustees attending was from out of town. Early orders of business were to choose a building site and to appoint two Methodist clergymen to stump the state for construction funds. The trustees also began hiring faculty and laying out curricula.

Meanwhile a "preparatory department" was opened to give prospective students further training needed to qualify for enrollment in college-level courses. The preparatory department was necessary for college-level work at the time because high schools as now known did not then exist. Pre-college preparation was required of most students who had not attended private academies.[8] The preparatory department taught English grammar, geography, book-keeping, arithmetic, beginning algebra and rudiments of Latin and Greek.

The first full school year for Indiana Asbury at the college level was 1839-40, with 22 students enrolled in freshmen through senior classes. Most came from nearby homes. The preparatory department had 58 students. There were four faculty, including an acting president, for the college and preparatory school. The first commencement in 1840 graduated the three seniors.

The new institution began in the county seminary, a two-story brick building located on a plot south of the town square. By September 1840 the new college classroom building – a large (for its time) three-story brick structure with bell tower, called

West College, built to replace The Edifice which burned in 1879.

the Edifice – was completed enough to move into. The Edifice was sited near the seminary on what is now college grounds. It was an outstanding building for its day, with more than enough classrooms for teaching needs, a large chapel, a library, three recitation halls and two halls for student literary groups.

Indiana Asbury's first professor was the Rev. Cyrus Nutt, a Methodist minister recently graduated from Allegheny College in Pennsylvania. Nutt began in June 1837 as director of the preparatory department. As with so many of Indiana Asbury faculty after him, he went on to a distinguished career. After becoming a regular faculty member for the full college in 1838, he served also as acting president until the first president was appointed in February 1839. Eventually in 1860 he became president of Indiana University, a post he held until his death in 1875.

Simpson, the first president, was a Methodist preacher who was a professor of natural science at Allegheny College when chosen by the Indiana Asbury trustees. After successfully

Matthew Simpson

guiding the school in its early years of growth, Simpson resigned in 1848 to become editor of a church magazine. He subsequently became a nationally prominent Methodist bishop and an adviser to Abraham Lincoln. He was chosen to deliver the address for Lincoln's funeral at Springfield, Ill.

As was customary for established colleges at the time, the curriculum at Indiana Asbury was heavily laden with classics such as Latin, Greek and mathematics for lower classmen, followed by subjects ranging from calculus and philosophy to astronomy, geology and rhetoric in the upper classes. The president taught seniors a course on Christian living. College tuition was $24 a year. Other student costs included a janitor's fee of $1.25 a session, several dollars for books, and $1-2 a week for a boarding house for those enrolling from outside the Greencastle area.[9] The president's salary was $1,000 a year and Nutt's $400, but the school often lagged in its payments to staff.

THE FIRST DECADES OF GROWTH

The same strong church base and enthusiastic sponsorship that gave Indiana Asbury its start continued to promote its success in the decades immediately following. Other factors contributing to the school's growth included outstanding leadership, an increasing and prospering population in Indiana who wanted to send its sons to college, and a growing number of influential alumni.

Enrollment and faculty grew substantially in the years leading up to the Civil War. Throughout the 1840s the students in regular college courses numbered about 50 and by the 1850s that number increased more than a third. Pupils came from more than a dozen different states, though still largely from Indiana.

Preparatory Department enrollment varied greatly but rose to as high as 404 during this period. The faculty doubled to six professorships plus some instructors and tutors.

Several ventures by Indiana Asbury for new educational departments in this period met with little success. One of these endeavors, Indiana Central Medical College in Indianapolis, opened in 1849 but suspended in 1852 with financial troubles after having granted Doctor of Medicine degrees to 40 students. A Law Department, begun in 1853, ended in 1862 with student departures for military service after having granted 54 law degrees.

In marked contrast to student life today, those attending Indiana Asbury and similar schools of the time had little opportunity to engage in activities, day or night, unrelated to the classical training laid out for them. The college gave no encouragement to sports. Prohibited were unexcused absences, disorderly conduct, irreverence, immoralities, absence from the living quarters in the evenings except for attendance at an approved event, leaving the Greencastle area or visiting shows or other places of amusement. With "frivolous" conduct made so difficult, it also was easier for Indiana Asbury students to live relatively inexpensively. An 1852 report said much of the student body was "batching" – boarding themselves – and were living on 50-75 cents a week. At the time, a chicken could be bought in Greencastle for four cents and eggs for three cents a dozen.[10]

The limits on outlets for extracurricular student energies gave added importance to two literary societies, the Platonean Society and the Philological Society, formed in 1839 and 1840 respectively. Featuring orations and debates, the societies had University endorsement and halls of their own in the University building, and membership included students, selected faculty members and Greencastle professional men. Other colleges of the time had similar societies.

Accompanying this literary society activity, which continued through the Asbury years, was a growth of the "secret societies" commonly called fraternities. A Beta Theta Pi chapter was formed at Indiana Asbury in 1845. A Phi Gamma Delta chapter was formed there in 1856 and a Sigma Chi chapter in 1859. The Greek system grew to be a permanent feature over the years with most of the student body belonging to one Greek house or another.

INDIANA ASBURY AND THE CIVIL WAR

American colleges lost much of their student bodies to one side or the other during the Civil War. Indiana Asbury was no exception. Indiana was a northern state and the college was unabashedly supportive of the Union cause. The preponderance of the student volunteers signed up with northern units, although some southerners went with the Confederacy.

Following the fall of Fort Sumter on April 15, 1861, President Lincoln called for volunteers for the Union as did the Governor of Indiana. Classes at Asbury were temporarily dismissed. A company called "Asbury Guards" was immediately organized and started drilling on campus. Students eagerly volunteered. The unit eventually became part of the Sixteenth Indiana Regiment. Meanwhile a second company was organized in Greencastle, also largely made up of Asbury students. It became part of the Tenth Indiana Volunteers.

The drain of students to the war was so heavy as to cause rumors that Indiana Asbury was closing. Thomas Bowman, then college president, denied that the trustees or faculty ever "entertained the idea of suspending the college exercises." However enrollment shrank to little more than subsistence levels. The low point was in 1862-3 when only 61 students remained in attendance. As the war entered its later stages, Asbury began offering various encouragements to veterans to return to the school. Once the guns fell silent enrollment soon reached pre-war levels and more.

ASBURY GOES COEDUCATIONAL

Even in more modern times, a proposal to admit women to a hitherto all-male college could be met with stiff opposition. Considering the social context in mid-19th century America, Indiana Asbury took this step with relative ease. A committee appointed by Asbury's trustees in 1860 favored admission of women. Action was delayed during the Civil War, but promptly afterward, measures to admit women were put in process to go into effect beginning with the 1868 school year.

A debate ensued along predictable lines. Opponents of Asbury going coeducational, including many Asbury students and alumni, until then all male, pointed out that famous eastern schools such as Harvard and Yale remained all-male. They argued that allowing women at Asbury would harm its reputation, that student morals would suffer, and even that women were not as capable of intellectual studies as men. Proponents among the college's broader constituency and its leadership refuted the more strident criticisms of co-education and noted that many prominent schools in the Midwest and elsewhere, starting with Oberlin in 1833, were co-educational from their beginning.

Opponents failed to derail the process and five females matriculated as freshmen in 1868. They quickly proved themselves in their studies and conduct. More women enrolled in 1869, and their numbers grew thereafter.

The first commencement in which women graduated was 1871, by which time the school

Bettie Locke Hamilton, the Indiana Asbury student who founded Kappa Alpha Theta there in 1870. It was the first college Greek sorority in the U.S.

had 35 women students. To the admiration of the college community, the 1871 graduates included four of the five original entrants. By 1882 Asbury faculty had its first female full professor, Alma Hollman, A.M., who was elected to the chair of the modern languages department.[11]

In later years, women came to outnumber men at the Greencastle institution, and they too became heavily involved in extracurricular as well as academic activities, including Greek social societies. Sororities soon appeared on campus and joined fraternities as a feature of DePauw life.

POST-CIVIL WAR ASBURY

After the war enrollment picked up again rapidly to reach a new high of 159 in the collegiate four-year course in 1865-66, plus 248 in the preparatory school. This compared with the pre-war high of 139 in the college and 268 in preparatory classes.

Changes that had begun before the Civil War or started shortly thereafter accelerated during the latter years of the 19th century on the Asbury campus as they did elsewhere in American schools. The arrival of women students was a reflection of the social progress of the times. On the academic side, important developments came in revision of curricula. Classical studies such as Greek, Latin, philosophy, and mathematics received less emphasis, and more was placed on subjects such as English literature, American history, French and German.

Liberalizing trends also were responsible for more electives for the students, particularly after the 1890s. Asbury widened its options for study to include subjects ranging from Spanish to Robert's *Rules of Order* to analysis of foods.[12] The school began an honors system for superior students. It brought famous speakers from around the nation to Greencastle.

Extra-curricular activities were becoming increasingly important on the campus scene. The number of fraternities multiplied in the postwar period starting with a Phi Kappa Psi chapter in 1865. Organized sports began to take hold. In 1866, Indiana Asbury played a baseball game against Wabash College, inaugurating the oldest intercollegiate athletic rivalry west of the Alleghenies.[13]

Barred from the men's literary and fraternal organizations, the women formed their own literary society, the Philomathean, in 1869. In 1870 they inaugurated what is generally considered the first Greek sorority in the U.S., Kappa Alpha Theta, that subsequently spread nationwide.[14] A chapter of the Kappa Kappa Gamma sorority came to Asbury in 1875.

With Asbury seeming to flourish as flagship of Methodist higher education institutions in Indiana, church leaders moved to bring other schools in the state into the Asbury sphere. In 1874 stockholders of the Indiana Female College of Indianapolis turned the college over to Asbury. In 1876, Battle Ground Institute near Lafayette was incorporated into the Asbury preparatory school. Subsequently another women's school, DePauw College in New Albany, a beneficiary of philanthropy from Washington C. DePauw, a member of Asbury's board of trustees, closed down and provided its assets to Asbury. Links also were established with some preparatory schools in the state.

By 1870 Asbury's enrollment included 254 students in the college and 90 in the Preparatory Department, a total of 344. Income was $8,000 a year. By comparison, the state university at Bloomington had 279 students and an income of $23,000 due to higher tuition fees.[15] Indiana Asbury Vice President John Clark Ridpath glowingly reported enrollment was 40 percent larger than that of Indiana University and more than double that of any other college in the state.[16]

By the end of the 1870s, Asbury was flourishing both in academics and in enrollment. Enrollment at Asbury climbed to 360 in 1872-3, to 450 in 1873-4, and 451 the following year.[17] The trustees voted in 1873 to remove tuition fees.[18] As of 1878 Indiana Asbury was by far the largest and most influential university in Indiana, with 431 students. Next was Indiana University with 311.[19]

FINANCES TAKE SHARP DOWNTURN DESPITE ENROLLMENT GROWTH

Unfortunately the enthusiasm for Asbury's growth had not been matched by increases in income needed to pay for it. The school was headed for financial crisis. A severe general economic downturn caught the institution unprepared.

An anomaly of Asbury's money problem was that the school actually had done better financially when its academic fortunes were low. During the Civil War years, when the University came close to closing down because its students were off to military service, it ran small surpluses. Tuition receipts were too small to make much difference and decreased faculty size cut salary costs. Fund-raising after the war brought in several large gifts that temporarily put Asbury on a better financial footing in the immediate postwar years.

However the economic depression of the 1870s hit the school's endowment investments heavily. Asbury began running large deficits each year. Railroad and other bonds held by the University went into default or yielded reduced interest. Tuition never had been a mainstay of the school's income, so the dropping of the nominal tuition of $10 a term starting in 1874 was not a significant factor. But the institutions merged into the Asbury family had been money losers. Some of the resources from donations to Asbury for other purposes were used up in building a main campus building, East College.

Many attempts to right the balance included a 10 percent cut in all salaries in 1878, but none were sufficient. There was talk that the school might have to shut down.

East College, DePauw's signature building at its campus center. Construction began in 1871 and was completed in 1882.

DEPAUW UNIVERSITY IS BORN

A search was on for a rescue for Indiana Asbury, and one of the searchers became the rescuer. He was Washington Charles DePauw, a longtime member of Asbury's Board of Trustees and the Board's president starting in 1881. DePauw was an active

Methodist layman. He was strongly interested in education. A native of Salem, Ind., he served as a trustee not only for Indiana Asbury, but also for Indiana University and for Indiana Asbury Female College in New Albany, the latter adopting his name in 1867 after he made a large donation.

DePauw was enormously successful as a business entrepreneur. He was reputed to be the wealthiest man in Indiana. One company he developed in New Albany eventually produced 60 percent of the plate glass made in the United States. He also owned farms, flour mills, iron-working plants, a woolen mill and substantial investments in banks, insurance and railroads.

Washington C. DePauw

DePauw wrote a will in 1881 bequeathing a large part of his estate after his death to the establishment of a "DePauw University." He had had in mind a new institution possibly in Indiana, or perhaps elsewhere in the country. Indiana Asbury's trustees, hoping to obtain DePauw's largesse for their school, asked him to divert his donation to Asbury and to make it available immediately, not posthumously. They proposed to rename Asbury after him if he did so, and offered a plan for University expansion to include new colleges of theology, law, and medicine, plus special schools of design, technology, music, and mining. There would be new professorships and the construction of new buildings to accompany the academic enlargement.

DePauw responded with a slightly revised proposal. He included requirements that Greencastle and Putnam County purchase needed land and that Indiana Methodists join in raising more funds for the endowment. The trustees agreed. On January 17, 1884, Indiana Asbury, which then had 532 students, ended 47 years of existence and DePauw University was born.

The new DePauw University promptly began on its ambitious expansion plans. Washington C. DePauw himself headed a building committee authorized to construct five new building projects - men's and women's dormitories, a law building, a theology building, an observatory, and an addition of a laboratory to the old Edifice, now called the West College building. Work was underway on all of these projects by the spring of 1884. DePauw personally supervised endless details of the construction, spending so much time in Greencastle that it was rumored he would establish residence there.

Then unexpectedly, on May 5, 1887, DePauw died from a stroke. This was a shock to the University not only because of the loss of the active leadership of its great benefactor, but also because the financial underpinnings for grandiose expansion suddenly became quite tenuous. Washington DePauw had a complicated will that clearly stipulated funding for the commitments he had made in the name-changing agreement with Asbury. However further large amounts had been expected also from his estate 10 and 15 years hence. Additionally, his oldest daughter was contesting his will, a suit eventually settled out of court.

Along came the financial panic of 1893 to devastate the Washington C. DePauw estate. Most of its business holdings were hit. The main plate glass works at New Albany shut down and moved to Alexandria, Ind., only to run at a loss there. Others of the DePauw enterprises went into receivership. What remained from the estate for the fledgling university in Greencastle was only a fraction of what had been forecast optimistically while DePauw was alive. Of an anticipated $1 million, the total actually received from him and other members of his family was approximately $300,000.[20] A major loss in income came from defaults totaling $5,250 on interest from I.C.& L. railroad bonds held by the school.[21] Other investment income for the school also decreased as did payment on pledges.

ANOTHER CRISIS – AND SURVIVAL AGAIN

Total enrollment dropped from 1063 in 1891-2 to 707 by 1894-5. The 1893 operating deficit was $15,000.[22] Once again, by the late 1890s, rumors were circulating that the University would have to close its doors.

DePauw University survived its financial crisis by belt-tightening and new funding drives. The trustees appointed a chancellor to raise money for the endowment and for current expenses. The fund-raising went reasonably well. After a new president was installed in 1903, further rounds of solicitations were so successful that the University was again expanding its spending for building, salaries, and other expenses. A drive in 1911 collected $550,546, described at the time as the largest amount yet raised for education in Indiana.[23]

More buildings went up. Andrew Carnegie contributed a munificent sum for a library at DePauw, as he did for so many other places. A long-awaited gymnasium was built, followed by a girls' dormitory, Minshall Laboratory and then an administration building constructed with funding from the family of Clement Studebaker, the famed wagon maker and a longtime trustee of Asbury and DePauw.

Studebaker Administration Building, built during the World War I era as a donation from the family of Clement Studebaker, renowned wagon and auto maker who had been an active DePauw trustee. The office of the President and a handsome paneled meeting room are on the second floor.

SUCCESSES AND FAILURES FOR DEPAUW SCHOOLS

Meanwhile the schools envisioned in DePauw's early ambitious days were, in most cases, not doing well. A School of Theology opened in 1884. At first it prospered, reaching a high of 100 students in 1892-3. But attendance shrank after that, the school ran deficits, and it closed in 1897-98 with enrollment down to 39. A School of Law also began in 1894. Its attendance climbed to about 50, but the school also contributed to the deficits DePauw faced in the early '90s and was shut down in 1894. A School of Art, opened in 1885, also rose in enrollment, then fell, disbanding in 1913.

A Preparatory School begun in 1884 was more successful. It was a follow-on to the preparatory department that had been an important feature of Indiana Asbury's education since the college's beginning. Attendance reached a peak of nearly 400 by 1892-3. The Preparatory School continued into the early 20th century but faded as high schools in Indiana and elsewhere began doing a better job of preparing their graduates for college. It phased out in 1914.

The one new school achieving lasting success was the School of Music. A fledgling music department was developing in the last days of Indiana Asbury. Washington C. DePauw had a special interest in the music school. Enrollment mushroomed and demand grew for use of its expanded physical facilities also for the University's daily chapels and a host of other events. Various groups from the music school began performing on trips throughout Indiana and the country. By May 1918 the school was presenting its 2,500th recital. The University choir was in national demand. DePauw's reputation for excellence in music continued throughout the 20th century and beyond.

With the closing of the Preparatory School, DePauw's remaining academic institutions were the Asbury College of Liberal Arts and the School of Music. Liberal arts remained at the heart of the University as they always had been. The curriculum was revised at the time of titular change in 1884 and periodically thereafter, reflecting both general education trends and the particular philosophies of those in charge of the school's course availabilities and requirements. The departments then were generally headed by a professor of long tenure, with assistants added as enrollment grew. The faculty core was about 20 men. The college president himself also taught courses.

EVOLVING INTO A MODERN SYSTEM

A much more "modern" system evolved in the early years of the new century with an expansion of offerings and departments. DePauw established a Department of Economics. The Department of Romance Languages expanded, as did the Departments of Sociology, Political Science, History and Philosophy.

Enrollment grew along with the expansion in facilities, faculty and course work, particularly in the first years after the turn of the century. The student body almost doubled from 1903 to 1909, when it reached nearly 1,000.[24]

Enormous changes in student extracurricular activities likewise evolved in the period between DePauw's birth and the end of World War I. The fraternities and sororities succeeded the literary societies as the center of the school's social life. Intercollegiate athletics took hold, spurred by alumni. DePauw's football team at the time became strong enough then for schedules that would have been unthinkable in later years. DePauw's gridiron "Tigers" took the field against such athletic powerhouses as the Universities of Indiana, Purdue, Notre Dame, Michigan and Michigan State.

New extracurricular clubs came on the campus scene. The various language departments had clubs, as did the social science and science departments. The national academic honorary society, Phi Beta Kappa, approved a chapter at DePauw in 1889.

Other clubs such as the YMCA and honoraries installed during this period included Tusitala for literary composition, Tau Kappa Alpha for oratory or debate, Delta Sigma Rho for public speaking, Duzer Du for drama, and a Press Club that initiated the Sigma Delta Chi journalistic society. Sigma Delta Chi in time spread nationwide.

WORLD WAR I

A campus attitude of indifference initially greeted the outbreak of World War I in 1914, but opinion became more pro-allies as the war went on. Germany's announcement in February 1917 of submarine warfare against all non-friendly shipping galvanized support for U.S. entry into the conflict. When President Woodrow Wilson declared war soon thereafter, the effect on the Greencastle school was to begin to denude it of men just as the Civil War had in the 1860s.

Student departures from school started almost immediately. Enrollment for the 1916-17 academic year was about 940. By the beginning of the 1917-18 year, registration was down 140 students from the previous a year and withdrawals were continuing.

In May 1918 the government began formation of a Student Army Training Corps program at DePauw. This involved

DePauw unit of the Student Army Training Corps (SATC) organized in the fall of 1918.

21

conversion of various college buildings into barracks, a mess hall, post exchange, and other accommodations for 500 men, who were inducted into the S.A.T.C. Oct. 1. The government paid tuition, lodging, board, and a monthly allowance to the students, plus uniforms and military gear.

However the entire S.A.T.C. operation at DePauw never amounted to much. When the World War I flu epidemic hit the campus in November, the men were quarantined and the women sent home. Then the World War I armistice was signed on November 11. S.A.T.C. was demobilized on December 14.

A RETURN TO "NORMALCY"

It did not take long after the armistice for DePauw to move back into a civilian mode and resume the advancement that had been underway since the turn of the century. Immediately following the departure of the S.A.T.C. the buildings put to military-related service were restored to civilian use. Incentives were offered to ex-servicemen to return to school, including special credits toward graduation, free tuition and easy loans, though many of the S.A.T.C. recruits were not academically interested enough to stay on. The disbanded S.A.T.C. was followed in January 1919 by a revived Reserve Officers' Training Corps unit at the school. Participation in R.O.T.C. training was required of freshmen and sophomore men but optional for juniors and seniors.

By the following school year, DePauw was back to "normal." Enrollment at the University for 1919-20 climbed to around 1,000, the largest total since 1914 when the preparatory school closed. About two thirds of the students came from Methodist homes, and most of them from nearby: 83 percent from Indiana, 9 percent from Illinois. About one-quarter came from farms.

The gender ratio soon returned to a more equal proportion after the war although women still outnumbered men. In the first school year after America entered the conflict, 1917-18, the

Meharry Hall, the chapel in East College, is also used as an auditorium.

enrollment of men dropped to 290 compared with 446 women. In 1919-20 the number of males in the student body was back up to 427 compared with 515 women.[25]

By 1918-19 the liberal arts faculty included 35 men and women of widely varying ages. The president no longer taught classes himself. The bachelor of arts degree was the only one granted. Graduation required 124 semester hours, including a major of 30 hours, 16 to 24 hours of foreign languages, 16 hours in English-related subjects and Bible, 15 hours in science or mathematics, 15 hours in social sciences, six hours of English composition, four hours of military science (for men), four hours of physical education and an additional three hours in education or philosophy. This left the students little time for pure electives, although they had a considerable number of options within the prescribed fields. The school hired a dozen new faculty in 1919, the largest number added in any single year in the school's history.

As part of a growing emphasis on raising scholarship standards, a point system was established in 1917. It worked to stimulate student interest in achieving good grades, though it did spawn cheating by some.

Daily attendance at chapel, which had been mandatory for students in DePauw's first years, was no longer required. Yet by 1919 two-thirds to three-quarters of the student body was still attending daily, partly because many Greek houses required their freshmen to go.

Interest in intercollegiate athletics was rising to new heights. The new gym was built in 1916, and the basketball team improved so greatly that by 1918-19 it had a 12-3 season with wins over Indiana, Michigan State, and Notre Dame. Meanwhile winning orators continued to come from DePauw. In 1919, David E. Lilienthal won the state competition again for the Greencastle school. As many students were traveling to Indianapolis to support DePauw orators as were going to the school's football games.[26]

In sum, as of the end of "The Great War" DePauw was a successful small Midwest liberal arts University with a Methodist sponsorship but not heavily sectarian in its operation. Its early emphasis on classical studies had evolved to a more wide-ranging curriculum as was the trend in other American universities.

Most of the students came from Indiana and nearby Midwestern states. Extracurricular interests ran the gamut from athletics to musical performances, debating, and religious activities. The Greek fraternity-sorority system played a large role in the campus social life. Women on campus outnumbered men and men who had been away in wartime tended to do less well academically on their return than the women.

This was the DePauw of 1919 to which an extraordinary benefactor made the contributions described in the chapters ahead.

***

Chapter 2

EDWARD RECTOR – A SON OF THE MIDWEST[1]

Edward Rector was driven by "vigor of mind, intellectual integrity, decisive convictions and a passion for humanity."
— Grose, *Rector*

The immigrant ancestors of Edward Rector came from the area of Siegen, Prussia, Germany, an iron-producing region. Virginia Governor Alexander Spottswood imported 14 heads of families from there in April 1714, 42 persons in all, to found an iron works industry in the colony. Among the immigrants was John Jacob Rector, a skilled iron worker, then age 40 and a native of Trupbach, Westfalen.[2] The craftsmen were placed on the colonial frontier in a fortified stockade on the Rapidan River. They named the settlement Germanna.

The settlers soon wearied of the struggle to establish an iron industry under inhospitable conditions. They moved somewhat north in the colony to what subsequently became Fauquier County and organized a farming settlement, Germantown, which proved very successful. From there, many thousands of descendants of the families spread throughout America in ensuing years.[3]

Jacob Rector, a son of John Jacob who was born in Germanna, and his wife, Mary Ann (Hitt) Rector, moved to Rowan County, North Carolina, for a few years, then returned to Virginia where they settled in Grayson County. A family story says that during that time the family freed all the slaves they owned, except for one negress who refused to leave until her mistress, Mary, died in 1813.

Jacob and Mary Rector had several sons, one of whom was Jesse Rector, born in 1759. Jesse was much admired within the family. Among other things, he had fought in Washington's army. As a private in the Fauquier County Militia in 1781, he was at the siege of Yorktown. After Cornwallis' surrender Jesse marched to Yorktown to participate in tearing down some breastworks, and subsequently assisted in the pursuit and capture of some Tories.[4]

Edward Rector never knew his grandfather Jesse, who would have been age 104 at the time of Edward's birth. However he heard many details of Jesse's military service as passed on by his own father, Isaac.

Jesse married twice and had large families both times. The first marriage produced nine children, the second eight. Families of such size were not uncommon in frontier days, though mortality rates were much higher than after the country matured.

Jesse's second marriage was to Margaret Winford, born in Flint County, Delaware, 1778. She was 19 years his junior. Their eight children were born while the family lived in Grayson County. However the age disparity between Jesse's first and second families was so great that they seemed almost a generation apart.

Isaac Rector, Edward's father, was born in 1816, the fifth of the eight second-tier children. Edward Rector knew little of his grandfather's first family except his father's recollection that there had been nine children.

WESTWARD HO! TO BEDFORD INDIANA

In 1821 Jesse Rector, at age 62, decided to migrate westward with his second family. The oldest child was age eighteen, the youngest a babe in arms.

The Jesse Rector troupe, including Isaac, traveled by wagon through Kentucky to southern Indiana, where they first settled at Palestine, the Lawrence County seat. However "the malaria was found to be so bad there" that in about 1825 the residents abandoned the town entirely and moved to virgin land five miles to the northwest, establishing a new County seat, Bedford.[5] Jesse cleared a forested track near Bedford and settled down to farming.

Of his father's siblings, Edward said "all of the family I ever knew"[6] was his father's oldest brother, Levi, who was 60 at the time of Edward's birth, and one sister, Rebecca, who was then 53. As a spinster, "Aunt Becky" lived in the Isaac Rector household.

Jesse's children grew up with both the joys and the rugged chores of a backwoods environment. The Indians by then were recently departed, but their image was fresh in the youngsters' minds. Edward Rector enjoyed telling a story about how his father carried "a big white scar" on his wrist all his life from an early "Indian fright": imagining himself to be pursued by Indians at the farm, young Isaac rushed into the house to save himself, stumbled and fell forward, wrist out, into "a skillet of hot lard in which his mother was frying doughnuts."[7]

Wild game was ample; the boys hunted and brought back to the dinner table venison, wild turkey, ducks, geese, squirrels and occasionally, bear. Isaac Rector grew to manhood on his father's farm, doing not only farm chores but also getting work in nearby Bedford. Subsequently he moved into Bedford, taking a job in a dry goods and general store, first as a clerk and later as a cashier at the local branch of the State Bank.

ISAAC RECTOR MARRIES

In Bedford Isaac met a Juliet B. Gardiner from Columbus, Ohio, who happened to be visiting relatives in town. Juliet was the fourth of 13 children of James B. Gardiner and Mary Poole, James being of English and Mary of Irish descent. An older sister, Harriet, had married Richard W. Thompson and the couple was then living in Bedford. Another older sister, Caroline, had

Isaac Rector

come to Bedford on a sisterly visit and met and married Daniel Dunihue of Bedford. Juliet had come to see both sisters, and Bedford being a small town, soon made the acquaintance of Isaac Rector, a Dunihue friend.

Edward recalled with interest and amusement stories Isaac told his children about his courtship of their mother. After Juliet returned to Columbus, Isaac made several trips to see her. Since there were then no railroads in the area, he first had to go by horseback from Bedford to Louisville, a wearing and lonely ride of some 75 miles. From Louisville to Cincinnati the travel was luxurious and congenial, by river steamers with staterooms and fancy meals. However the final leg of the journey, from Cincinnati to Columbus, was again arduous: a 24-hour ride by stagecoach for 120 miles.

Isaac Rector finally married his Ohio sweetheart on November 25, 1841. The wedding was at her family home in Columbus with a local notable minister presiding. Isaac was age 25, Juliet 24. He took his bride back to Bedford for their permanent home.

Isaac's marriage linked him to a prominent Ohio family. Juliet's father was a well known newspaper man who served as editor of the *Ohio State Journal* for many years.[8] Furthermore her brother-in-law, Richard Thompson, moved from Bedford to Terre Haute and went on to a highly successful career as an Indiana lawyer and politician. At one point Thompson was appointed by President Hayes to be Secretary of the Navy. A Methodist and supporter of Indiana Asbury, he was honored by Indiana Asbury with a Doctor of Laws degree in 1846 and served as a trustee there from 1874 to 1876.[9]

EDWARD RECTOR'S BOYHOOD BEGINS

Isaac and Juliet Rector had seven children, five boys and two girls, born over a span of 19 years. The youngest child was Edward Rector, born July 7, 1863. Isaac was then age 47 and Juliet 46.

By the time baby Edward was born two older brothers had died and two were soon to leave home. The oldest surviving brother, Jesse Winfield (nicknamed "Win"), attended Indiana Asbury. After graduation he went west to become a school teacher in Iowa, and later a lawyer in Manhattan, Kansas.[10] The other brother, Charles, left home in his early teens to make a living, becoming an expert telegrapher. One of Edward's two sisters died when he was 11. The surviving sister, Mary, was 14 years his senior.

Such large age differences meant that Edward Rector had little contact with the majority of his siblings. He got to know his two surviving brothers only in later years during their rare home visits.

Baby picture of Edward Rector, born in Bedford, Ind., 1863.

The only sibling with whom Edward developed a lifelong close relationship was Mary, who remained at home. She was his loving "big sister" in the household.

Isaac was a loving and caring father, and enormously successful in his initial business years. Following his banking employment in the 1830s he founded his own bank, and over the next two decades as a banker, he reputedly became the wealthiest man in the county.[11] Edward recalled his father as paying more taxes on property than any other man in the county.[12]

In 1853 Isaac Rector bought a spacious tract on the south edge of Bedford, about a mile from the Court House, and built a beautiful brick and stone home. It was surrounded by acres of large forest trees, and overlooked a meadow of several more acres stretching to the nearest neighbor's house. Isaac was an avid gardener, cultivating roses and other flowers and ornamental shrubbery, raising vegetables and growing and grafting fruit trees. Collecting sugar and molasses from a hundred or so maple trees was an annual spring rite. This homestead, in which Edward Rector was born and raised for the first years of his boyhood, made a lasting impression on him. In his memoirs written more than a half century later and in other comments, he seemed able to recall the residence, its rooms and furnishings, and the land in great detail, even though he only lived in it himself until age four.

Rector family home in Bedford, Ind.

FINANCIAL CALAMITY STRIKES ISAAC RECTOR

The reason for Edward's short tenure in the first family mansion was a financial catastrophe which struck his father shortly after the Civil War. According to a local historian, "a trusted employee embezzled bank funds. Rector deliberately and unnecessarily bankrupted himself to make good his bank's debt but it failed despite his valiant efforts."[13] Being an outstandingly honorable man, he gave up his house and its grounds towards satisfying his creditors. The property sold for $5,450 at public auction in 1867.[14] Also sold were most of the furnishings, including cherished items such as a grand piano played by his daughter Mary.

Isaac moved his family into a small frame house nearby which he rented. The traumatic change in circumstances and his father's rectitude left a lasting impression on Edward.

The original home remained on site until well into the 20th century. It and the surrounding area were acquired by the city in 1908 to become Bedford's first city hospital.[15]

By the time of Bedford's sesquicentennial observance in 1968 the old hospital had been succeeded by a large modern hospital. In an adjacent parking lot stands a single marker erected by the sesquicentennial commission at the site of Rector's original home. It bears a plaque which reads:

> Birthplace of Edward Rector, attorney (1863-1925) … Lawrence County's greatest philanthropist, he endowed the Rector Scholarship Foundation at DePauw University with $2,250,000 in 1919. To date 5,100 awards have been made, 22 to Lawrence County natives.
> "To youth of ability and courage in America Edward Rector is a shining example."

A DIFFERENT BOYHOOD THEREAFTER

In the late 1860s, with the town still very much a rural community, young Edward's shift of residence meant growing up with new neighbors and playmates. There were large families with many children both older and younger than he. One neighbor was Dr. Isaac Denson, the Rectors' family physician, with a son Joe who became Edward's close friend. Another was a German farm family, the Clouseys, whose children helped their family income by working at various jobs. Edward, also needing money, would join the Clousey children in farm work.

Edward recalled arising at 3 or 4 a.m. to go out and gather blackberries. His father would pay him market price for those berries the family consumed; the leftovers were traded by Edward to another neighboring farm family, the Mitchells, in return for milk from the Mitchells' cows, a quart of raspberries for a quart of milk. However the Rectors' milk consumption was usually less than a quart a day, while Edward's raspberry harvest in season was a lot more than that. Therefore young Rector kept an account book in which he recorded the Mitchells' milk paybacks against the raspberry surplus in the months following the end of the berry season.

Isaac Rector encouraged industry and thrift in his son from an early age by paying small amounts for particular jobs. Besides buying raspberries from the boy, Isaac paid for removing potato bugs from potato vines and for cutting rail fence into stove wood length. A boyhood friend remembered Edward's selling debugged potatoes at the rate of 10 cents per 100, earning him the nickname "Taterbug."[16]

Isaac Rector offered Edward a dollar to read the Bible all the way through, but according to the son the father did not pay because "I accomplished the task so quickly that he was doubtful of the thoroughness of the job."[17]

One childhood lesson that influenced Edward for life was unplanned. The older Clousey boys both chewed and smoked tobacco. Wanting to be "manly" too, Edward borrowed a "chew" from one of the brothers during a berry gathering session. After some chewing young Edward felt too ill to go on with berry picking and had to lie down during the rest of the outing. On another summer day Edward tried smoking. He bought a clay pipe and green tobacco from a Clousey brother for 25 cents. After puffing on that Edward had to lie down for several hours in the tree shade, then sneak home and go to bed, skipping supper.

Edward Rector never again used tobacco. Interestingly for those accustomed to more recent anti-smoking campaigns, Rector never took any credit for being a non-smoker. He said he avoided tobacco after his boyhood experiences only because he did not have the "perseverance and determination" to acquire the smoking habit. By lacking those two admirable qualities, he said "I ... have no doubt missed a great deal of pleasure and comfort which it affords its devotees."[18]

EDWARD STARTS SCHOOL

Edward Rector began his formal schooling in Bedford before grade schools were established in the Indiana town. First, at around age six, he began attending a private one-room school where his sister Mary was the teacher. Then he went to a similar school at which a Miss Sue Borland taught.

In 1871, when Rector was eight, Bedford opened its first public grade school. The school marked a milestone in the growth of the southern Indiana town. It was built to two stories, with a cupola and four large rooms on each floor to accommodate both grade and high school classes, and it was run by professional educators. The high school superintendent and principal was a Professor James H. Madden, educated at a normal school at Lebanon, Ohio. Madden brought a corps of five teachers, including his wife.

Edward began in the new school building in September 1871 as a student in a class equivalent to seventh grade. He continued through the equivalent of eighth grade, being taught most of the time until high school by a Miss Frances C. Simpson. The new school building was destroyed by fire in November 1871. It took two years to be restored, and the classes were scattered about town during the interim. In September 1874, at age 11, Rector entered high school.

Edward Rector's memoirs speak little of his course work but more about Professor Madden and his wife, who "hold a very large place in the memory of my school days." He portrays the superintendent as tall, bearded, "dignified and stern," respected but not widely liked, "with very definite and excellent ideas about the organization and administration of the school, which devolved entirely upon him." His wife, by contrast, was sweet and beloved by all.[19]

Rector graduated with his class in May 1878 at age 14, the youngest ever from Bedford High School[20] and among the brightest of the 11 who graduated with him.[21] The graduates included six girls and five boys. He remembered the valedictorian then as a "fiery" red-headed named Arista B. Williams, who later, like Rector, became a Chicago attorney, by which time he was "subdued and successful."[22]

Two aspects of the class are worth noting. One was the distinguished careers of all the boys – girls of the time were expected to become homemakers. Williams and Rector went on to become successful attorneys in Chicago. While one of the three other boys died in law school, the other two entered the teaching profession. The second aspect was the formation of enduring friendships. The Bedford schoolmates, boys and girls, remained lifelong friends. Rector himself returned to Bedford for high school reunions a number of times.

Six members of Rector's class – more than half – went on to an institution of higher learning which later became Valparaiso University. At the time it was a normal school, established by a Professor Henry B. Brown, an acquaintance of Madden at the Lebanon Normal School. Brown came to Bedford to recruit enrollees for Valparaiso from Rector's graduating class.

"I was naturally very anxious to go, as so many members of my class were going, but was unable to do so for lack of means," Rector recounts. "Perhaps I might have managed to have gone, and to have worked my way through, as did at least one member of my class, if I had been a little older and had a little more strength and determination, but I was not quite fifteen and rather under-size for my age, and it did not seem feasible for me to undertake it. That was my last opportunity, however, to secure anything beyond a high school education, for I shortly afterward went to work, to try to earn some badly needed money, and have continued at the job ever since."[23]

ALTERNATIVES TO COLLEGE

Unable financially to go on to college, Edward Rector in the summer of 1878 cast about for full-time employment. Earning money was hardly a new undertaking for him. Since childhood, with encouragement from his father, he had worked at odd jobs whose proceeds he spent to meet various desires. For example, at age 10 Rector saved up enough to buy his then-heart's object, a shotgun displayed in a hardware store window for $3.75, which he paid for entirely in nickels.[24] During high school one of his summer vacation occupations had been to re-bottom cane-seated chairs.

Another summer vacation project, which had some bearing on Rector's later profession, was copying a manuscript for a prominent local citizen, Moses F. Dunn. After an unsuccessful foray as a Republican politician, Dunn, a man of inherited wealth, turned to the practice of law and literary pursuits. Since Dunn's handwriting was almost illegible, he hired young Rector, trained to bold penmanship by Miss Simpson, to inscribe a 1,600-page manuscript one summer. His promised fee was $50.

Rector did such good work that Dunn paid him 10 dollars extra – the $60 total amounting to more than Rector ever had at one time before. Rector forthwith opened his first bank account, depositing the full $60, which he later in half-jest said "laid the foundation of my fortune".[25]

Yet as a 15-year-old high school graduate Rector had no carefully thought out career progression in mind. He had toyed with the idea of becoming a shoemaker. A local shoe shop run by two brothers was a favorite schoolboy hangout. While socializing there with friends and listening to the brothers' stories afternoons after school and on rainy Saturdays, Rector noted the shoemakers seemed to have steady work day after day, without the weather and seasonal disruptions of farming or other outdoor activities.

However Rector never pursued an apprenticeship that would have led to a career as a shoe-making artisan. Instead, his first full-time employment was as a soda-jerk at a local drugstore. The proprietor was an Enos E. Johnson, a prominent member of the church to which the Rectors belonged.

Rector did not like his boss, who he implies was hypocritical despite his "sanctimonious character" and a severe demeanor in business. Rector noted that Johnson included a "girlie magazine," the *Police Gazette,* then regarded as scandalously racy, in his magazine racks. He complained also that his pay, at $10 a month, fell short of the $3 a week a competing drug store paid a friend who worked there. He did enjoy sampling the soda fountain in summer and reading magazines other than the *Gazette*, but his job ended after a year when Johnson's business failed.

FAMILY DWINDLES AND EMPLOYMENT GROWS

Edward Rector's home life underwent a major change shortly afterwards. His mother died unexpectedly in December 1879, after a brief illness, at age 62.[26] Rector was then 16. Shortly following her death, Isaac Rector got a federal job in Washington, D.C., through his brother-in-law, Richard Thompson, who was then Secretary of the Navy. Isaac's move to Washington reduced the Rector household remaining in Bedford to three – Edward, his sister Mary, and Isaac's sister, Becky.

The three moved into a small frame house in Bedford. Mary spent part of the winter visiting maternal relatives in Cincinnati. "Aunt Becky," then 70, managed the household and cooked for Edward, who recalls "a very happy and comfortable winter together."[27]

Rector's next job, in 1879, paid less than his drug store job but was more congenial for him and more beneficial for his eventual career. He went to work for $1.50 a week as an all-purpose assistant in the printing office of Conner & English, among other things learning to set type and writing news items for the firm's country newspaper. This business also failed, but by now interested in becoming a printer, Rector gained employment with the town's leading newspaper, the Bedford *Star*. There he became a proficient typesetter, a good friend of the politically-prominent publisher Johnny Johnson, a Democrat, and increasingly well acquainted around the county seat.

Then another friend, William Erwin, the county recorder, hired Rector at a pay increase to record deeds and mortgages in "long-hand" because of Rector's good penmanship. That position led in turn to a transfer to an office across the hall in the court house, where Rector signed on in 1881 as an assistant to the county auditor. There he made long-hand duplicates of the property and tax records vital for the auditor and treasurer.

Thus by age 18 Rector was achieving much success in Bedford employment. His official salary was increased over the next two years at the court house to $60 a month. He also had opportunities for outside employment. He made money on the side by doing tax duplicates for the city clerk and by helping on the books of a local sawmill.

Rector's boyhood home life effectively ended in his latter teenage years. In early spring of 1882, the two women remaining in the household, his sister Mary and aunt Becky, left Bedford permanently to join Isaac Rector in Washington. Isaac Rector continued with his employment with the Navy

Department there until his death in 1899 at age 83.[28]

Edward, then 18, went to board with Miss Miranda Rawlins. "Aunt Miranda" kept a large house just off Bedford's public square, and she enjoyed having compatible "paying guests" even while she personally was financially well off.

Rector made more acquaintances while at Aunt Miranda's. A long-term boarder was a Judge Gideon Putnam, one of the town's best known lawyers and a leader of the bar. A new boarder was Homer Fisher, a farm boy who lacked formal education but had native intelligence and humor. Fisher worked in the office of the Bedford railroad station agent. While boarding at Aunt Miranda's he and Rector went on a train excursion to Niagara Falls. The two remained lifelong friends.

THE LAW BECKONS

Meanwhile Rector continued his search for a career path. He had well demonstrated by now his self-reliance, intelligence, proclivity for hard work, skill in a variety of pursuits, an interest and ability in making money, and a capability for getting along with people in all walks of life, particularly with those of importance. He seemed likely to succeed in whatever occupation he chose, but he was still moving *ad hoc* from one opportunity to another.

The law was one option. He had relatives in the legal profession. His uncle Richard Thompson was a prominent Indiana lawyer who had lived in Bedford. A cousin, Arthur Stem, practiced in Cincinnati. But it was one of his Miranda acquaintances, William H. Martin, who had the strongest influence in persuading him.

Martin, a Rawlins relative who visited and sometimes boarded at the home, was a dedicated lawyer who later became a judge. "It was he who led me astray from my earlier resolves to be a shoemaker, and later a printer, and inveigled me into the law," Rector recalled.[29]

Martin urged young Rector to study law and loaned him a law book. In those days an aspirant could be admitted to the bar by passing an exam, without going to law school. Rector struggled through the book when he could spare time from his busy Court House duties. However he lacked the supportive environment of a law office which would help him pursue his study.

Rector decided that to become a lawyer, he would have to go to a law school – which he could not afford – or seek placement in a law office. His solution was to get a job as a clerk in the office of Arthur Stem in Cincinnati and use this as a base for entering (and paying his way through) law school.

The aspiring youth still was only nineteen when he arrived at the office of Stem & Peck in Cincinnati in November 1882. The firm specialized in patent law. Much of the newcomer's work initially was taking dictation in long-hand, transcribing it, and taking down testimony from witnesses in depositions.

To facilitate matters, Rector taught himself shorthand from a textbook. Soon he was so proficient that he took all dictation in shorthand, including from the firm's partners. Later, during his three years with Stem & Peck, the office acquired a then-new device, a typewriter.

Rector's arrival in Cincinnati in 1882 had been too late to enroll in law school for that academic year. While working, saving his earnings, and waiting for admission to school the next year, the young law clerk boarded at first with his Cincinnati aunt and uncle, the A. M. Stems, parents of his cousin Arthur. Their home was in Mount Auburn.

Edward had previously visited the Stem home at age 11 with his sister. Arthur's mother was a sister of Edward's mother. The senior Stem had been a U.S. Sub-Treasurer at Cincinnati as an appointee of President Rutherford Hayes, a close friend, and subsequently went on to the Internal Revenue Department which was then headed by another Cincinnatian and future president, William Howard Taft. The Stem and Taft families were friends and neighbors at Mount Auburn.

In the fall of 1883, then age 20, Rector entered the University of Cincinnati School of Law. To be closer to school and have more time for study, Rector moved into a nearby boarding place with a fellow student. His routine over the next two years was heavy with work at Stem & Peck, attending a law school lecture each day, studying in the evenings and early mornings, and daily workouts at a gym to maintain health.

Rector recalls that there were 62 students admitted to the law school in the fall of 1883, and 62 graduated in the spring of 1885. Edward tied for second-place honors scholastically, winning $50 in gold. First place went to Robert B. Bowler, a wealthy Cincinnatian who later became Comptroller of the Treasury under President Cleveland. However Rector, in contrast with his high school experience, formed few lasting friendships among his law school classmates. One exception was his Cincinnati roommate, Charles Pleasants, from Vevay, Indiana. The two kept in touch and visited each others' homes throughout succeeding years.

Edward Rector at twenty-one, as a law school student in Cincinnati.

VALUABLE EXPERIENCES AS CLERK

Rector's duties as a clerk in Stem & Peck had entailed, among other things, a considerable amount of business travel which the partners felt could be entrusted to junior aides. Rector enjoyed the journeys as a tourist while gaining valuable experience as what today would be called a paralegal in handling matters for his firm.

One early visit was to Detroit, where the young clerk was sent to settle Stem & Peck's suit against the City of Detroit for infringement of a patent relating to desks used in the city's public schools. Rector dealt with the city's law firm headed by Don M. Dickinson, later Postmaster General in President Cleveland's cabinet. What Rector remembered most from his visit was not the case or its participants so much as the electric street car line that he encountered on the Canadian side of the Detroit River, running from Windsor to Walkerville.[30]

In connection with a trip to northern Indiana to take depositions from witnesses Rector made acquaintances with, among others, Francis E. Baker, who subsequently became U.S. Circuit Judge at Chicago. Rector later argued many cases in his court.

A Stem & Peck suit related to ice-making and refrigerating machinery in New Orleans gave Rector his first taste of the storied city in December 1885. He was then a junior attorney fresh out of law school. The other side's lawyer, Philip H. Dyrenforth, head of a large Chicago firm, took a liking to his youthful opponent and together they visited the old St. Charles Hotel and the French quarter, and attended an opera at the French Opera House. The two remained lifelong friends.

An assignment to Rector to go to San Francisco in connection with an alleged patent infringement relating to distilling apparatus turned into a series of train adventures marked by stoppages due to floods and then heavy snow. Rector struck up a friendship with a fellow passenger, Samuel S. Fifield, a newspaper editor from Ashland, Wisconsin, and former Lieutenant Governor of the state, and his wife.

Rector altered his itinerary to sightsee with the Fifields at Salt Lake City and then ride together to San Francisco. Waiting for Rector in San Francisco was Edward's law school roommate, Charles Pleasants, then based in San Diego. By now a party of four, the group spent a "delightful week" touring famous places and hitting night spots. At a light opera performance of "Erminie," which Rector had previously seen in Cincinnati, Rector delighted in recognizing "old friends" from the show - Alice Vincent, Rose Beaudet, and "a very charming little soubrette and dancer, Fanny

Rice."[31] Despite the diversions, Rector managed to accomplish his business mission in San Francisco. He found evidence of prior importation and use of the distilling apparatus that his Cincinnati client was using. The fact of previous existence of the device prior to the issuance of a patent for a similar apparatus defeated the suit alleging patent infringement. As for his new train companions, "Governor" Fifield and his wife, they joined the growing ranks of Rector's lifelong friends, periodically coming from Wisconsin to visit with Edward at his subsequent home in Chicago.

Notwithstanding the experience Rector gained in patent law during his clerkship at Stem & Peck, he had no intention then of specializing in that field as a career. "On the contrary, by the time I had finished my course in the law school I felt that I knew entirely too much law to ever confine my activities to one narrow branch of it. Rather, like Lord Bacon, I would take all law, if not all knowledge, for my province."[32] As for staying in Cincinnati, the fledgling attorney - now age 22 - had caught "Chicago fever" from his visits to the big city and contemplated hanging out his shingle there.

PROMOTION TO PARTNERSHIP

But for the time being, at least, Rector decided on a different course after receiving a flattering offer from Peck after he had graduated and passed the bar exam in mid-1884: if Rector would stay with Stem & Peck through 1885, Peck would then leave the firm and set up a new partnership with Rector. Rector was assured a livable salary immediately without the risks of starting out alone. Thus the new Peck & Rector office on Fountain Square in Cincinnati opened for business in January 1886.

A major client of Peck & Rector from day one was the National Cash Register Co. of Dayton. Peck had been counsel for the company from the time of its formation several years earlier. Peck entrusted the National account largely to Rector.

Rector devoted a great deal of work to an important suit brought in National's behalf against a Boston firm. The case eventually reached the U.S. Supreme Court and provided Rector with valuable experience and important new contacts. Peck and Rector retained a Boston associate, William A. MacLeod, who became another one of Rector's lifelong friends.

Rector spent much time in Boston over a period of several years during the protracted litigation. During the winter of 1890-91 he was stricken by typhoid fever. The hospital rooms were full due to a flu epidemic. MacLeod's personal doctor had Rector stay at the doctor's home for six weeks. Rector's sister Mary came from Washington to serve as nurse. The illness ran its course without complications, and in convalescence Rector went with his sister to Washington for several weeks before returning to Cincinnati.

Another lasting friendship Rector formed during his protracted visits to Boston was with Frederick P. Fish, a prominent New York lawyer who headed the firm representing the other side in this case. Rector worked with or on the opposing side to Fish in a number of cases over the ensuing decades, with Fish referring many valuable clients to Rector.

One professional whom Rector particularly admired from his Boston experience was Henry B. Renwick of New York City, a scientific expert in patent litigation. Rector saw in Renwick qualities to which Rector himself aspired and for which he later became known himself during his legal career. Rector said he learned, or thought he learned, from Renwick "thoroughness, and intellectual honesty or integrity." Renwick, he said, "examined the cases laid before him with the utmost thoroughness, and if he felt that the case was not a good one, on the side presented to him, he would not take it."[33]

The partners in the Peck & Rector firm got along well. As time passed Peck turned over half or more of the business to his younger associate. Rector's income by 1892 had climbed to

$4,000-$5,000 a year. Yet for him Chicago still held its allure. He perceived Cincinnati as comparatively stagnant in his field, and Chicago as energetic, rapidly growing, and with a far larger market locally and nationally for the services of a patent attorney then approaching 30 years old.

A MOVE TO CHICAGO

Edward Rector parted ways amicably with Peck, who generously allowed his junior partner to take with him a number of accounts he had handled for the firm. Among them was National Cash Register Co. Thus with some business income assured to start with, Rector opened an office in downtown Chicago on April 1, 1892.

Rector's new quarters were in part of a suite rented by a fellow former Cincinnati law school student, Albert H. Meads, in the then-new Chamber of Commerce Building at LaSalle and Washington Streets. Rector joked later that he would not have started his Chicago venture as he did had he been superstitious, by opening on April Fool's Day, a Friday, in office number 1314 on the 13th floor of the building.[34]

In actuality, Rector's move to the "Windy City" proved to be an almost-instant success. The clients he brought from Cincinnati gave him more business than ever. More clients came in to his Chicago office. He doubled his income in the first year, making $10,000.

A HAPPY MARRIAGE BEGINS

A year after his arrival in Chicago, Rector married Lucy Rowland of Cincinnati. The pair had known each other for some years, but Rowland delayed the marriage out of a sense of obligation to help care for a brother's orphaned children. The marriage appears to have been exceptionally happy and successful, and she strongly supported his philanthropies.

REACHING A PROFESSIONAL PINNACLE

Rector's career as a patent lawyer proceeded in high gear. He was admitted to the Illinois Bar in 1892 and joined the Chicago, Illinois and American Bar Associations. His growing list of clients came to include corporations that were or would become prominent and outstandingly successful nationally. He became director on the boards of a number of major companies.

Among those employing Rector's counsel in the patent field were: American Telephone and Telegraph Co., Boyer Machine Co., Burroughs Adding Machine Co., Chicago Pneumatic Tool Co., Detroit Lubricator Co., Firestone Tire and Rubber Co., General Electric Co., General Motors Corp., National Automobile Chamber of Commerce, National Cash Register Co., Packard Co., Studebaker Corp., Splitdorf Co., Todd Protectograph Co., Toledo Scale Co., Thompson-Houston Co., Tiemens-Halske Co., Westinghouse Electric and Manufacturing Co.[35]

As his practice grew, Rector took on partners. The first was Samuel E. Hibben, the firm becoming Rector & Hibben. Then came Frank Parker Davis and Rector, Hibben & Davis. Later with John B. McCauley, it was Rector, Hibben, Davis & McCauley, along with junior partners and a sizeable office staff.

Over his 30 years of active practice following his move to Chicago, Rector came to be known as one of the best patent attorneys in the nation. He was a member of the bar of the U.S. Supreme Court, of most U.S. Courts of Appeal, and of many U.S. District Courts. He participated in a number of prominent cases, usually on the winning side. A Philadelphia lawyer, Henry N. Paul, who had sided both with and against Rector in different patent cases, gave this appraisal of the Chicagoan's performance:

"As an antagonist I found he always knew the weakest point of my case and made his attack directly upon it. As a colleague, I found that he always brushed aside all side issues and technicalities and went directly to the main issue. These are habits of mind which are acquired only by long trial experience. Courts learn to know these men and to trust their arguments as they do not trust those of other lawyers. This was pre-eminently the case with Rector. He never tried to fool the Court. And the Court knew it.

"He also had the rare faculty of making an intricate subject clear and simple. Another great gift was that he could be very persistent in enforcing his point without irritating the judge on whom he was endeavoring to impress his view. Likewise he could tell a client that his case was a bad one without the client feeling aggrieved."[36]

SOME PERSONAL TRAITS

As he climbed in wealth and fame, Rector remained a tireless worker. "Leisure" in the sense of inactivity was not entertainment for him. He took joy in industriousness, whether on a patent case or in a non-business pursuit. He seldom took a vacation. He frequently traveled on business, with books and legal briefs.

Rector occasionally would get out on the golf course. He had a locker at the South Shore Club,[37] but he was not a frequent player. A senior DePauw official, Henry B. Longden, recalled many years later that he had been traveling with Rector in northern Michigan and the two had agreed to play golf in a resort area there every August –"there were six courses around the bay and we'd go around the courses during the week."[38]

He liked artistic performances, as noted in autobiographical references to his attending shows ranging from the night club scene to operas. In Chicago he enjoyed spending the evening with wife and friends at a good play or musicale.

He took pleasure in a certain amount of driving, both on short recreational trips and longer jaunts. When George R. Grose was DePauw president, he recorded one occasion when the Rectors arrived in Greencastle from Chicago in a new Peerless car, rather than aboard their more customary Monon train. Before Rector finished this DePauw visit he took a side trip to Indianapolis in his Peerless with a car-full of riders including his wife, Grose, Longden and Katharine Alvord, dean of women. The trip back to Chicago of somewhat less than 200 miles took 7½ hours under road conditions of the time.[39]

Rector was slightly shorter in stature than many of his peers and was notably clean in his personal habits. Longden observed that Rector was always immaculately groomed, as befitting his status as a Chicago lawyer. Rector hadn't smoked since his boyhood mishaps with tobacco, and Longden said Rector didn't swear, drink, or even use slang, perhaps because he spent so much time in a court room.

Also among Rector's lifelong traits were a comparative frugality and simplicity of living reflecting his meager beginnings, despite his accumulation of wealth. He did not spend ostentatiously for apparel, food, or lodging. Upon his arrival at the big-time scene in Chicago he made $10,000 his first year, while "his total personal expenditures for clothing, incidentals, etc. did not exceed fifty dollars."[40]

One humorous story about Rector's aversion to spending much for personal items relates that he was shopping with his wife and saw a pair of shoes that he liked. However the shoes were priced higher than the amount he was accustomed to paying, so he had his wife buy the shoes for him instead.[41]

His generally non-lavish lifestyle by no means meant penny-pinching on items he deemed worthwhile, nor was he personally aloof. On the contrary, he was extraordinarily generous to those whom he perceived to be in need. He was gregarious, with many lasting friendships. He liked giving presents to children. He paid well for works of art, he was fond of good books and he decorated his house in good taste.

The Rectors' first family residence in Chicago in the 1890s was at 4411 Berkeley Avenue in the city's south side near the

A 1908 snapshot of the Rector's home at 4917 Greenwood Avenue, Hyde Park Station, Chicago. The building looks much the same in a snapshot taken a century later.

University of Chicago.[42] In 1907 the Rectors moved to another house in the same area, at 4917 Greenwood Avenue, Hyde Park Station, that Rector bought for $35,000, a substantial sum in those days.[43] They lived there for the rest of their lives.

The Rectors were known for their hospitality to visitors. Their Greenwood Avenue home was a comfortable, three-story brown brick town house, large but not grandiose. It had 14 rooms and was sited on a 50' x 200' lot in a residential neighborhood.

Many friends over the years dined there. Some stayed overnight or sometimes much longer. Senior DePauw officers found it congenial to visit there on University business.

On the social level Rector has been described as a good listener with a hearty laugh. He did not appear supercilious. He did not use profanity. His humor tended to be self-deprecating. However in personal discussions he could be as articulate and brilliantly analytical as he was in arguing a legal case.

Grose, a Methodist minister who was president of DePauw for a dozen years (1912-24) until being elected Bishop, came to know Rector well and became a fervent admirer. In a short biography, Grose said Rector had "an insatiable craving for friends." He rated Rector's "genius for friendship" as being the largest factor in Rector's success. The lawyer's clients and fellow workers became friends who lavished affection toward him as he did toward them.[44]

Rector's friendly approach and a remarkable memory for names were recalled by one of the students to whom Rector was introduced when he first came to DePauw. The student, who also became a fervent admirer of Rector and his wife in later years, said they were "wonderfully friendly and personable people" and that Rector always called her by her first name after the first meeting. Furthermore, she said, he would ask about her two brothers, by name – "I've never seen such a memory in my life."[45]

Rector did not wear religion on his sleeve. His unpublished autobiography does not mention church work. Bishop Grose described Rector as a trustee and generous donor to St. James Methodist Episcopal Church, which is in the Chicago University neighborhood near the Rector home. He said Rector "revered God, loved men, and cared for noble causes … He had no sympathy with sectarian narrowness or with religious bigotry."

Rector was driven, the Bishop said, by "vigor of mind, intellectual integrity, decisive convictions, and passion for humanity."[46]

RECTOR'S UNEXPECTED DEATH

Rector first became involved with DePauw in 1915 spurred by Roy O. West, a close Chicago friend who was a DePauw graduate and enthusiastic supporter of his *alma mater*. Over the next decade Rector devoted himself and his fortune increasingly to the Greencastle school, his philanthropy highlighted by an historic scholarship program.

Rector was in the full swing of things – many things – in the summer of 1925 when disturbing word came of an illness he suffered while on a business trip to Cleveland. He was stricken while in a courtroom there on June 29[47] with what was described as an attack of acute indigestion. His wife, with him in Cleveland, wired Longden on July 1 that Rector was "ill in Huron Hospital here" and could not attend a forthcoming meeting, though in another Western Union telegram the following day she said her husband "is getting along nicely. His condition is most encouraging."

Rector himself was not as sanguine about his condition, telling Longden July 6 that he was "improving slowly" but would have to stay longer in the hospital.[48] He returned to Chicago and at first entered a hospital there. He was removed to his Greenwood Avenue home a few days later and was believed to be recovering when he suffered a heart attack and died at his home around 5 p.m. August 1.[49] He was 62 years old.

A brief funeral was conducted at his home the afternoon of August 4 by the Rev. Edwin Holt Hughes, Methodist Bishop of the Chicago area and a former DePauw president 1902-09. Rector was buried initially at Oakwood Cemetery in Chicago with expectations that the body would be taken to Greencastle later for burial at a lot he had purchased at Forest Hill cemetery in Greencastle.[50] A great memorial assembly for Rector was convened at DePauw after classes resumed following the summer recess. The formal service was held in Meharry Hall, a chapel, on October 16. Hundreds of friends and admirers gathered for the occasion. West, presiding over the service, called it "a day of sorrow" but also a "day of thanksgiving" for Rector's life and all he had done for the University. Eulogists included DePauw President Murlin; Bishop Hughes; Rector's longtime law partner, Frank Parker Davis; Frederick D. Leete, Bishop of the Indianapolis Area of the Methodist Church; Hugh McGlasson, a Rector Scholar class of 1927; and Longden. There were 508 Rector Scholars on campus at the time.

In 1931 Rector was reinterred in Forest Hill Cemetery "overlooking Greencastle and the DePauw University campus where his heart always was." Six Rector Scholars served as pallbearers at a short afternoon service July 8. It was conducted by Bishop Hughes, who had preached at the first memorial service.[51]

The fact that Rector had bought the burial plot at Forest Hill several months before his death[52] was further evidence of the fullness of his devotion to his "investment." His tombstone, and subsequently that of his wife, stands among others in a section where lie others of DePauw's most honored dead. Nearby is that of Longden, and also those of Grose and Hughes.

***

The Rector grave site at Forest Hill Cemetery.

3 Chapter

EDWARD RECTOR –
GREAT BENEFACTOR OF DEPAUW

*"...chance plays a major role in everyone's life and in
the case of Edward Rector and DePauw University, the
lines of fate crossed ..."*

Edward Rector continued an active law practice literally to
his final days before his unexpected death. He was paid
handsomely for his legal work and for his directorships
on major corporations. He invested well. He lived comfortably
but not lavishly, continuing his youthful habit of keeping a close
watch on expenditures.

Yet as Rector progressed to the top of his field as a patent
lawyer and adviser to major firms, he was not content just with
accumulating wealth and prestige. In the early years of the 20th
century, after he had become established in his Chicago practice,
he began to develop an interest in charitable activity, particularly
in the educational field.

Several factors fostered Rector's increasing ventures into
philanthropy. He was imbued with a humanitarianism that
reflected tenets of the frontier religious society in which he was
raised. Friendships were a key element of his life. He liked
people and was excellent at analyzing personalities. As he grew
older, he became increasingly interested in younger generations.

His interest in youth was magnified by the fact that he and
his wife Lucy had no children of their own. And, at least partly
because of his own searing experience of being unable to attend

college due to finances, he saw education as a prime instrument for helping those whose adulthood still lay ahead.

That Rector should have focused his philanthropy on a small Methodist institution of higher learning in Greencastle, Ind., was not surprising, either, given his Indiana background, although there could have been a number of alternatives. There were many other opportunities in the Midwest to advance education. But chance plays a major role in everyone's life, and in the case of Edward Rector and DePauw University, the lines of fate crossed at a point in Rector's life when he was increasingly devoted to improving the schooling of youth.

As a boy in Bedford, Rector of course had known of what was then Indiana Asbury, a leading college in the state, subsequently renamed DePauw. Greencastle was about 65 miles north of Bedford. He was aware that his oldest brother Jesse Winfield Rector had gone to school there, though with the 19-year difference in their ages, Edward was too young at the time for this to make much of an impression on him.[1] His father Isaac was a member of Indiana Asbury's Board of Trustees in 1865-66, but Edward was still in his childhood and apparently unaware until later of his father's membership on the Board. Grose, president of DePauw during most of the years of Edward Rector's association with the University, said Edward did not learn of his father's service on the Board until he was on his first visit to the school.

According to Grose, this disclosure "greatly intensified" Edward's interest in DePauw. Further, with the period of his father's Board membership spanning approval of the first admission of women to Indiana Asbury, Grose said Edward "took great satisfaction in the fact that his father was an ardent believer in the higher education of women and as a member of the corporation vigorously supported their admission to the college."[2]

As a Methodist and Indiana native, Rector also was exposed to DePauw in other ways through various contacts. Lemuel H.

Murlin, a DePauw graduate and Methodist minister who later became president of DePauw, recalled meeting Rector and his wife for the first time in May 1912 at Saratoga Springs, N.Y., where the Methodists were holding a General Conference. "We were staying at the same hotel and frequently dined together," Murlin said. "They were then beginning their interest in DePauw, and seemed to regard it as a high privilege to share in its life."[3]

ROY WEST INTRODUCES RECTOR TO DEPAUW

Probably the single most important instigator of Edward Rector's interest in DePauw was Roy O. West, an eminently successful Chicago attorney. West was active in Republican politics and was appointed Secretary of Interior in 1928 during the latter part of the Coolidge administration. He was also a prominent Methodist and interested in helping the education of the next generation. He and Rector, likewise a leading Chicago lawyer, Republican, and Methodist church trustee, formed a fast friendship.[4]

West was an 1890 graduate of DePauw and one of the institution's most enthusiastic supporters of all time. Throughout the period of his friendship with Rector, and long thereafter until his own death in 1958, West was active in University affairs, including fund-raising for the school as well as donating substantially donor. He served on DePauw's Board of Trustees from 1914 on through the rest of his lifetime. He became President of the Board in 1924, a post he held for 26 years. DePauw's excellent Roy O. West library was named in his honor.

Roy O. West

With West's devotion to DePauw and with Rector entering a stage of his life in which he was increasingly interested in

George R. Grose, DePauw president from 1912-24, associated closely with Edward Rector.

advancing education and educational opportunities for the young, it is easy to understand why the friendship was an important stimulus leading to Rector's gifts to DePauw. West in effect introduced Rector to the Greencastle school and to its go-getter President, George Grose. West gave Grose a letter of introduction to Rector, and Grose followed through by calling on Rector at the lawyer's Chicago office.[5]

West became a DePauw trustee in 1914. The Board decided the college needed a gymnasium to attract male students, whose attendance was declining compared with that of women. It mounted a $100,000 campaign to construct the gym. Without yet having grown close enough to DePauw to visit the campus, but listening to his friend West, Rector donated a modest (for him) $100 toward the campaign. Later that year he gave another $500. The gym, named the Bowman Memorial Building after Bishop Thomas Bowman, an Indiana Asbury president 1858-72, was built in 1915.

Rector followed through on his initial "investment" in DePauw by paying his first visit to the school in 1915. He showed the same thoroughness as he did in preparing law cases: upon arriving in Greencastle he "inspected the plant, became acquainted with members of the faculty and met the students with keen personal interest."[6] Among those with whom he met was Salem B. Town, financial secretary of the University and a DePauw alumnus. Rector told Town he was glad he had something in the gym "but felt he did not have as much as he should have, and on returning to Chicago, sent Dr. Town a check for $400" – making his total contribution to the building $1,000.[7]

In chatting with President Grose, by Rector's account, Rector asked Grose whether there was a loan fund available for "worthy and needy students who required some financial help" in getting through college. Grose said there was a fund provided by the Methodist Church, but it was limited to Methodist Church members and thus not available to the many students at DePauw who were not. Rector put up another "small" amount for loans without restriction as to race, color, or creed.

The "Edward Rector Fund" for needy students, as described in a University document a couple years later,[8] grew successfully as a revolving fund over the years. The students receiving the loans were allowed to set their own time of repayment and were charged low interest rates. The fund became self-sustaining and required no replenishment because of the high rate of repayment of principal and interest by the borrowers.[9]

"MY INVESTMENT IN DEPAUW" CAPTIVATES RECTOR

After his first visit, if it had not happened already, Rector's attention to DePauw became his prime interest and continued as such for the remaining decade of his life. "As an avocation I practice law," he told a DePauw dinner audience some years later, but "my investment in DePauw ... is the thing of greatest interest in my life today."[10]

After a member of the Board of Trustees died in late 1915, Grose nominated Rector at a January 1916 Board meeting to fill the vacancy and West joined in Grose's "high commendation of Mr. Rector's qualifications." Rector was identified as a Chicago lawyer "about 52 years of age and a son of Isaac Rector, who had been a Trustee of Asbury University from 1858 to 1861,"[11] and as "a member of the same Methodist church of Chicago" (St.

James) as West. Rector had already told Grose and West that he would serve. The Board unanimously approved his nomination. Rector was sworn in at the next meeting, June 6, 1916. After that Rector never missed a regular meeting of the Board during his lifetime.

The new trustee promptly began applying both energy and means to upgrading school facilities and the level of instruction. According to then-President Grose, Rector and his wife were at Saratoga Springs in May of 1916 at the same time Grose was there. Grose recalled that the prospective new Board member asked what DePauw's immediate needs for its best development were. Grose said he replied that the three most urgent needs were student housing facilities, adequate endowment and "provision for free scholarships for the promotion of higher scholastic standards." Before the conversation ended Rector said that he had decided to give $100,000 immediately to the University for purposes to be determined later.[12]

At his first Board meeting the following month, Rector made a motion, unanimously adopted by the Board members, for a campaign for $600,000 for endowment of the University and $400,000 for buildings. He proposed that $750,000 be raised by the University starting with his $100,000 for buildings and that $250,000 come from the Methodists' General Education Board. Rector also gave a small sum for scholarships, and in soliciting for the endowment, obtained gifts of $60,000 from personal friends during the campaign period in addition to the large donation of his own.[13]

Grose's biography documented Rector's assiduousness in cajoling other donations beyond his own. In one instance, when the DePauw president visited Rector at his Chicago office, the attorney handed him a letter just received from a prominent firm for whom Rector had just won a lawsuit. The grateful company paid his contract fee, and added: "We know that you will not consent to receive more than the amount agreed upon in our contract. But we are enclosing an extra check of two thousand dollars with instructions that you send it to your Greencastle Pet."

On another occasion Rector received a $5,000 bonus check for winning a case for Firestone Tire and Rubber. Rector returned the check, saying his services had been duly rewarded "but there is a poor college at Greencastle, Indiana, in which I am greatly interested, whose president never refuses any gift." Grose of course accepted Firestone's.

In still another instance, the president of Burroughs Adding Machine, for whom Rector was a longtime chief counsel and member of the board, told an individual soliciting a donation to DePauw that "I am not particularly interested in colleges. But what does my friend Edward Rector think?" The visitor said he had been sent by Rector to ask for $50,000 for DePauw. "Well, then," Gross said the company executive replied, "before New Year's Day I'll send you fifty thousand in United States gold bonds."[14]

A BRICKS AND MORTAR DONATION: RECTOR HALL

The trustees' building program encompassed constructing Bowman gym, which had just been completed, a women's dormitory, and an administration building. Rector's $100,000 committed to Grose at Saratoga Springs was earmarked for the dormitory, and work was started on it almost immediately.

Rector's donation for a major women's residence hall illustrated not only his generosity but also his vision and a painstaking attention to detail in the achievement of his objective. He wanted more than routine living quarters. He envisioned an edifice that would not only be pleasant for the girls, but also architecturally outstanding, and of multiple uses for the University. It would include spacious dining facilities and some comfortable accommodations for distinguished visitors.

The architect selected for the project with Rector's approval was Robert Frost Dagget, son of the founder of the well-known Indianapolis firm of Robert P. Dagget, who had studied at the École des Beaux-Arts in Paris. Building began with a ceremonial ground breaking in October 1916, with Rector helping Grose hold the plow.

It is difficult to overstate the energy Rector applied and the detail into which he delved in his oversight of the design and construction. Rector visited other campuses and inspected their dormitories to gather ideas on what should, or should not, be incorporated in his Greencastle edifice. Rector, and also his wife, paid the closest personal attention to such matters as design, materials, furnishings, decorations, and costs as the building proceeded.

For example, after a weekend in Greencastle inspecting the premises, Rector wrote Dagget on Nov. 5, 1917, that he had concluded that there should be some lamps at the foot of the lower terrace because "all of the steps are very dark at night, and somewhat dangerous." He said two lamps at each end of the lower steps would provide enough light for all of the steps. Then he went on to discuss extensively how the lamps should look, what height they should be, the type of supports to be used, and so forth. Other letters on the subject went to Grose, the University president, and Henry B. Longden, a senior professor who also held administrative posts. As Grose put it, Rector "put himself into every brick and stone of Rector Hall."[15]

Not surprisingly, changes and additions added to construction costs. Rector gave another $100,000 out of his own pocket for additional expenses for the building and its furnishings, doubling his original donation.[16]

The result was a building widely regarded at the time as one of the best women's dormitories in the Midwest. Grand in concept and design, it adjoined the campus center in a U-shape with a frontage of 193 feet and a north wing of 115 feet. A plaza and steps led toward the campus.

Isaac Rector Hall, built in 1917 and one of the finest women's dormitories in the Midwest, was named for Edward Rector's father.

The stately residence featured a sweeping first floor drawing room 56 feet by 40 feet with gracious furnishings. Nearby was a magnificent paneled banquet-size dining room capable of seating 275. Stairs and passageways led to women's dormitory rooms and guest quarters.

The building was formally dedicated in the fall of 1917 about a year after its start. At the dedication ceremony Rector officially presented the completed building to West, who by then was acting president of the Board. Rector had the building named after his father, Isaac Rector, who had supported the admission of women during his trusteeship.[17]

Rector Hall immediately proved popular with the women students. There was a waiting list for occupancy. The structure remained in active service until the end of the century,[18] and especially in its earlier years was used also for social occasions and distinguished guests. Rector and his wife were among those who overnighted at the guest quarters during visits to the University, as was Grose after he became a bishop.[19]

Edward Rector was so pleased by the impacts of his donations to DePauw as he observed them to date that he was stirred to give even more, then more yet. His further gifts included provisions for more dormitories, although he died before he could oversee their construction personally as he had Rector Hall. His will contained money for another women's residence,

Lucy Rowland Hall, completed in 1928 and named after his wife, and Longden Hall, a men's dormitory completed in 1927 and named after the professor/administrator whose devotion to Rector's scholarship program (see below) Rector credited largely with its success.[20] Rector avoided having any building named after himself.

Rector's philanthropic ambitions for DePauw extended well beyond bricks-and-mortar donations, however. He was interested in educating youth, and eventually the great bulk of the wealth he had built up over the years went to the small Greencastle school for this purpose.

RECTOR'S SCHOLARSHIP BOMBSHELL

The desire that grew into Rector's greatest donation to DePauw, with enormous impact on the school, had been with him for years. As a bright youngster he had been denied an opportunity for a college education because of financial misfortune. He wanted some day to have part of his own fortune used to provide this opportunity for others. His first gift for scholarships and his active role in establishing the student loan fund, as it turned out, were just the beginning.

As Rector's University-related activities grew, his active mind seized on a grander concept to be carried out on a much larger scale. In order to bring it to a practical possibility, he thought through various goals he wanted to accomplish. He applied his growing knowledge of the state of education of his time and of DePauw's needs. He weighed what mechanism would be most effective in carrying out the objectives. He discussed his ideas with, among others, West and Grose, and with Longden, whose experience with the school dated back more than 40 years.

Rector concluded that the best way to help DePauw and future generations of students who, like him, lacked the financial wherewithal for college education, was to establish an endowment for scholarships. The scholarships were to be based on excellence.

The program would be administered through a foundation. And while the immediate beneficiaries would be worthy young men from Indiana, the program would also elevate DePauw overall as an educational institution.

As with so much else that Rector did, it would be on a grand scale. And he was not averse to some showmanship in presenting it.

The Chicago attorney dropped his philanthropic bombshell on Greencastle at a chapel exercise April 30, 1919: he announced that he was offering to provide enough money to *establish 100 full tuition scholarships for male students annually at DePauw in perpetuity.*

One hundred annually would have been a very large number of scholarships for any university at the time. For DePauw, it was an enormous quota, especially for its male student population that had been temporarily decimated by World War I military enlistments. After the Student Army Training Corps closure at the end of 1918, enrollment was on the rebound though still only up to 942 in the 1919-20 school year, including 427 men in all classes.[21] Assuming illustratively that the freshman male intake rose to 200 a year in the future, that would mean half of the men would be matriculating as Rector Scholars.

Rector followed through with a letter to the University president and Board of Trustees dated June 6, spelling out his offer. (See Appendix B) He proposed to "establish and endow" 100 scholarships a year at DePauw for the best graduating Indiana high school male students.

The scholarships would be for full tuition from matriculation to graduation. Tuition at DePauw in 1919 cost $75 a year, $300 for four years. Rector did not attach a specific dollar figure to his proposal, but Salem B. Town, the University's financial secretary who kept track of donations, reported in 1925 that Rector by then had provided $1,069,000 to the foundation running the program.

There is no definitive method for calculating the value of the Rector scholarship gift in latter-day dollars. One generic table for economists is a composite price index table issued by the U. S. Office for National Statistics, which pegs a 1919 dollar as worth $30.68 in 2000. Under that formula Rector's original scholarship donation would equal $32.8 million in 2000, and his total scholarship donation of $2.7 million including the bequeathal in his will would be worth $82.8 million in 2000.

Another comparison might be through the number of scholarships provided. Rector's $1 million bequest in 1919, with an approximately 4 percent annual return on principal, amounting to $40,000, could finance 100 new full, four-year tuition scholarships a year, since tuition then was $75 per student and Rector added a $25-a-year loan cushion as part of his plan. In the year 2000, tuition was $20,200, approximately 200 times the per-pupil dollar amount in 1919. Assuming the same rate of return from principal, a donation in 2000 would have to be about $200 million for 100 new scholars a year, provided tuition remained stable.

Whatever measurement is attempted, it is hard to overstate the impact of Rector's magnanimity in the eyes of the recipients of the time. It was one of the biggest in history to a small liberal arts college. The Rev. Edwin Holt Hughes, a Methodist bishop and former DePauw president, described it as the largest gift ever to a school in Indiana and as the largest ever by an individual to a Methodist college.[22]

Compared with the year 2000, the effect on DePauw was all the greater for the relative size of the school in 1919 (947 students in 1919 compared with more than 2000 at the end of the century) and particularly for its male student population that made up less than half the total. It should be stressed further that in 1919, there were far fewer scholarships generally than was the case 80 years later.

DePauw historian George Manhart has observed that the Rector scholarship program was probably the one feature most sharply distinguishing DePauw from other colleges,[23] and that after Rector's philanthropies began "the history of DePauw University was to be in considerable part the further story of the gifts and the vision of Edward Rector."[24]

RECTOR'S ZEAL EXTENDS TO UPPER MANAGEMENT

Rector's zeal for DePauw continued without letup following his historic donation. While at the same time he was maintaining his law practice, he was in frequent touch with the school through visits, correspondence, trustee meetings, and contacts ranging from the president to incoming students. He became extraordinarily immersed personally in the scholarship program and the progress of its scholars. And in a commitment with permanence, he bought a burial plot in Forest Hill Cemetery on a hillside overlooking the town and the University.[25]

Along with his charities Rector played a role in DePauw's senior management. As an activist on the Board of Trustees since joining the group in 1916, his efforts ranged well beyond raising and donating money. He was close to Roy West, longtime Chairman of the Board and friend from Chicago. He was in frequent and friendly contact with Methodist minister George Grose, DePauw's president until 1924 when Grose was elected bishop.

While Grose went on temporary leave for research and writing in China in 1922, the Board appointed Longden, a close associate of Rector as administrator of his Foundation, as acting president of the University. At a June 1922 board meeting, on Rector's motion, the Board elected Longden as University Vice President and praised him for his work during Grose's absence.

Following Grose's resignation in 1924, the Board again made Longden acting president and Rector headed a search committee for a new president. Three months later Rector's committee proposed Rev. Lemuel Murlin to succeed Grose.

Rector had met Murlin first at a Methodist General Conference in Saratoga Springs in 1912 when they stayed at the same hotel there, and their friendship grew thereafter. Murlin was a DePauw graduate who had been president of Drake University in Kansas and of Boston University. His selection received unanimous Board approval.

Rev. Lemuel Murlin

HIS GREATEST FINANCIAL GIFT
COMES AT THE END

Rector kept furnishing further financial aid for DePauw programs along with his personal time and effort. By the time of his inauguration in 1919 of the scholarship program, with a gift valued at $1,069,000, he had already donated $1,000 toward construction of Bowman gymnasium, $200,000 to build Rector Hall and $50,000 to the University's endowment fund. In 1920, he was the first to subscribe to a $100,000 pension fund for teachers' retirement, contributing $10,000. In another University endowment drive in 1923, he donated $35,000. These amounts by 1923 totaled $1,365,000.

Correspondence relating to Rector's activities indicates he made further monetary and other contributions that were not recorded as he pursued his DePauw interests. He sent thousands of dollars worth of books, furnishings and supplies for Rector Hall, for the library and for other buildings, which the recipients did not know were coming until they were delivered. Town said he believed Rector's total gifts to the University before his death totaled at least $1.5 million.[26]

When Rector died of a heart attack in 1925 at age 62, his final great financial gift to DePauw was in his will. The document happened to have been freshly signed only about a month before his death.

In his will,[27] after some comparatively small secondary bequests, Rector assigned the remainder of his estate to the University. The will's total for DePauw came to more than $2.3 million. That included $150,000 for the teachers' retirement fund, $250,000 to build Lucy Rowland Hall and $250,000 to build Longden Hall.

The balance of the estate was for the Rector scholarship endowment itself. This balance was calculated at the time at around $1.7 million, more than $600,000 above the original 1919 bequest. That would bring Rector's total donation for the scholarship program to around $2.8 million.[28] Lucy Rowland Rector willed another $136,000 for the scholarships from her estate following her death in 1948.[29]

In sum, Rector's monetary gifts to DePauw added up to at least $3.8 million, and probably more – a huge sum for that era. Of this, slightly more than two-thirds was for the scholarship program.

The local newspaper, the Greencastle *Banner*, commented following the filing of Rector's will: "The immense amount of money Mr. Rector left the university was a genuine surprise in Greencastle. Some felt that he would make additional provisions, but probably only those who knew him best realized his complete interest in the school, which only could have brought his entire fortune, with small exceptions, to the university."[30]

***

Chapter 4

LUCY ROWLAND RECTOR

She was a "perennial queen, for whenever she visited the campus she was always surrounded by a group of Rector scholars and other admiring DePauw friends."
— DePauw President Clyde W. Wildman

George R. Grose, president of DePauw 1912-24, was closely associated with Rector's activities and wrote a short book about the great benefactor after his death. About Rector's wife, Lucy Rowland Rector, Grose's remarks were relatively brief, but he did say that "The spirit and magnitude of Edward Rector's benevolence would not have been possible had Mrs. Rector not cooperated sympathetically in all his plans."[1]

The marriage of Edward and Lucy took place in Cincinnati on Oct. 24, 1893.[2] Edward had moved to Chicago the year before to start a new law practice there, and therefore the couple established residence in the big city. Friends of the Rectors regarded them as a devoted pair and many enjoyed the Rectors' hospitality at their southside Chicago town home. Rector also took his wife on many trips.

Mrs. Rector was regarded as a gracious and proper lady. She was eight years older than her spouse, but she was not one to upstage him in the presence of others. In speaking of Edward to others, she referred to him formally and respectfully as "Mr. Rector." Edward likewise referred to her as "Mrs. Rector" in his conversations with others. She invariably supported his proposals in public.

In private, Rector apparently shared many thoughts with her because he generally seemed aware of her opinions. Lucy Rector for her part apparently had no problem in telling her husband "everything that is on my mind."[3]

A memorial for her in the *DePauw Magazine*[4] said the Rectors "had an intellectual comradeship, a oneness of purpose and an equality of social exchange which made their home life ideal. They had no children and this seemed to strengthen even further the bond between them."

Lucy Rowland was born in England on January 20,1855.[5] Details in the DePauw archives on her family life are sparse. The DePauw archivist provided the following response in 1976 to a Welsh inquirer, based on information from Mrs. Hazel D. Longden of Greencastle, a daughter-in-law of Henry Longden and longtime admirer of Mrs. Rector:

Lucy Rowland Rector

"Lucy Rowland came to America and directly to Cincinnati, Ohio from (we believe) the Isle of Wight when Lucy was in her teens. The mother ran a boarding house in Cincinnati and Lucy had a milliner's shop in their home.

"Edward Rector went to Cincinnati to Law School and lived in their boarding house. She did not marry him when he first asked her because Lucy and her mother were supporting her brother's orphaned children in Salt Lake City, Utah.

"There were three of these children, Mary, Lucy and Richard E. Jr. Mary Rowland married a Sweet – nephew of W. W. Sweet, a DePauw professor and he was a world famous brain surgeon. She lives in a suburb of Boston, Massachusetts. Lucy married a Mormon and lives in Salt Lake City, Utah. Richard E. Jr. went for a year or two to DePauw University but did not graduate."[6]

Rector's own unpublished and incomplete autobiography does not mention Lucy Rowland before their marriage even though it covers some years when he must have known her while he was studying and practicing law in Cincinnati. Nor does he speak of any other romantic attachments while describing numerous friendships made in his younger years.[7] He makes only a couple of references to "Mrs. Rector" in his memoirs[8] written later, and both references referred to mutually pleasurable visits with friends.

(Edward Rector's unpublished autobiography makes no mention of boarding with the Rowlands. He speaks of boarding during his first year in Cincinnati in 1882 with his aunt and uncle, the A. M. Stems. Then upon entering law school in 1883 he said he joined with a fellow law student in rooming together with "the family of a Mrs. Bonner, which consisted of herself and daughter and a brother and sister." He speaks of the two students working and studying diligently while rooming there until earning their law degrees in 1885. Rector does not refer further to his living quarters before moving to Chicago in 1892, nor does he speak of acquiring a personal residence in Chicago after arriving there.)

After the marriage, Hazel Longden described Edward and Lucy as inseparable and happy – "the only disappointment of their marriage was that they had no children of their own."[9]

When Edward Rector became interested in DePauw, Lucy was widely regarded as completely supportive of his DePauw activities, but not assuming a leading role. She modestly said she herself "had nothing to do with" originating the scholarship plan; "I was only happy that Mr. Rector had the wish to do it."[10]

She accompanied him to Greencastle on numerous occasions while he was alive. Thereafter, her health permitting, she made many appearances and/or statements in behalf of the scholarship program over the ensuing decades until she died two dozen years later. DePauw president Clyde Wildman remembered her as a "perennial queen, for whenever she visited the campus she was always surrounded by a group of Rector scholars and other admiring DePauw friends."[11]

A common stop for the Rectors during their Greencastle visits was at Rector Hall, the handsome girls dormitory built with Rector donations and named after Edward Rector's father Isaac. The couple would overnight at the building's guest accommodations.

The Rectors knew many of the female students by name. Any girl so greeted by the Rectors at Rector Hall was of course pleased and flattered.

Lucy Rector herself was the honored guest at a number of teas and dinners with the women of the dormitory. The tables were set with vases of yellow roses, her favorite flower and one that her husband had given to her for years.[12]

Winona Welch, a 1923 DePauw graduate and subsequent long-time professor at the University, said that when she entered college as a freshman in 1919 the then new Rector Hall had a reputation as a "Rector baby" because of the close attention given to it by the Rectors. Reservations for students living at the women's residence were much sought-after because it was rated as "one of the best dormitories in the middle west,"[13] and Welch managed to secure one.

"Mr. and Mrs. Rector came to the campus frequently to visit friends but especially to become better acquainted with the girls in Rector Hall," Welch said in recollections written years later. "Gradually, the expression Rector Baby was forgotten and all of us girls became Rector Girls because Mr. and Mrs. Rector adopted all of us, figuratively speaking, and we spoke of them, informally, as Daddy and Mother Rector. Their photographs were always on the mantle room in Rector Hall.

"Mr. and Mrs. Rector rarely missed Old Gold Day [an alumni homecoming day], May Day, and Commencement, on campus. We students looked forward with *much pleasure* and were *so thrilled* to greet them on every occasion.

"I can see them clearly in my memory as we girls waited for them to go into and out of the dining room with Miss Alvord [Katharine S. Alvord, dean of women], whose table was at the west end of the dining room. ... Mrs. Rector, as you well know, so gracious and charming and always wearing a smile and Mr. Rector with pleasing dignity, pride, and poise."

While she was self-effacing and unassuming in comparison with her husband in public appearances, Lucy Rowland's interest and support for DePauw and the scholar program was far from passive. One story told by a DePauw professor was that when he was new to the faculty he attended a

Katharine S. Alvord, dean of women at DePauw, 1915-36

social occasion in honor of the Rectors. As he was meeting Mrs. Rector, he of course called her by name and she, to his surprise, spoke his name. He asked her how she happened to remember his name. After joking briefly, she answered his question. She said she had studied the school yearbook, the *Mirage*, on the train all the way while coming to Greencastle from Chicago, so that she would be able to call by name the faculty and administration members as she met them at the reception.[14]

Edward Rector's unexpected death had a traumatic emotional effect on Lucy, which she kept suppressed in her public appearances. Her marriage and loving bond with her husband had been the center of her life. Grose in his diary told of stopping at the Rector home in the spring of 1926 during a cross-country return trip from a stay in China. In a March 30 entry, Grose said:

"What a welcome – sad but genuine from dear Mrs. Rector. She is indescribably stricken. I have never seen more pitiable grief. Now and again she breaks down in uncontrolable [sic] sobbing. And yet she is trying to be brave ... .

"Instead of going on to Greencastle, as I had planned, I stayed with Mrs. Rector. I could not leave her, she is so solitary."

The former DePauw president, by then a Methodist

Bishop, finally departed for Baltimore two days later but left his daughter Virginia, who had been traveling with him, behind with Lucy for a couple more days.[15]

Grose returned to Chicago in late May by train – "met by Mrs. Rector" – and spent several days at the residence working on correspondence and Rector files, for a forthcoming biography on Edward Rector.[16] On one of his evenings the widow hosted a dinner party at the house attended by, among others, Roy West and Chicago's Bishop Hughes. "Bp. Hughes spent the night with me at the Rectors," Grose recorded. "Fine evening. How I did miss my dear Mr. Rector ... ."[17]

The following day Grose noted that he "Took drive with Mrs. Rector. She is having hard time to be brave."

Grose was back in Chicago at the Rector house again a couple of times the following month, and found some relatives staying there - "Mary Rowland and her fine brother Richard from Salt Lake City."[18] The siblings were children of Lucy Rowland Rector's brother, Richard E. Rowland, whom she had helped in her earlier years. She also had Rowland cousins from England who had visited in 1920[19] but files do not show subsequent visits.

Helping with the Rectors' home life was a faithful housekeeper who immigrated from Sweden as a young woman around 1911. She remained with Lucy after Edward's death, through the rest of Lucy's lifetime, for some 38 years all told.[20]

Notwithstanding her grief after Edward's death, Lucy Rector continued to be interested and involved in the scholarship program, although not as a hands-on manager in her husband's style. Her contribution lay more in being available for consultation with the University leadership and as an inspirational image for the students when she visited the campus.

"She loved to come back to see people and how things were changing," said a DePauw alumna of 1918 who joined the University staff after graduation and recalled Lucy Rector's visits. "She never lost her love of the place."[21] In her later years and in poor health, Lucy no longer physically came to DePauw but she still kept in touch with its affairs.

Shortly after Edward Rector's death, DePauw's trustee board chairman Roy West and some others sought to persuade the widow to accept a seat on the all-male board on which her husband had served for so long. She demurred. It would have been uncharacteristic of her more backstage manner to take on such a role.

A discussion ensued at the first Board meeting after Edward Rector died, in September 1925, on the pros and cons of allowing women to serve on the Board. On the question of inviting Lucy Rector to serve, according to the Board minutes, "practically all felt that it would be an exceedingly courteous thing to do ... yet this was coupled with the feeling that she would decline to serve because of her belief that her husband would have opposed any such invasion." Therefore no official invitation was issued.[22]

However the University leadership continued to consult with Lucy Rector on major matters involving the scholarship program. She was named to the governing committee of the Foundation, succeeding her husband. The committee was headed by the University president and included the Foundation director and the comptroller. Available records do not show to what extent she personally attended its periodic meetings but West, fellow Chicagoan and longtime Rector friend, was often in touch with her. University president Murlin and Henry Longden, director of the Rector Scholarship Foundation, also stayed in communication with her.

In general, Lucy Rector took the position on pending scholarship issues that West and Longden "know better than anyone else" what her husband wanted done. She once told Longden, "I tell you and Mr. West everything that is in my mind as I used to tell Mr. Rector and I'm sure that you and he understand that I do not want to meddle now ..."[23]

She did keep up on campus developments, however, and

the leadership continued to consult her. For example, according to Board notes, in 1926 Murlin said he had Mrs. Rector's support in promoting Longden from secretary to director of the Foundation.[24] In 1928 West conveyed to the trustees Lucy Rector's agreement that Foundation holdings of Kellogg Switch-Board Co. stock, which had been donated by her husband, should be reduced.

In 1929 she volunteered a strong opinion against women smoking after reading a student opinion column in the DePauw newspaper. She wrote Longden that Edward Rector had an idealized view of women – he "placed woman on a pedestal" – that included an avoidance of smoking. She quoted Rector as once saying during a dinner table conversation with guests that "voluntarily, I do not associate with any woman who smokes."

She said that at another time her husband indicated he would be in favor of refusing residence in Rector Hall to any woman who smoked there or anywhere else. For herself, she said that since many colleges do allow women to smoke, why should any female smoker choose DePauw "whose ideals are higher?"[25]

In 1930 the committee awarding Rector scholarships wanted to know her opinion about some conditions in making the awards to women. As she put a question in a Feb. 17 letter to Longden, "should the *women* students receiving the fellowships pledge themselves to remain single for life – or for a long term of years?" She answered unequivocally: "I should say – certainly not – I can speak definitely not only for myself, but for Mr. Rector – we would not deny 'our girls' that which Mr. Rector and I both realized was the greatest happiness in life – moreover – the years training which they will receive and have earned – will undoubtedly be of service to them after they are married."

She added: "If it is *settled* in their mind – when applying for the fellowship that they intend marrying *soon* – I think that should be taken into consideration – I don't think that you should want them to take the money for an wedding trip or to marry within the year – " And she reiterated opposition to

Lucy Rector with picture of her husband, Edward.

female smoking, extending it to scholarship recipients: "When awarding the fellowships – I am very sure that Mr. Rector would not want a Fellowship given to any woman who smokes ..."[26]

Concerning the 1919-32 study showing that fewer than half of the Rector scholars who had matriculated actually graduated, and the financial difficulties impacting the scholarship program during the early 1930's (see Chapter 8), West wrote to DePauw president Oxnam that he had conferred with Mrs. Rector. "She feels that the scholars must be selected with greater care at this

Lucy Rector, center, in her later years, conversing with Dr. Henry Longden, on left. Robert Farber, later to become a dean at DePauw, is on the right.

time," West said. "She is quite willing for the number of scholars to be reduced during the depression. She will be glad, however, when we can admit one hundred annually, that having been Mr. Rector's plan. She does not object to the payment of higher tuition by the Rector Scholars than by the others provided that the Rector Scholarship Fund shall not be charged for the excess. As usual, she is in a reasonable frame of mind and wishes to cooperate in these strenuous times."[27]

After her husband's death Lucy Rowland Rector continued to live in the same spacious south Chicago brick town home where the couple had lived happily together over the years. The comfortable three-story edifice was located in Hyde Park[28] near the University of Chicago. She expressed sadness at reminders around the house of her bereavement, but she did not intend to move elsewhere. "A million dollars would not tempt me to sell this dear home," she said.[29]

The upscale décor at the Hyde Park residence included objects d'art collected by Edward and admired by guests. Lucy herself was so interested in the Art Institute of Chicago that she would drive visiting relatives and friends to the museum in her electric car.[30]

One of the most esteemed decorations at the Rector home was a display of cut glass in the built-in china cabinets of the circular dining room. Edward Rector's library with its books and leathered furniture was where he posted his map with the pins showing the hometowns of each Rector scholar.[31]

Another attraction was a large picture of Rheims Cathedral hung on a wall alongside a landing in the stairway. One visiting relative, Virginia Lyon, a cousin, recalled stopping to admire it as she was proceeding upstairs. Lucy took mental note of her cousin's interest and with typical generosity and thoughtfulness, bequeathed the painting to Virginia in her will.[32]

Lucy Rowland Rector continued entertaining at her home as a widow though less formally and less frequently. While she had household help, she liked to join in preparing the meals herself even though that could involve a lot of work. She maintained that "I was going to give up housekeeping when I couldn't serve my guests."[33]

Her niece Mary Rowland, who had visited periodically earlier from Salt Lake City, decided in 1930 to return to Chicago for a more extended stay.[34] Mary continued to provide companionship for her aunt in ensuing years.

Lucy Rowland Rector did a fair amount of traveling while she was still physically able, in addition to continuing her trips to Greencastle. Her correspondence indicates visits to her family in Salt Lake City and to Cincinnati. In the touring and recreation category were visits to the Boston area and to Europe.

She and her husband had gone to Europe in 1922. In the summer of 1929 she went again, this time with Mary. She said the food and service on the German ocean liner *Berlin* was good "but I did get tired of the German jabbering – the passengers were nearly all German." Places they visited included Geneva and Nurenberg. Counting the seagoing travel time, it was a long excursion. According to Lucy, Mary "loved the ocean trip, which was too long for me."[35]

Lucy Rowland Rector did a lot of letter writing from her home. By her own account, she arose early in the morning – 4 a.m. or earlier – and worked on her correspondence "before the house is stirring". Some of her letters are undated.

She had a chatty style and a habit of stringing her remarks out with dashes between thoughts, not separating sentences with periods or question marks. She told Longden, a major DePauw correspondent, "you have discovered before this that I never punctuate. I only *dash* – Mr. Rector used to make fun of me – but he didn't want me to change."[36]

Some of Lucy Rowland Rector's letter writing involved plans to re-inter her husband's body at the Greencastle cemetery plot bought shortly before his death. He was originally buried at Chicago's prestigious Oak Woods cemetery in 1925. The widow wrote to Longden about the style of lettering she wanted on the new tombstone and the location she preferred for Edward's grave and for hers alongside, where she was to be buried later.[37] Edward was reburied there in 1931.

Lucy Rowland Rector continued to journey to DePauw on special occasions during the 1930s and visit with students and University officials. A 1937 film of the school's centennial celebration shows her emerging from Longden Hall erect and smiling with West. She was then 82.

However the widow's personal travels to Greencastle dropped off years before her death as illness set in and she became increasingly homebound in Chicago. In responding to an invitation to a Rector Hall dinner in October 1942 she wrote to the Dean of Women, Helen Salzer: "I am better but not well. How I wish that I could be with you all. For the dinner. ... I am thinking that when I get a *lot* better – I'll just have a little visit – all my own at DePauw ... [signed] Lovingly yours, Lucy Rowland Rector"[38]

Letters became all the more important to her during her period of ill health. Some of her correspondence during this time was penned by others because, she said regretfully, of her "inability to write at present time".[39]

Sylvia C. O'Connor, a 1956 DePauw graduate, recalled Lucy Rector as "tiny, old, and frail" in her later years. A granddaughter of West, O'Connor and her sister, Louise Cannon Francis, a 1952 DePauw graduate, said West always called on Lucy Rector on Sunday mornings while on his way to nearby St. James Methodist Church. O'Connor's recollection of intriguing treasures at the Rector home was that of a stereoscope kept on the parlor table.[40]

Helen Salzer, dean of women at DePauw, 1936-43

Mrs. Rector continued to be listed on the Rector Foundation's governing committee until her death at her Chicago home on Nov. 6, 1949, at age 94.[41] She had recently sent greetings to DePauw through West on Old Gold Day that fall.

Services were held for Lucy Rowland Rector at the DePauw campus Gobin Memorial Church on Nov. 30. She was buried beside her husband at the Forest Hill cemetery in Greencastle.[42] The main beneficiary in her will was his scholarship program, which received $136,000.

***

Chapter

HENRY B. LONGDEN –
EXECUTOR EXTRAORDINAIRE[1]

"… the interests of the Foundation are inseparably bound to the best interests of DePauw."
– Henry Longden

I n his final will and testament, Edward Rector said the success of his DePauw scholarship program was "largely due" to Henry Longden. Rector's description was appropriate. Not only is the size of a donation important to an institution, but also what the gift accomplishes may depend heavily on how well it is administered. Rector – and DePauw – were fortunate to have as the first administrator of the program one of the outstanding figures in the history of the school.

While Rector himself was an impelling force in the early days of administering the scholarship program because of his intensive personal involvement, he died in 1925 while the program was still young. Longden was involved with the program from its start in 1919 as Secretary of the Edward Rector Scholarship Foundation. After Rector died Longden was appointed Director of the Foundation and he guided it energetically until he retired a decade later in 1935 at age 75.

Rector's passing did not alter the policy direction of the scholarship program. He and Longden were only three years apart in age – Longden was the older – and in pursuing the goals of the Foundation they shared in their commitment to excellence in education and in their compassion for those lacking means.

All told, Longden was linked to DePauw for 73 years beginning with preparatory school at Indiana Asbury. He served in many capacities including as acting president. Upon his death he was mourned as "DePauw's Grand Old Man." One of his most cherished posts was with the Foundation. Rector donated a dormitory in Longden's name that continued to function into the 21st century as a major University hall.

Henry Boyer Longden was born September 13, 1860, in Vevay, an Ohio River town in southeastern Indiana, the son of Samuel Longden and Sarah Boyer Longden.

Samuel Longden had immigrated to the American Midwest from England. He was a Methodist preacher whose ministries moved from place to place. Young Longden's upbringing therefore was in a religious family but itinerant. The family "lived in rapid succession in Moorefield, New Washington, Vienna, Carthage, Greencastle, St. Louis, Ind., Hope, Greenwood, Castleton and Milroy," Longden later recalled. "Father superannuated in the fall of 1875 and we moved to Greencastle."

Greencastle was of course the site of then Indiana Asbury, the leading Methodist college in the state. In 1875, at age 15, Longden enrolled in the preparatory school of Indiana Asbury. He had the financial advantage of living at home, but his family was poor. He saved $40 as a field hand for four months at a farm near Milroy, working for $10/month to bankroll his start at Asbury. Then as a student he worked at a variety of manual jobs to pay his college costs and stay on in school. He hired out as a laborer in building construction. He sawed wood, shoveled coal and worked as a field hand at harvest time.

ACADEMIC EXCELLENCE

Longden excelled scholastically from his first year at Asbury onwards. He graduated from the preparatory school in two years to enter the University where he studied four more years. He achieved high marks in science and also in languages. He won first class honors in German. He joined the Delta Kappa Epsilon fraternity in his junior year. He was a commencement speaker for his graduating class of '81. He later was awarded a Phi Beta Kappa key for academic excellence after the honorary fraternity established a Phi Beta Kappa chapter at DePauw in 1889.

Upon graduation Longden first was interested in becoming a physician. However he lacked funds to go to medical school.

An often-told story about Longden is that his career was literally decided by the toss of a coin. According to Longden, he and a fellow student set off from Greencastle with another student to earn money by selling books. As he later told one of his students, "When they [the two young men] came to a fork in the road, being hot and weary, and not too enthusiastic about their undertaking, they decided to toss a coin to settle whether they should go ahead, or return to town. The flip sent them back to town."[2]

When he returned home after the coin toss, Longden found waiting for him an offer by Indiana Asbury President Alexander Martin to teach Greek and science in the preparatory school at

$500 a year. That invitation "brought to me one of the happy moments of my life," Longden recalled. On September 21, 1881, just turned 21, he began teaching in his new job. That launched a career with the University that lasted for more than half a century, until his retirement from active service in 1935.

Alexander Martin

Longden immediately proved successful as a teacher. After a year as instructor in Greek and science, he was appointed as an instructor of Latin and given a $100 raise. He also did course work toward a graduate degree. For the following year, 1883-84, his teaching salary was increased to $800. He spent part of that on a summer trip to Amherst, Mass., his first venture to the East Coast. Besides doing graduate study at Amherst, he went sightseeing in such places as Boston, New York, and Old Point Comfort. The University, by then renamed DePauw, awarded Longden an A.M. degree in 1884.

By this time Longden was becoming well established as a member of the faculty of the College of Liberal Arts of the University. He was made adjunct professor of Latin in 1885-86 and an associate professor of Latin the following year, with a salary of $1,200 – double his pay of four years earlier. With his department head going on two years' leave, Longden was put in charge of the department. This assignment included teaching all the Latin classes in the absence of the department head.

In July 1886, at age 25, Longden married Mary Louise Johnson. The two had been sweethearts when they were youngsters in school at Greenwood, Indiana. The newlyweds spent the summer in Chautauqua, New York. Back on campus in September, the young professor plunged again into a heavy schedule of teaching plus administrative duties imposed by the sabbatical absence of his department head.

Longden also was showing skill as an administrator. In addition to his duties running the Latin department, he also was assigned to fill in as acting librarian for the school. Further non-teaching assignments went to him as his career advanced. Over time, his administrative talent carried him to the top ranks of the University leadership.

TEACHING GERMAN

While Longden was forging ahead in his career as a professor of Latin, his stronger academic interest was in German language and literature, a subject in which he had starred as an undergraduate. When his turn for a two-year sabbatical came up in 1888, he sailed with his wife for Germany. He studied the country's language and assimilated its culture. He enrolled in university courses first in Göttingen, then in Leipzig.

While in Leipzig in 1890 Louise gave birth to twins Beatrice and Grafton. Longden brought back from Germany a nurse and helper for his wife, who had been ailing. Shortly after their return to Greenwood in July, 1890, the twins took sick of cholera. Beatrice died.

The Longdens next moved to Greencastle, where the couple bought the first home of their own. The German nurse stayed on with the family for 17 years.

Longden resumed his work as a Latin professor following his return from Germany. In 1892 he was awarded the academic position he coveted most: chair of German Language and Literature. The position remained his primary appointment at DePauw for the rest of his career, until his retirement 43 years later in 1935.

While Longden's academic standards were high for himself and for his students, research and writing scholarship were not his prime interest. He may not have fared so well under a "publish or perish" regime at another university. Although he

Henry B. Longden in his office in the Studebaker Administration Building at DePauw University. Edward Rector's picture is in the background.

undertook further graduate studies over the years, among them at the University of Berlin and the University of Chicago, he did not pursue them to the extent of earning a Ph.D. degree. His one doctorate was honorary, bestowed by DePauw in 1925.

Ironically, a characteristic of Longden was lack of enthusiasm, bordering on disdain, for purveyors of advanced formal education. His diary comments about two of his professors at the University of Munich in 1897 provide an illustration. One professor, Longden wrote, "is learned and as usual with such men, dry as dust." He found the lectures of another professor to be "interesting," adding "he has some enthusiasm which is very rare among scholars."

RELATING TO STUDENTS

Henry Longden's strength lay in his love for teaching, rather than research, and fortunately for him and DePauw, the small liberal arts school provided both a setting for close contacts between professors and students and a broad interpretation of what constituted acceptable methods of teaching. He had a style and a personal interest in students that endeared him to successive generations of classes at DePauw.

A part of Longden's attraction for students came from his deliberately formal appearance and manner. His bearing was erect and trim. He was bald for much of his adulthood, but he nurtured a mustache with goatee as a facial trademark. His attire in public was at a minimum, businesslike, and as men's clothing fashions changed more than his over the years, his dress in later life could be described as "old-school gentleman."[3]

Typically he wore coat, tie, vest, white starched collar shirt, often a hat, and sometimes a pince-nez. Small wonder that as a professor of German, with his manner and his enthusiasm for German culture, his students nicknamed him "Der Kaiser."

In contrast to his formal attire, Longden's teaching manner was unconventional. While he focused on certain substantive aspects of the course at hand, he also sprinkled his lectures with personal observations delivered with a wry humor. He was disseminating his broader wisdom to his students along with the immediate subject. "Though he didn't realize it, Dr. Longden didn't teach Goethe so much as he taught Longden," was a description from a "Der Kaiser" pupil in the class of '27.[4]

Another alumnus, E. L. Olcott, '16, a grandnephew of Reuben Andrus, a Methodist pastor who was president of Indiana Asbury in the 1870s, was himself studying for the ministry and had no ambitions to become a German teacher. But he signed up "for two whole years of really tough work under Dr. Longden" because "I loved the man." Longden, he recalled, would say: "I don't feel like teaching German today. I want to talk about life." Olcott added: "Dr. Longden was to me, the prime example of that of which we stand in dire need today: Professors who can teach not only their subject, but life itself."[5]

Longden's advice on how to succeed in getting an education was summed up in a telegram he sent an entering student: "Choose men, not subjects; attend chapel daily."

A SENSE OF HUMOR

Longden's sense of humor was an important ingredient in his bonding with students. Displaying an irreverence for academic routine, he was known to show up for class without a book. Instead of calling roll, a student recalled that "Der Kaiser" might merely say: "If anyone isn't here this morning, let him speak up."

The same student, who credited Longden with making him a better-than-average pupil, remembered Longden including him among three in an advanced German class whom he told "I don't think you've earned an 'A', but I'm giving you one anyway."[6]

Longden was the personification of punctuality, except on a day when four tons of dynamite blew up at a local quarry. Longden had been sitting near a window at the time of the blast. Longden's bald head was gashed from splintering glass. He arrived at class late, wearing a skullcap, looking like a rabbi. The students tittered, but he took it in self-deprecating stride.[7]

On another occasion, a student waiter was serving a table at Longden Hall at which one of the diners was Longden, then age 70 and one of the most distinguished and dignified personages on campus. The building was named after him. It was a Saturday evening, and the young waiter was in a hurry to meet his date, so he spun around the table sliding the deserts at the guests rather than serving each carefully. The desserts were Dutch apple pie, with cream on top. Unfortunately the student server shoved too hard on Longden's dessert plate, which swooshed beyond the table's edge, landing upside down in Longden's lap. Longden "pushed back from the table and let loose a roar of laughter that could be heard all over both the dining room and the recreation room."[8]

A SENSE OF COMPASSION

Probably the single strongest link between Longden and the students was his compassion. Mindful of his own poverty when he came to Asbury, he was known to dig into his own wallet to tide over a penniless student. He was expert at finding jobs for those who needed them to stay on in school.

Students sensed that Longden was interested in them personally and in their problems, and that he was a good listener. Many are the alumni who recalled Longden as a father figure to whom they would go for advice on personal matters. They included the homesick and others with emotional disturbances of youth. Longden told of an incident in which a 220-pound football tackle came to his office, burst into tears, and said "I want my mother."[9]

In his 54 years on the faculty, Longden taught more than 5,000 students. Among them were many who went on to prominent careers, and one who became a member of his family. She was Hazel Day, class of 1916, a good pupil whom he would address (to her dismay) as "Fraulein Day" rather than using nicknames which he employed in calling on the men in the German class.[10] She graduated with *Phi Beta Kappa* honors, married his son, Grafton (class of 1913), and remained involved in DePauw activities.

Another student was Roy O. West, class of 1886, who took Latin under Longden before Longden became "Der Kaiser" professor of German. Longden "graded closely but fairly," recalled West, who later came to know Longden well during West's lengthy tenure as Chairman of DePauw's Board of Trustees.[11]

A DEPAUW TRADITION

Longden loved DePauw traditions. Over time, he became one himself. One of the Longden traditions was a welcoming chapel address he gave to all the students at the start of each new school year. He was an outstanding speaker and through the years the chapel was well-attended. He delivered this annual address for more than 50 years, continuing past his official 1935 retirement year until 1942.

Longden's longevity and the high regard in which he was held made him an authority on much of DePauw's early history. He personally knew DePauw's first graduate and 11 of DePauw's first 14 presidents.

Since Longden's time in Greencastle began well before DePauw acquired its name in 1884, the Longden "tradition" arguably predated the renamed school itself. By 1884 he was an established member of the faculty. One of the campus witticisms he enjoyed was that he had been there longer than anything else at DePauw except the monument to Bishop Robert

Roberts memorial

R. Roberts, who died in 1843 and was buried on campus.

Longden liked to talk about what he termed "the DePauw romance" that groomed youths for successful lives. Among his favorite examples were Sutemi Chinda and Aimaro Sato, Japanese students who were in Longden's class of 1881 at Asbury. They roomed in a garret room in return for doing janitor work. Upon returning to Japan, both rose to top positions in the Japanese diplomatic service including ambassadorships to the United States and other major posts, treaty negotiating assignments, and counsellorships in the Imperial Court.

Longden, who maintained personal friendships with his classmates, would cite this as a "DePauw Romance" with a rise from "janitor to Lord Chamberlain."

ADMINISTRATIVE SKILL

Longden's skill in administration and rapport with students, combined with his ability to work with the University leadership and faculty, kept him involved in important duties at the school through his long service. In addition to having served as a librarian, he also was appointed registrar early in his career.

In 1922 he was named vice president of the University, a post he retained for 13 years until his retirement. The position made him acting president during presidential vacancies in 1921-22 and 1924-25.

From the standpoint of DePauw's development, none of Longden's appointments was more important than that of director of the Rector Scholarship Foundation. The scholarship program and its huge funding were a major element in the school's life for years to come. As Longden put it, "the interests of the Foundation are inseparably bound to the best interests of DePauw."[12]

Roy West was chairman of the Board of Trustees at the time Rector made his historic donation in 1919. West said that

"When Mr. Edward Rector had established his scholarships, he [Rector] said, "Now who will look after my boys?' I said, 'Dr. Longden. He loves boys. He is an excellent student. He is patient. He knows human nature and boys. He is just.' Mr. Rector said, 'I will ask him to serve.'"

Longden accepted with enthusiasm and administered the Foundation with untiring dedication until his retirement 16 years later.[13] His active interest continued literally up to the time of his death in 1948 at age 88, when he was still listed as a member of the University Corporation Committee overseeing the Foundation.[14]

When Longden finally retired in 1935 at age 75, the turnout in his honor was on a scale rarely seen at DePauw. A special train carried alumni from Chicago to Greencastle for a memorable chapel at which he was made vice president emeritus and acclaimed as DePauw's Grand Old Man. Among notables attending were U.S. Supreme Court Justice Willis Van Devanter; World War I hero Maj. Gen. Omar Bundy; former U.S. Senator James E. Watson; David E. Lilienthal, head of the Tennessee Valley Authority; three former DePauw Presidents – Bishops Edwin Holt Hughes, Francis J. McConnell, and George R. Grose; and Edward Rector's widow, Lucy Rowland Rector.

***

Chapter 6

THE GRAND SCHOLARSHIP
PROGRAM BEGINS

"… I always afterwards had a notion that if I were ever able I would like to help some fellows to go to college who were in the fix I was in at that time."
– Edward Rector

Professor Henry Longden once asked Edward Rector, "when you get a little spare time," to set forth for historical purposes a fuller account of the origin and purpose of the scholarship program. Longden said he often had been asked "as to how you came to fix on this particular thing, and how long it was until you had the matter clearly established in your mind, and had made up your mind to establish the Scholarship Foundation."

It is interesting that Longden should have made this request in a letter to Rector dated September 30, 1922, more than three years after the undertaking began. Longden was present and very much involved in the official birth of the program in the spring of 1919. He had been Secretary of the Edward Rector Scholarship Foundation, created to administer the program, since its inception. He had innumerable contacts with Rector as its administrator and otherwise. In many respects, his views on aiding college education were similar to Rector's. Why would Longden feel a need for further explanation from the benefactor this long after the original gift?

One answer is that while Rector had put forward general

principles for the scholarship program, he originally left open many details on how they might be administered. Rector was willing to be flexible in its actual operation. The program would be fine tuned as it went along. Particularly since Rector was very much a hands-on donor, and the estimable Longden was in close consultation, Rector seemed to prefer some evolution of the program through practical experience rather than laying out all particulars in advance.

Further evidence of Rector's expectation of some future changes in program administration lay in the wording of his will.

Edward Rector Scholarship Foundation medallion

In bequeathing the remainder of his estate for "the purposes of the Edward Rector Scholarship Foundation," Rector gave Foundation authorities broad administrative leeway to offer scholarships to Indiana high schools "upon such terms and conditions as the authorities ... may determine, and also to enable such additional scholarships to be offered, either within or without the State, as those authorities may deem advisable."

Rector's DePauw philanthropies clearly were heavily motivated by his boyhood experience, his humanitarian urge and his substitution of DePauw's young people for the attention and affection he would have devoted to his children had he had his own. As to how he "came to fix on this particular thing," his concept took shape as his interest in DePauw grew. He had the wealth and was willing to apply it. With his lawyerly penchant for examining a case to see how his client might benefit most, the use of scholarships was an obvious option.

By 1919 Rector was gratified with the results from his first "investments" in the Greencastle school that started in 1914. These gifts included various sums for building projects and a loan fund for needy students. Next would come his grand donation for scholarships, which would be his response to the circumstances of his own boyhood that had denied him a chance to go to college.

What Longden called a "partial answer" to his request for a Rector explanation of the genesis of the program came in Rector's "Investment in DePauw" speech four months later, though he never received a full account. Rector said in that speech:

"When I graduated from the Bedford High School forty-odd years ago, nearly all of my class went off to college, at least we called it that, and considered it so, although the institution was not a college but the school then being conducted by Mr. Brown and Mr. Kinzie at Valparaiso, later known as Valparaiso University. I felt very much abused that I did not have the means to accompany my classmates, and I always afterwards had a notion that if I were ever able I would like to help some fellows to go to college who were in the fix I was in at that time. Finally the opportunity seemed to present itself, and this Scholarship Foundation at DePauw was established." (See Appendix A)

WORKING OUT "DETAILS"

Rector's plan was still evolving both before and after his announcement of his funding offer at an April 30, 1919, chapel meeting. He made that clear in a lengthy letter he wrote the following day to the University president, George Grose. "I have not worked the details of the matter out satisfactorily in my own mind as yet," Rector said, "and shall want to give it further and careful consideration in conference with you."[1]

Rector had offered to fund 100 full tuition scholarships a year. The focus was on students from Indiana high schools, but "details" remaining to be resolved were significant. He discussed them in his correspondence with Grose. Why should the scholarships be limited to men? How could the best scholars be attracted? How would the extra amount Rector proposed for a loan fund be handled? Would the scholarships be for one year or for four? Should the monetary amount of the scholarships be announced? Should their duration be dependent on student performance? How should the awards be distributed among the state's high schools?

Rector explained to Grose what he had in mind by proposing a $100 per year/per scholarship donation, when DePauw's tuition was $75 annually. The $25 "surplus" was not for distribution to each scholar, he said, but for a fund for aid to those scholars who could not afford books and incidentals. Rector expected fewer than one half of the scholars would need this aid, therefore leaving well more than $25 apiece for those who did. If this format were to be adopted, Rector said, it would be a mistake to announce an amount in connection with the Scholarships beyond saying it would cover all required college fees.

Rector believed the duration of each scholarship should be for four years, in order to attract the best scholars and keep them until graduation. However the continuance of a scholarship from each semester to the next should be made dependent "on the work and character of the student." Rector expected that half of each new 100 freshmen scholars would lose their scholarships some time after entering the college. "I suppose we probably would never have in the University more than approximately two hundred scholarship students," he said, but if by good fortune a larger number stayed through the four years, a "determined effort to take care of them in some way" would be made notwithstanding the extra cost above projections.

A more difficult issue was scholar selection. Indiana had 600 high schools in its 92 counties. One option Rector suggested would be to limit scholarships to the honor students in each high school. This might bring to DePauw 100 of the best from Indiana's high schools each year; but then, the actual number probably would vary widely, causing serious administrative problems. Another option would be to assign one scholarship a year to one high school in each of the 92 counties, with students in each school to compete for the award; the other eight scholarships would be awarded "as might seem advisable."

While in general the scholarships "should be awarded primarily, if not exclusively, on scholarship records," Rector told Grose, "we shall have to consider very carefully the ultimate plan and basis upon which the scholarship shall be awarded." As for timing of the initial awards, he added in a May 31 letter to Grose, "let's go slowly and carefully and surely in the matter, and work it out just right."

Indiana's 92 counties

Rector from the beginning was clearly uncomfortable with limiting the awards to men. He was hardly anti-feminist, having just donated to DePauw one of the finest women's dormitories in the Midwest. The handsome building, Isaac Rector Hall, was named after his father. Isaac Rector had been a trustee when the process of admitting women to the previously all-male Indiana Asbury, DePauw's predecessor institution, was underway.

Rector justified limiting the scholarships to men on grounds that women at DePauw largely outnumbered men, and that living quarters for women were still insufficient despite his gift of the new dormitory. The only gender-neutral policy in the scholarship awards would apply to students already enrolled: any one, male or female, achieving the highest grades in each of the pre-graduating classes – freshman, sophomore and junior – would qualify for a Rector Scholarship.[2]

While he did not mention poor male academic performance at DePauw, where women outdid men in achieving scholastic honors, Rector's presumption was that bringing in Indiana's brightest male students would do more toward raising the overall academic level than adding more women since the women were already doing well. Still, absent those two factors, he told the University president that "I should much rather make it a 'free-for-all', and thereby bring to the University the best scholars obtainable" based on "merit alone."[3]

A FOUNDATION CHARTER – BY LETTER

By the time of formal presentation of his proposal in a June 6, 1919, letter to the President and Board of Trustees, Rector had settled on enough principles and detail to set up a workable program, particularly since he himself would be active in supervising its implementation. The June 6 letter was promptly approved by the trustees and became a form of charter for administration of the Edward Rector Scholarship Foundation.[4] The "Foundation" itself was an administrative creation for carrying out the program, there appearing to be no evidence of its establishment as a legal entity.[5]

The key statement of purposes in Rector's gift letter was in the following paragraph:

"I have several objects in view in making this offer. One is to afford an opportunity to some of the young people of the state to secure a college education of the kind that can be had at DePauw, who might not otherwise be able to do so. Another is to bring into the University in each freshman class, a hundred of the brightest high school students of the State, with a consequent raising of the standard of scholarship in the University. Another is to link up and connect the high schools of the State with the University as closely and permanently as possible, for it is upon the high schools of the State that we must primarily rely for the future students of the University. Another is, by a wide distribution of the scholarships in all parts of the State, to create an interest in and active support of the university in some localities where it does not now exist."

To summarize the offer in scholarship terms:

- 100 "free scholarships" for attendance at DePauw would be "distributed among the High Schools" of Indiana each year.
- The scholarships would be awarded to the best male students in the graduating classes of the respective schools.
- Each scholarship would be for $75 a year, covering the cost of tuition charged by the University.
- Additional "incidental fees" which the University levies on students would be absorbed in the $75 tuition cost.

Also, a pool of money for loans to needy students would be made available from the scholarship funds. While the income from Rector's donation would amount to $100 per scholarship, $25 of each scholarship would be reserved for a fund for those who might be awarded a scholarship but lacked the financial means to take advantage of it.

The objectives were to:

- Provide for young Indianans, who might not otherwise be able to do so, an opportunity to get a good college education.
- Raise DePauw's scholarship level by bringing into each freshman class 100 of the brightest from Indiana's high schools.
- Link Indiana high schools with DePauw "as closely and permanently as possible," because the University would be relying on state high schools primarily for its future students.
- Create an interest in and support for the University in parts of the state where it did not currently exist.

Rector suggested in his letter to the trustees that perhaps up to a quarter of the Scholars would be dropping out of college, a more optimistic projection than his private projection of a 50 percent discontinuance rate made a month earlier. He also held out the possibility that if the plan worked well, he would add to his donation so as to increase the number of scholarships above 100 a year.

On the issue of awarding scholarships to men only, he again defended his conclusion "with some reluctance," citing an imbalance in the student body gender ratio and "overtaxed" living quarters for women. He said the policy was being established, "for the present and perhaps permanently," to help "reestablish an approximate equality in the number of men and women students at the University, while at the same time raising the standard of scholarship."

The goal of raising academic standards at DePauw was fundamental to Rector's proposal. The academic standing of male students, or lack thereof, during the war and immediately after was an "awful educational nightmare," according to Longden who had lived through this period at DePauw as a professor and administrator. "Scholarship on this campus and everywhere else, for that matter, was at a pitifully low ebb," Longden said. "The work had been so interrupted and broken that the students came up to the senior year without a modicum of the training that one about to graduate was presumed to have."[6]

Rector's emphasis on linking up with Indiana high schools was directed at a problem peculiar to DePauw at this time. The University's relationships with the public school system in Indiana, DePauw's primary area of supply for students, were at a low state. DePauw was a private school, with a reputation for elitism in some public school circles.

For example, high school graduates could enter state colleges without freshmen examinations but not DePauw; and even after agreeing to drop this requirement, DePauw still refused entry to those who could not pass a special exam in English and in reading Latin at sight. To further compound the issue, nearly all the public high school teachers in the state were graduates of state institutions, not DePauw. An impression was widespread that DePauw regarded itself as superior to the state schools and was unwilling to cooperate with them.[7]

THE SCHOLARSHIP PROGRAM GETS INTO GEAR

Rector and others in the University high command lost little time in moving forward with the grand project following trustee approval in June 1919. On July 25, an organizing committee met to arrange for officers and administrative process for the new Edward Rector Scholarship Foundation. Longden was appointed secretary as per Roy O. West's recommendation (see previous chapter).

The initial meeting was attended by all the officers involved – Rector, Grose, West, H. H. Hornbrook, and Longden – and it proved instrumental in setting operational policy and direction for the new enterprise in the years ahead. The typewritten minutes are preserved today in the DePauw archives on five small loose-leaf notebook pages.[8] For the public, an announcement was promptly issued to declare availability of the new scholarships: any male student with first or second standing in any high school graduating class in Indiana would be automatically eligible for an award. From schools in which the top two graduates did not apply, applications from any males in the upper 10 percent could be submitted for consideration.

President Grose was already on the path to recruiting scholars even before the program was approved by the trustees and officially instituted. While not knowing what the specific ground rules would be for scholarship awards, he sent letters to Indiana high schools saying a "limited number" of "free scholarships" would be available at DePauw for Indiana high school male honor students that fall. He invited personal applications from the students through their schools.

The original class of Rector Scholars enrolled in 1919. Henry Longden stands in the rear.

Neither Grose nor Rector expected a large list of applicants the first year. The timing of the formation of the Foundation was late in the season for entries in the upcoming 1919-20 school year, and few male students stood at the head of their class in Indiana high schools. This did not concern Rector, who was more interested in getting off to a sound start than in speedy initial recruiting success.

As it turned out, 48 applicants were accepted as the first round of Rector Scholars enrolled at DePauw in September 1919. A subsequent survey showed that all but six of the 48 could not have attended college without such aid, and that the students went on to distinguish themselves in many fields after leaving DePauw.[9] (See Chapter 12)

Detail of pin given to Rector Scholars.

RECTOR DEVOTES HIMSELF PERSONALLY
TO THE PROGRAM AND "MY BOYS"

In discussing administration of the scholarship program in the immediately ensuing years, it cannot be stressed too much the extent to which Rector personally applied his own time, energies and supportive attention to the undertaking and to the young men it brought to DePauw. A subsequent DePauw president, Lemuel H. Murlin, said that "while Mr. Rector was living, he was practically Director of the Rector Scholarship Foundation; Mr. Longden was Secretary."[10]

Not only was Murlin's statement about Rector's role in the Foundation true in an administrative sense, but also Rector's contributions were far beyond that of Foundation manager. In addition to what time he could spare, Rector gave away much of his wealth to the Foundation during his lifetime, and in the end, after his death, the entire remainder after certain bequests in his will.

Rector devoted himself personally to the program in a measure rarely seen from large financial benefactors. While Rector still carried on an active legal practice, his philanthropy was becoming his highest interest, and the students winning Rector Scholarships were becoming his family. He was immersed in the program both generally and in person. In this embracing of "my boys" at DePauw and afterwards, he was fully joined by his wife, Lucy Rowland Rector.

Rector's personal interest in each scholar started from the time the student was picked by DePauw. After receiving word of the boy's selection, Rector would send him a letter of welcome along with a booklet entitled "Should Students Study?" stressing the value of a college education.

As Rector put it in a typical letter to the newcomer, "I am old-fashioned enough to still believe that the main purpose for which a young man should go to college should be to get an education, and that an education of the right sort cannot be had without hard work and diligent and conscientious study ... the vast majority of the really successful men of the world are those who have done good work and attained high scholarship in school and in college ... The Edward Rector Scholarship Foundation is intended to be exactly what its name implies, a Foundation for Scholarship, and its success and usefulness will be measured by the degree to which that end is attained. I earnestly hope, therefore, that you will come to the University with a firm resolve to make the highest and best use of your scholarship of which you are capable."[11]

At his Chicago home Rector kept a map of Indiana with pins showing the home towns of all Rector Scholarship holders. The Scholar's class in school was indicated by the color of the pin head – for example, green for freshmen, blue for sophomores.[12] In time Rector came to call it a "porcupine" map because of the increasing number of pins each year, and he had to increase the map sizes.[13]

During his automobile travels if he passed through one of the Scholars' home towns, he would stop to visit with the Scholar's parents and have a friendly discussion on how the Scholar was doing in school.[14] When he went to Greencastle, which was several times a year, he not only met with the University leadership but he also particularly enjoyed associating with the students. He made a special point of chatting with his Scholars, many of whom he could call by name.[15] Customarily each fall, he enrolled symbolically as a DePauw freshman and attended the semester's first chapel service.[16]

Rector followed the Scholars' progress in part by keeping with him a little pocket notebook. In it he kept track of the grades of each scholar each semester. His record-keeping was so meticulous that he would note absence of some grades in the data provided him by the Foundation.[17] To the extent he had time, he would commend personally those who did well and console those who did not.

CONCERN FOR THOSE STRUGGLING – AND ENCOURAGING THE SUCCESSFUL

Rector was particularly concerned about those who did not maintain the grades required to keep their Scholarships, and perhaps were leaving college as a result. He once told Longden: "It is perhaps more important that I should write a letter of interest and encouragement to the boys who failed to make the required grade than that I should write letters of congratulation to those who distinguished themselves."[18] Sometimes he consulted also with parents too about their son's scholastic troubles.

For those successful in school, a letter from Rector would convey his pleasure and encouragement. To a senior about to graduate with the first class of Rector Scholars, Kenneth Buchanan, he wrote:

> "I well remember the occasion of my first meeting with you – when I dropped in to Crawford's for a piece of pie on arriving at Greencastle too late for luncheon – as well as the fact that you were the first one of the scholarship students whom I met. I have watched your work during the succeeding years with special interest, even if I have not seen you as often as I should have desired, and have been greatly pleased at the fine record you have made. Professor Longden tells me that you are going on with your work when you leave DePauw, and my interest and good wishes will follow you."

In a humorous way, Rector referred to A. Dale Allen as "high" man among his scholars because, enrolling in the original class of 1919, Allen was listed first alphabetically. At one point Allen decided to take a year off from college, and Rector was unable to persuade him otherwise. However Allen did return to graduate in 1924 and went on to a successful career thereafter, as

Certificate of Scholarship

THIS IS TO CERTIFY THAT DALE ALLEN

OF GREENSBURG, INDIANA HAS BEEN GRANTED A SCHOLARSHIP
ON THE

EDWARD RECTOR SCHOLARSHIP FOUNDATION.

ON PRESENTATION OF THIS CERTIFICATE TO THE TREASURER, OF
DePAUW UNIVERSITY, CREDIT WILL BE GIVEN FOR ALL REGULAR TUITION
AND FEES IN THE COLLEGE OF LIBERAL ARTS.

THIS CERTIFICATE IS VALID FOR EIGHT SEMESTERS, PROVIDED IT IS NOT RECALLED BY
THE STUDENTSHIP COMMITTEE. THIS COMMITTEE RESERVES THE RIGHT OF RECALL AT THE END
OF ANY SEMESTER.

(SIGNED) *George R. Grose*
PRESIDENT

DePAUW UNIVERSITY

September 9, 1919.

Henry B. Longden
SECRETARY

*Rector Scholarship certificate for A. Dale Allen, "high" man among the
original class of 1919 because he was listed first alphabetically.*

noted in the final chapter.[19]

Rector did not live long enough to follow the progress of
his Scholars' post-college careers for any extended period. He
died in 1925 – shortly after the third class graduated.

In the time he had, he was as interested as any parent in
job success for his boys. In some cases he paid the hotel bills
for graduated Scholars who had come to Chicago, until they
found employment.

Rector's business contacts could open doors for the young
graduates. In one example, he recalled that the president of
the Standard Trust and Savings Bank in Chicago stopped by
his table during lunch to praise a young Scholar graduate who
had recently joined the bank. He quoted the bank president
as saying, "Well, if you have any more like Barth [the DePauw
graduate] you can send them along to me – I can use them."
Rector added, in a letter to Longden, that "it is certainly very
pleasing to see how each of our fellows who makes good opens
the way for others to follow."

AIDING THE NEEDY

Complementary to Rector's personal devotion to his scholar family was his compassion generally toward financially strapped young people entering and in college. Before launching his grand Foundation venture, he had been active in promoting a loan fund for needy students. The Edward Rector Fund, as it was called, prospered as a revolving fund over the years with students repaying their low-interest borrowings on schedules of their own choosing. Rector's similar accommodation for needy Rector Scholars put $25 per scholarship annually into a revolving loan fund available to any Scholar needing financial aid.

Rector's promotion of the two financial-aid funds are one answer to arguments that he overstressed scholarship, accompanied by "character," as the basis for the Rector Foundation selections, with no consideration of an applicant's need for financial assistance as a criterion for an award. "The scholarships are awarded upon the basis of scholarship and character, and nothing else," he said in his principal speech reviewing the program.[20]

He noted in this speech that many of the Scholars – in one informal sampling, one-half of them – could not have afforded to enroll at DePauw but for the Scholarship. Under his scenario, those not academically successful enough to win or maintain a Scholarship could receive financial assistance from another Rector-aided fund, while Scholars without means could borrow from the pool set up by the Foundation. At its inception a rule had been laid down that the student could borrow no more than $100 a year, for a potential total of $400 over four college years.

No one familiar with Rector's dealings with young people could doubt his empathy for those who were poor. The story which touched him most was Longden's account of a young Scholar who had come to the Foundation director to ask if it would be justified to borrow money from the loan fund to buy an overcoat. The student had not had one in high school, but when he came to DePauw he found most men there owned overcoats. Longden paid him $24 out of University funds to buy one. In another instance, Rector fully approved of a Foundation loan made to a student to pay for a surgical operation.

To make the financial assistance available under a wide variety of circumstances, some unforeseeable, Rector favored giving the director broad discretion to make his own judgment. He once wrote to Longden: "We did not attempt to formulate any definite rules and regulations when we started it [the Loan Fund], but have felt our way along as it progressed, and the results have been so exceedingly gratifying, and so far beyond our highest anticipations, that I think we should continue the administration of it as far as possible without arbitrary rules and regulations, leaving it as flexible as possible to meet conditions and developments as they arise."

Rector in fact was surprised and disappointed that the scholarship loan fund was not used more.

After two years, Rector wrote Longden that while he had originally feared demands on the loan fund would place a greater burden on his finances than he anticipated, so far "exactly the opposite" had happened. He felt that needy scholars had been burdened with too much outside work to earn money, instead of taking advantage of the subsidized loans.

Two years later, in a 1923 letter to Longden, he was still of this opinion. "I am surprised that the aggregate amount of the loans is not larger than it is," he said. "I should not feel at all concerned if, with 400 or 500 scholarship students on Campus, the aggregate amount of loans should ultimately reach two, or even three times the present amount of them."

The amounts did in fact increase as college costs went up. From $5,488 in 1921-22, Scholar borrowings from the fund climbed each year to $11,398 by 1924-25. By then the total funds distributed since inception had reached $34,932, of which

$18,763 had been repaid and $16,170 was still outstanding.[21]

WOMEN, OUT-OF-STATE SCHOLARS, BOOKWORMS AND PICKING A UNIVERSITY PRESIDENT

Notwithstanding his original "reluctant" adoption of a male-only policy in awarding scholarships for incoming freshmen, and subsequent reaffirmations of that policy, Rector took delight when women won scholarships under the one exception to the men-only rule – the provision for scholarships for students ranking first in their college class scholastically, regardless of gender. These awards did not detract from the number of men who might be coming to DePauw under his Scholarship program, and they reinforced his emphasis on academic excellence.

Women began winning Rector scholarships early in the

Edith M. Richards, pictured front row center, was the first Rector Scholar to graduate.

Rector Scholars program. In the first year after the original entering class of 1919, Edith M. Richards, of New Castle, Ind., made the highest grades in the class of 1921. She was a senior, thus graduating two years ahead of the first all-male Rector class. Since she no longer needed tuition payments, she was given $100 cash as her Rector scholarship award.[22]

A Rector award during the 1920-21 academic year also went to a woman then a sophomore, Harriet Geiger, of Hartford City, Ind., for winning top honors in her class. She graduated

Lucy Rowland Hall, also a handsome women's dormitory, built adjoining Rector Hall in 1928 under a donation from Edward Rector's will. Rector named the residence hall after his wife.

in 1923 with Phi Beta Kappa honors after a distinguished undergraduate record including Mortar Board membership and class secretary. Two other women with subsequent Rector awards also graduated that year.[23]

Rector was disappointed when he did not have female Rector Scholars on campus. According to Longden, Rector was hoping that some other donor might step in with scholarships for women. This was not to be, though Rector continued to help them in other ways. His will included $250,000 for an additional women's dormitory, to be named Lucy Rowland Hall after his wife.

Meanwhile the males-only policy on scholarships for new students soon proved successful in its goal of helping to reduce the gender gap of the immediate postwar period when the women on campus substantially outnumbered men. Before the Rector fund started in 1919 women outnumbered men by a ratio of 2-1. By the 1921-22 school year, more men were enrolled than women, and by 1929 men outnumbered women by a ratio of 2-1.[24]

The Foundation also was awarding scholarships to men already on campus. In 1920-21 it offered Scholarships for the 10 freshmen who ranked highest in their class exclusive of existing

Longden Hall, a men's dormitory built in 1927 under a bequest in Edward Rector's will, was named for Henry Longden, a longtime DePauw administrator and devoted manager of the Rector Scholarship program.

Rector Scholars. In subsequent years, it awarded Scholarships to freshmen achieving grades at the honors level. The practice waned in later years when funding for the scholarships tightened.[25]

The question of geographic distribution of scholarships also kept arising. While the express goal of Rector's original proposal was to award scholarships to students from Indiana, it did not rule out students from other states.

As time went on, Indiana counties were not supplying enough applicants who could fill the requirements for available Rector scholarships. Over the first three years two non-Indiana applicants were accepted from contiguous states. Thereafter the number of out-of-state Scholars increased substantially, particularly after more funds entered the program following Rector's death.

Rector's acceptance of out-of-state awards was consistent with what he regarded as DePauw's natural source of supply for students; he favored high schools in nearby cities, such as Cleveland, Columbus, Cincinnati and Louisville, which he viewed as sufficiently proximate to be considered as "tributaries" to Indiana colleges.[26] In his will written in June 1925 shortly before his death, he still wanted a Rector scholarship to be made available to every high school in Indiana, but he also favored such additional scholarships "either within or without the State," as the Foundation's administrators "may deem advisable."[27]

As for extracurricular activities by "my boys," Rector had been concerned when they first started arriving on campus that they would suffer an image as bookworms with little interest beyond studies. That concern soon proved unfounded. As the number of scholars grew, so did their presence on athletic teams and in the other campus pursuits outside the classroom.

For example, the 1925-26 annual report of the Rector Scholarship Foundation said 10 of 15 of DePauw's football lettermen were Rector Scholars, as were six of the eight on the basketball team, and 15 of 16 on the track team. The captains of all these teams were Rector Scholars.[28]

Rector liked to tell of one of his Scholars, Rufus Scales, a farm boy from southwestern Tennessee, who was working in Greencastle during summer vacation to earn money for the next school year. A carnival came to town with a professional wrestler who offered $5 to anyone who could throw him. Scales succeeded, though "it took me sixteen minutes to throw him, and I was pretty tired when I got through." Word of Scales' strength persuaded a local cement mill manager to give him a summer job at the then-handsome rate of $25 or $30 a week.[29]

Aside from the scholarship program, Rector was proud of DePauw graduates from wherever they came. As with Longden, among his favorite examples were those of two Japanese graduates of the class of 1881, Sutemi Chinda and Aimoro Sato, who went on to distinguished diplomatic careers for their country.

RECTOR'S UNEXPECTED DEATH A SHOCK

Because of his vigorous participation in University affairs both in the Scholarship program and as an active trustee, Rector's unexpected death caused far greater shock in Greencastle than had he been absent since his major bequest a half dozen years earlier. The mourners at his massive memorial assembly focused on the greatness of the man and his contributions to DePauw. A subsequent tribute from L.E. Mitchell, DePauw publicity director, which appeared in the *Western Christian Advocate*, typically pointed to Rector's personal role in the scholarship program. It said:

"The [Rector] plan was put into operation with 48 Rectors in the fall of 1919, and from that hour Mr. Rector himself was on campus in spirit all of the time, and in person whenever his important duties in Chicago would permit him to bring Mrs. Rector to meet his boys. He knew each young man by name, where he came from and what were his ambitions and plans for the future; he helped many graduates to find good positions; he sent copies of good books to be distributed to all members of the Foundation, and in every way showed his deep personal interest in his gift."

BUT THE PROGRAM CONTINUES TO ADVANCE

Yet the impact of Rector's death on continued progress of the Scholarship program was mitigated by some important factors.

One was the extent of institutionalization of the program that had taken place over its first six years. Systems for selecting those eligible, awarding the Scholarships and administering them in operation had been developed and were maturing further with each year of experience. While certain of Rector's personal practices – such as symbolically "enrolling" himself as a DePauw freshman each year – died with the death of the benefactor, other activities supportive of the program were continued and new ones begun.

For example, Rector and his wife had an annual campus reception for Rector Scholars. The Rectors had last received the Scholars at this yearly affair on April 23, 1925. The annual event continued for a number of years thereafter with Lucy Rector attending. And with the growing total of graduated Scholars, alumni activities were getting underway, including formation of a Rector Alumni Association and introduction of a newsletter named *The Rector Record.* (See Chapter 10)

Another major factor in program continuity was the continued full-scale devotion by Longden as its administrator and University vice president. Longden's title with the Foundation had been "Secretary." In 1926 President Murlin recognized Longden's dedication to the program by proposing, with trustee approval, that with the departure of Rector, Longden's title now be changed to "Director" of the Foundation.[30] Lucy Rector also continued personal and active support for the Scholars for years thereafter.

What would change radically following Rector's death were funding aspects of the program, as noted in ensuing chapters. While there was a substantial increase in scholarship moneys from Rector's will, control passed from his hands in Chicago to the DePauw administration and trustees in Indiana. And when particular problems or projects arose on campus with a need for financial remedy, Rector was no longer on the spot to pull out his wallet.

ASSESSING THE SCHOLARSHIP PROGRAM

There is no doubt that Rector himself regarded his scholarship program as an outstanding success. As he put it after the first four years, "the experiment has proved satisfactory and successful beyond our highest anticipations."[31] He had reports that the Rector Scholars had made scholarship fashionable on campus, tending to raise the academic standards throughout the student body, and that by taking leadership roles in extra-curricular activities Scholars had dispelled fears that they were bound to books.

Following Rector's death impressive statistics were cited on what the program had achieved during his lifetime. As of the last scholastic term before his death in the summer of 1925, the student grade level at DePauw averaged 47.4 credit points. This was more than double the 20.8 point average for the University's student body in the year before the Foundation was established at the start of the 1919-20 year. In 1918 five students out of a class of 86 graduated *cum laude*; in 1925, out of 244 graduates, 104 earned *cum laude*. Of the 244, 109 went into graduate studies, compared with 20 percent or less in earlier years.

And of course, because of the Scholarship program, DePauw's great leap in scholarship was among men, who

David E. Lilienthal

previously were well behind DePauw's women students in academic achievements. Men's grades on average rose above those of women by 1925. A fraternity, not a sorority, had the highest scholastic standing among the Greek units. Two-thirds of those elected to the scholarship honorary, *Phi Beta Kappa*, were men.

A few months after Rector's death an assessment of the impact of the program on scholarship at DePauw was penned by David E. Lilienthal, who himself in later years became one of DePauw's famed alumni in roles such as chairman of the Tennessee Valley Authority and of the Atomic Energy Commission. Lilienthal was a senior on campus when the first Rector Scholars arrived in 1919.

Lilienthal recalled that the Scholars initially were coolly received because of their lack of more popular credentials, such as athletic prowess. They had come with financial backing "simply because they had led their fellows in the wholly incidental and irrelevant matter of studies!", Lilienthal said in an essay entitled "Making Scholarship Popular."[32] But Longden as a highly respected "father confessor" to many DePauw students, and Rector's active participation, held the Scholars to their scholarship goals and gave the program momentum by the end of the first year.

Lilienthal's assessment was that the momentum continued to grow, given further impetus by more Scholars arriving each year, with scholarship becoming a campus badge of honor. The Scholars showed one could be a good student academically and at the same time enjoy other aspects of college life.

"Today their spirit completely dominates the college," Lilienthal said. He concluded, "It is, of course, too early to prophecy as to the future of the Rector Idea. The facts of accomplishment cannot be denied: in seven years it has wrought a scholastic revolution upon a typical campus; it has created a general interest in scholarship; it has gone very far in overcoming undergraduate hostility to the notion of scholastic achievement as a worthy ambition. It has done what other scholarship schemes have been unable to do: *create a tradition favoring scholarship* which is able to compete successfully with the athletic tradition, the 'campus activity' tradition, and the 'college-life' tradition."

***

Chapter 7

A DECADE OF UPS – THEN DOWNS

",,, the scholarship program continued to flower during the Roaring '20s with money being a limitation mainly in the eyes of those who would like to spend more of it."

The death of Edward Rector in 1925 removed the financial benefactor, the spiritual father and the active superintendent of the scholarship program. But enough had been achieved institutionally over its first half-dozen years to assure that the venture would move forward; and with the energetic Henry B. Longden continuing as dedicated foster father, more years of vigorous use of Rector's philanthropy were to be expected. Lucy Rector remained actively involved. Rector's old friend, Roy West, could be counted on for strong support as president of DePauw's Board of Trustees.

The first year following Rector's death saw further growth in Scholarships. Longden noted in his 1925-26 annual report on the Foundation that with the fall semester there were 510 Rector Scholars on campus, 35 more than any previous year. The incoming freshman class had 170 Rectors, far above the 100 that was Rector's initial target number. There were 149 sophomores, 113 juniors and 78 seniors.

The impact of the program at DePauw was so great that the college almost seemed like a "Rector school," at least as far as the male student body was concerned. The group's academic credentials were, by definition, excellent because good grades were required to receive a scholarship and also to retain it after entry. Longden reported that all of the 77 men on the mid-year honor roll were Rector Scholars. All of the 18 men elected to Phi Beta Kappa in the year, were Rector Scholars.

Among other activities of the Scholars, Longden, as had Rector, took delight in reciting their athletic achievements. The Scholars were not to be tainted with an image of involvement with books and little else. Rectors captained all of the varsity squads that year and provided many of the best players.[1]

While saying that Rector's will added about $1.1 million to the endowment, doubling it to $2.2 million, Longden nonetheless regretted that "the increased income will little more than take care of the increase in tuition." He said it "will not permit the carrying out of the plans for the Foundation cherished so long by Mr. Rector and those in charge."

Longden apparently was referring to their hope for granting scholarships to "deserving applicants" well beyond the 100 annually for Indiana high school honor graduates, the primary purpose of Rector's original donation. "The number of applications is increasing rapidly with the years making it necessary to refuse each year a still larger number and draw the lines still closer," Longden said. He expected this trend to continue as the Foundation became better known and the expense of a college education increased.

THE PROGRAM SOARS

Notwithstanding such concerns the scholarship program continued to flower during the Roaring '20s with money being a limitation mainly in the eyes of those who would like to spend more of it. By the summer of 1928 the 240 scholarships awarded to incoming freshmen marked a new high. When these freshmen awards were added to the 350 upper classmen already holding scholarships, the possible total of Rectors on campus for the 1928-9 year was nearly 600, half again larger than the 400 envisioned in Rector's original proposal. At this point the scholarships were valued at $1,000 apiece, paying all tuition and fees for the four years at $250 a year.[2] The following year a still higher record was set, with 270 new scholarships granted.

The actual numbers of scholars on campus were always somewhat lower than the total scholarships awarded, for various reasons. Some recipients of the scholarships decided not to come to DePauw. Some left during the school year or lost their scholarships because of failure to maintain the necessary grades. Some were on leaves of absence. The actual count for Rectors in attendance at the opening of the 1928-29 year was 540.[3]

As of the start of the 1926-27 year following Rector's death there were 230 Rector graduates, a number which would be growing annually. The spirit of the scholarship program was enhanced by the formation of the Rector Scholar Alumni Association. Chapters of the Association were formed in several major cities and held periodic gatherings locally.

In Greencastle a reunion of the Scholars and a banquet were held each year at commencement. Typically the honored attendees were Lucy Rector, West and Longden. The first Tuesday in November was fixed as Rector Day on campus.[4]

At Longden's suggestion, the graduates in 1927 began publishing *The Rector Record*. It was a chatty newsletter intended to "keep alive ... the personal element, the memories of old association with each other and with Mr. Rector."[5] Its first editor was Coen G. Pierson, a graduate among the original Rector Scholars enrolling in 1919 who went on to a distinguished career as a DePauw history professor.

Coen G. Pierson

Several other Rector graduates from the class of 1923 also joined the DePauw faculty. Samuel T. Hanna managed the DePauw Bookstore and taught at Greencastle High School. William H. Strain served on the English department staff before going to Indiana University. Harold Robbins became DePauw treasurer.[6] Many other Rector graduates served the University with distinction in teaching and administrative positions in subsequent years.

Starting with the original 48 Rector Scholars who entered in September 1919, by the end of the first decade of the program there were 434 Rector graduates. The geographic distribution of awards, their number, their monetary value and their scope all had expanded greatly beyond the 100 annual scholarships for Indiana high school students worth $400 for a four-year attendance at DePauw, which Rector had originally proposed.

Illustratively, as of the fall semester in 1929 there were 524 Rector men on campus – 215 freshmen, 130 sophomores, 89 juniors and 90 seniors – whose full-tuition scholarships were valued at $250 a year, up to $1,000 over a full four years. There were two women who won Rector Scholarships in post-freshman years by standing highest in their respective classes. While the largest contingent of the Scholars, 86, came from the 92 counties in Indiana, they comprised less than one sixth of the total. The others came from nine other states and from several foreign countries. The first recipient of a Rector award outside the continental United States was Peter Hyun from Lihue, Hawaii, in 1929. He was soon followed by scholars from Austria and Korea[7] and in later years from around the world.

LONGDEN'S GRANDER VISIONS

Meanwhile Longden's visions for Foundation activities on a grander scale were taking shape. A new feature added in 1929 was a scholarship to be offered each year to the American School of Japan, located in Tokyo, and

Left, Edward Rector at twenty-one, as a law school student in Cincinnati.

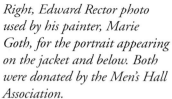

Right, Edward Rector photo used by his painter, Marie Goth, for the portrait appearing on the jacket and below. Both were donated by the Men's Hall Association.

"Edward Rector" (1863-1925)
by Marie Goth (1887-1975)
Presented by Men's Hall Association, 1928

Right, Plaque in Bedford, Ind. at Rector's birth site; below, Edward Rector playing golf with Harvey S. Firestone, founder of the Firestone Tire and Rubber Co.

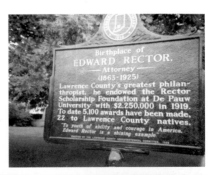

Above, Lucy Rector; at left, left to right, Roy O. West, Lucy Rector, Henry B. Longden.

Rector Hall first floor drawing room.

Rector Hall dining room was capable of seating 275.

A 1908 snapshot of the Rector's home at 4917 Greenwood Avenue in Hyde Park Station, Chicago (left) and the house (right) as photographed in 2008. See Chapter 2, page 48.

The Lemuel H. Murlin inauguration in 1925 brought together top row, left to right: Edward Rector; Bishop Frederick Leete of the Indiana Methodist Episcopal Church; Roy O. West, president of the board of trustees; seated, left to right: Vice-president Henry B. Longden and new president Lemuel Murlin.

Henry B. Longden

to the American School in Shanghai. These institutions provided pre-college education mainly to children of Westerners living in those countries.[8]

With what he called a "surplus" of Foundation money available, Longden was especially enthusiastic about increasing graduate work being done by the Scholars. A study of Rector graduates in 1921-23 through 1929 showed nearly half – 229 of 540 – had attended or would enter graduate school.[9]

A special post-graduate Rector Fellowship for graduating DePauw seniors, men or women, to study elsewhere at home or abroad, was introduced in 1929. There were to be six of these "traveling fellowships" bestowed annually. The stipends were $1,200 and good for one year. They were to be available to outstanding graduates to pursue further study in their chosen fields.

The first of these postgraduate awards were granted to a half dozen Rector Scholars in May 1929. Three of the fellows went to European universities and three to American universities.[10] The program was discontinued in 1935 under financial pressure during the Great Depression.

In his 1930-31 report as Foundation director, Longden floated the idea of a Rector-type scholarship program for women, perhaps more wistfully than pragmatically because there was no accompanying proposal for funding. After noting that all of the new Phi Beta Kappa men were Rector Scholars, he reported that there were now four women on campus who had won Rector Scholarships by ranking first in their classes academically – a senior, two sophomores, and one freshman – with "an exceedingly high" average grade of 2.792 on a 3.0 scale. "The high character of their work only shows what a splendid thing it would be to have a Foundation corresponding to the Rector, for young women," he said.[11]

The upward trend over the first 14 years of the program is shown in the following table:

Year	No. Entering Rector Scholars	Total Rector Scholars in College
1919-20	58*	58
1920-21	102	155
1921-22	145	242
1922-23	151	319
1923-24	156	411
1924-25	189	477
1925-26	215	516
1926-27	200	535
1927-28	198	540
1928-29	209	550
1929-30	203	535
1930-31	235	561
1931-32	271	620
1932-33	283	700
(1933-34	77)**	

(*includes the original forty-nine plus nine who earned Scholarships during the year.)

(**figures are from the Foundation's 1936-37 annual report, except those in parentheses which came earlier from Longden. See DC 577 Folder 1)

As the program headed into its second decade its supporters were not bashful about its accomplishments. "The Edward Rector Scholarship Foundation is the biggest and finest thing of its kind in the world," said *The Rector Record* in November 1929. Longden's report to the University president on the Foundation for the 1928-29 year noted that as of the fall opening, the 540 Rector Scholars on campus were an all-time high. He recited the by-now familiar litany of scholastic and extracurricular activity achievements of the Scholars.

Indeed the athletic accomplishments of the Rector Scholars were impressive enough to provoke suspicion from DePauw's sports rivals. University president G. Bromley Oxnam spoke proudly in January 1932 of DePauw's "most successful athletic year in history" with only one defeat in football and a perfect basketball season so far including wins over Indiana University and Ohio Wesleyan. He reported that the North Central Association conducted an investigation, but found "no special inducements" being offered to athletes notwithstanding "a most unusual number of scholarships" at the school. Oxnam noted that while 65.6 percent of the men at DePauw had scholarships, mostly Rectors, only 48 percent of the football squad were Rector Scholars.[12]

The number of scholarships awarded annually continued to rise for several years after the mid-'20s. From 198 new Rectors and 540 total in college in 1927-28, the count increased to 209 new entrants and 550 total on campus in 1928-9. There were 203 freshmen and 535 total respectively in 1929-30; 235 freshmen and 561 total in 1930-31; and 271 freshmen and 620 total in 1931-32.

The all-time high historically was recorded in 1932-33 when new Rectors were 283 and the total number on campus reached 700. The total approached one-half of the entire 1,552-member undergraduate student body, and nearly 70 percent of the 1,000 men.[13]

But behind these seemingly flourishing statistics significant problems were developing for the program, administratively and particularly financially.

SIGNIFICANT ADMINISTRATIVE FLAWS EMERGE

Not surprisingly, the relative scholastic superiority of Rector Scholars compared with the University average as a whole showed a downward trend as the program's numbers swelled. This was explainable at least in part by the improved level of scholarship at DePauw generally as a result of the Rectors' presence.

Some criticism came in a survey of Methodist educational institutions conducted by the church in 1930-31. It said DePauw had "done very well in some ways" by the Scholars, but not in others. It specifically criticized as "inexcusable neglect" the University's lack of "differentiated curriculums for brilliant students."[14] Yet it regarded the Foundation generally as well run and said "the director has done an excellent piece of work, perhaps better than anyone else could have accomplished."[15]

Of far greater concern to Longden was another review of the Foundation's operation given to him in 1932 covering the period 1919-32.[16]

This "exhaustive study" (Oxnam's description) of Rector Scholar enrollment since the start of the program was performed by G. Herbert Smith, DePauw's new dean of freshmen and an assistant to the Foundation director, following the Methodist survey.

Smith's study concluded that only 43.34 percent of the total 2,106 scholars to enroll in 1919-32 actually continued in school through the four years needed to complete their studies. "It is very startling to learn that less than 50 percent of all those who matriculate with Rector Scholarships stay through graduation," Longden quoted from the study's summary.

The results raised further concerns upon analysis. By subtracting the 5.5 percent who remained to get a degree despite losing their scholarship because of low grades, the completion rate for those originally awarded scholarships was only 37.84 percent, or closer to one-third of the total. "In other words, 62.16 percent of the Rector scholars fall by the wayside for some cause or other," the summary said. "This is an extremely high mortality rate." Longden judged it to be "particularly alarming" when compared with the all-student graduating percentages from similar Midwest colleges such as Allegheny (49.20), Dickinson (48.80), and Ohio Wesleyan (46.60).

The reasons for the low Rector Scholar graduating percentage were varied. The survey indicated that some Scholars left because of finances or conditions beyond their control, but many had come to DePauw with no intention of staying on for four years. The Rectors had a 25.40 percent withdrawal rate. Another 31.25 percent lost their scholarships because of insufficient grades, primarily in their freshman year.

An important factor was the uneven quality of the recipients' high school preparation. The selection process in general required that an applicant be at least in the upper 10 percent of his class and that he receive a recommendation from his principal. The study showed, for example, that of four Rector scholars from Summitville High School, all lost their scholarships by the end of the first year. On the other hand 17 of the 21 Rector Scholars from Connersville graduated with good grades.

LONGDEN PROPOSES REMEDIES

Longden's response to the "alarming" findings in the study was to advocate a number of partial remedies. He made the following points in his summary of the study:[17]

On the disparities among high schools in the records of the Rectors they sent to DePauw, Longden said "no hard and fast rules can be laid down" but a school's past scholarship achievement record should be considered in selecting new applicants. "It is evident that some high schools deserve little consideration," he said.

On the high rate of Rectors who were withdrawing in good standing (25.4 percent), Longden noted some colleges require that scholarship recipients who leave to go to another school pay tuition for the time they were enrolled before leaving. He declined to go that far but advocated greater care in ascertaining an applicant's intentions to persist to graduation before awarding a Rector Scholarship.

On the high loss rate due to failure to make grades (31.25 percent), he strongly opposed any lowering of scholastic standards for maintenance of Rector Scholarships. Instead, he advocated holding "rigidly" to "respectable" standards throughout the four years in order to maintain the scholarships' standards. He proposed that all Rectors be required to carry a full schedule of classes each semester and that any senior who lost his scholarship the last semester be required to pay his tuition for that semester. "This would serve to keep a high standard of work through the eight semesters," he said.

On the problem of Rectors leaving because of inadequate finances, he recommended care to award scholarships to those with enough money to pay for their expenses beyond tuition. He contended that to not only provide a scholarship, but also to help find work for and lend money to a Rector, is "eliminating the chances for other boys who might be willing to pay their tuition provided they could find jobs to help them along." He said that by paying more heed to a Rector applicant's financial situation, "we may be able to have two students, when otherwise we could have only one."

These Rector Scholarship problems were sufficiently severe to cause review by the University leadership. President Oxnam sent a summary of the scholarship study to Lucy Rector. She conferred with West, the chairman of the trustees and her husband's old friend.

West told Oxnam in an April 1933 letter that Mrs. Rector felt the Scholars must be selected with greater care. She would accept a temporary reduction in their number because of financial constraints and an increase in tuition provided the amount of increase not be paid by the Foundation.[18]

THE FARBER THESIS

A definitive analysis performed later in the decade by Robert H. Farber tended to support the study's findings. Farber, himself a Rector Scholar, joined the college administrative staff at a junior level in 1935 and went on to an outstanding career with DePauw. He subsequently became Director of the Rector Scholarship Foundation and Dean of the University. His master's thesis at the University of Chicago in 1940[19] evaluated DePauw's

Robert H. Farber

Rector Scholar selection system. His data included the 3,245 scholarships awarded 1919-39, with detailed sampling from the files on 654 scholars receiving awards over the five school years 1932-33 through 1936-37.

The Farber thesis found that aptitude tests provided by the American Council on Education proved exceedingly reliable in predicting the academic ability of Rector Scholars, but were not used by the Rector Foundation at DePauw in making its awards. More than one-third (1,166) of the Rector Scholars lost their awards due to low grades. The ratio of students in the lower five deciles in mental ability, on the basis of DePauw norms in the aptitude tests, who lost their scholarships because of poor grades was nearly five times as large as that of students in the upper five deciles.

With regard to high school size, Farber found the Rector award process to be very unreliable in selecting students who would do well at DePauw. Among scholars chosen from classes of less than 50 high school graduates, more than two-thirds did poorly at DePauw.

As for the Foundation rule that applicants be in the upper 10 percent of their high school class scholastically, Farber reported a definite relationship between the percentile rank in high school class and success at DePauw. Below the top six percent, he said, the number who did poorly in college was three times the number who achieved superior grades there. On the other hand, those in the top three percent in high school were three times more likely to achieve B averages or better, the requirement for retaining a Rector Scholarship. He recommended that the high school percentile criterion for Rector applicants be changed from the upper 10 percent to the upper five percent.

The high school principals' recommendations, another of the Foundation requirements for awards, were of little worth in picking capable students. "It was found that in the group rated 'high' there is no difference in the ratings for successful scholars and for those who lost their scholarships due to low grades," Farber said.

Another criterion taken into account in the Rector awards was participation in high school extracurricular activities. It had been presumed that a certain amount of such activities indicated that a candidate was a well-rounded person. The Farber survey showed not much difference in the college grades of Rectors between those who had engaged in extracurricular activities in high school and those who had not, except in sports and literary activities. Those who engaged in sports had a somewhat less favorable showing academically after entering college, while those who were into literary activities such as college publications tended to get very good grades.

Much more significant was an applicant's financial situation. For those who needed to work for only a small part of their college expenses, there was little relative impact on their scholastic record. But among applicants who indicated they would need a large amount of financial help outside of the scholarship, the number who failed to hold their scholarships was nearly double those who made good enough grades to retain them.

Farber examined two other factors in his study, without conclusive results. One was the level of parental education, although the data did indicate that students whose parents had been to college did better than those whose parents had not. The other was student age: since most of the applicants were age 18, there was not much basis for evaluation, though those who entered DePauw younger than 18 made better grades than those who were over that age.

THE PROGRAM PLUNGES WITH FINANCIAL PROBLEMS

Coinciding with the heightened recognition of problems in the scholar selection and retention process was the drastic financial situation caused by the Depression. The Foundation's financial difficulties are addressed in greater detail in the following chapter (Financing Through Crisis Times).

The financial crash caught up with the Foundation award volume in the 1933-34 year. Going into the 1933 fall semester, by Longden's count, 100 scholarships were offered to high school applicants of whom only 77 accepted and entered college. Thus from a record high of the previous year, the number of new scholars dropped to a record low since the initial 1919-20 year when recruitment was just beginning.[20] The drop in entrants from 283 in 1932-33 to 77 the next year was a plunge of nearly 73 percent.

The combination of administrative and financial problems added up to a difficult situation for Longden, by then in his seventies and approaching the end of his distinguished career. Longden's last annual report as Foundation director was for its 15th year, 1933-34, the year of the great retrenchment in the scholarship program.

Longden was deeply disappointed by the setbacks in the program, yet proud as ever of its achievements. He showed both minds in his assessment for his final year as director. Beginning his report, he stated: "The work of the present year in general has been good and compares very well with that of any other year, though in many regards it has been the most discouraging of all the years of the Foundation."

The economic situation underlay much of his description. He was discouraged "first, because we were compelled through the lack of income to cut down the number of freshmen, which caused a decided lessening of enthusiasm on the part of everyone connected with an institution that must retrench." At another point he stated: "The social and economic conditions of the times have influenced greatly the mind and enthusiasm of the scholars."

His report for the year went into some detail on the subject of the Scholars' personal financial needs. Since the great majority of the Rectors depended on themselves wholly or in part for their finances, he said there was a constant temptation for them to take on too much outside work, to the detriment of their studies; or else to deprive themselves of sufficient nourishment and an environment for good work, which also could cause them to lose their scholarships.

Longden also criticized over-involvement by some Scholars in campus activities as a cause for "not a few" to have lost their scholarships. At the same time he pointed with pride to leadership roles of his Scholars that year: 78.3 percent of the athletes in DePauw's major sports teams were Rectors, as were 15 of the 18 fraternity presidents, the top editorial and business managers of the University annual, the *Mirage*, and of the *DePauw* newspaper, and all the senior Cadet Officers.

Meanwhile the Scholars as a whole were maintaining good grades, he said. The Rector Scholar average points-per-hour in grades was 1.730 (on a 3.0 scale), well above the 1.419 average for all men in the University and 1.254 for the women. All of the men elected to Phi Beta Kappa were Rectors, as were all twelve elected to Blue Key, a senior honorary for outstanding men.

"It is this attempt to encourage character, scholarship,

activities and leadership on the campus, at the same time seeking out young men from all classes and environments principally in Indiana, and contiguous States that makes the Rector Scholars unique among all the scholarship foundations of the United States," Longden stated. "The only other foundation that has attempted anything like this is the Rhodes Scholarship, which has not been too successful." The Rector Director did not elaborate further as to why he thought there was lack of success by the Rhodes program.

LONGDEN'S FINAL RECTOR REVIEW

For his final document about the scholarship program as he was stepping down in 1934, Longden wrote a 32-page essay entitled "Inspiration, Origin and Purpose of the Edward Rector Scholarship Foundation."[21] Over the years since the start of the scholarships there had been suggestions for a more formal in-depth description of the program than provided by scattered references in publications and speeches. Longden's essay provided an authoritative report on the origins and intentions of the Rector Scholarship program; however, this document was not published nor officially acted upon.

Longden's review recounted Edward Rector's views and activities in setting up the program and getting it underway. He concluded:

"From the foregoing and from the many conversations held with the director (Longden), it may be fairly concluded that what Mr. Rector primarily intended in the establishing of the Rector Scholarship Foundation was:

(1) That most of the scholarships go to Indiana.

(2) That the chief, invariable and constant requirement should be scholarship.

(3) That the Rector Scholars be not considered as a Brahman sect or group of geniuses but merely

a cross section of the best young men that the high schools can produce.

(4) That it should be used as a means of popularizing and advertising the University.

(5) That it should never be used merely as a dole to help those without means.

(6) That it should not be over regimented and a wide margin of authority be left to the director in selecting scholars and in making loans.

(7) That the office of the director be the depository for the post-collegiate records of attainment and a bureau of employment for Rector Scholars out of work.

(8) That there should be created and maintained an 'esprit de corps' whereby the members might be of help to each other.

(9) That only the income should be used and great care and foresight exercised in the management of the principal.

(10) That through both the warp and woof of the whole fabric there should run the thread of friendly, personal interest and altruism."

Longden's conclusions may have included some embellishment reflecting his hands-on experience as administrator, but by and large they faithfully reflected Rector's views and deeds. Longden himself followed these principles during his tenure. After Rector's passing, Longden continued to refer repeatedly to the benefactor's vision and to praise his many acts of goodness.

***

Chapter 8

FINANCING THROUGH CRISIS TIMES[1]

"It is difficult to overstate the importance of the role of the Rector endowment in DePauw's struggle for financial survival during the depths of the Depression."

While Henry Longden could carry on the Rector Scholarship program in spirit and in its student administrative aspects with great ability after Edward Rector's death, dealing with its finances was another matter. As time went on, the scope of the program became more dependent on decisions made by the trustees charged with handling the University's finances.

DePauw in its earlier years was relatively informal in the administration of its endowment funds. Minutes of a December 20, 1920, meeting by the Board of Trustees executive committee indicate that the Union Trust Company of Indianapolis long had been a custodian of the school's endowment moneys, without a written contract setting forth the relationship between the two parties. A contract was then written which named Union Trust as the main custodian of the University's "Endowment Funds."

Among the provisions of the 1920 contract between DePauw and Union Trust was one which gained prominence in later years. It said:

"All cash turned over to the party of the second part [Union Trust] by the party of the first part [DePauw] and all amounts collected by the second party on investments held by it as a part of such Endowment

Funds shall be invested in first class real estate first mortgage notes which have been first approved by the first party; provided, however, the second party shall make investments of any cash coming into its hands as a part of said submission thereof to the first party acting through its proper officers or committee, any such investments so made pending such approval which are not in fact approved by the first party shall be immediately repurchased by the second party at the price paid therefore plus accrued interest; and, provided further that the total amount of any such investments so made which have not been first approved by the first party shall not exceed $25,000."

Trustee committeemen periodically reviewed the Union Trust administration of the endowment funds and made recommendations. One of the earlier recommendations came in February 1921 when the Committee on Investments and Real Estate rejected a proposal by Union Trust for 6 percent mortgage loan yields, saying equally good loans could be obtained which paid 7 percent.

The committee decisionmaking did not appear to encompass the Rector funds, which at the time were held in a Chicago asset management firm with which Rector dealt. Minutes of a May 1, 1924, meeting report that a proposal for "the merging of all University securities in one common fund for the purpose of investment, was briefly considered and by consent action was deferred." Rector at the time was a leading trustee.

RECTOR MANAGED FUNDING HIMSELF

During his lifetime it was Rector himself who did the major decision making on the handling of funds for his scholarship program. He made clear he did not want the fund management falling into the hands of a trustees committee. Notwithstanding that the assets were in the school's name, they were kept by the Chicago Title and Trust Company under a contract arranged by Rector with the University Board of Trustees.

Rector reserved for himself such supervision over the holdings of his endowment as he deemed necessary. At one point, when Longden as Foundation secretary suggested that the trustees' investing committee pass on a stock transfer that Rector planned for the Foundation portfolio, Rector told Longden:

"I do not intend that the investing committee shall have anything to say about the investment of the Scholarship Funds so long as I am able to actively look after the matter myself. In particular, I do not intend to allow the Scholarship funds to be invested through the same channels and in the same way as the general endowment funds of the University. I think it would be a mistake to put both of our big eggs in the same basket, besides which I should prefer to have the Scholarship funds invested in some such way that the returns, by way of interest or dividends, would come to the University automatically, as they have been doing from its holdings of Burroughs stock."[2]

Furthermore, Rector continued to give additional amounts for various other DePauw causes during his active involvement with the University. When unanticipated needs arose, Rector was generous to a fault. His style was to dig into his own pocket and supply any amount he deemed justified. One instance occurred in the fall of 1924, when an unexpectedly large number of scholarship applicants could not be accommodated from available Foundation funds. Rector gave an additional $50,000 for 75 more scholarships, while requesting no public announcement of his donation.[3]

The large unannounced gift illustrates also a degree of informality in funds sourcing for the scholarships. Behind the amounts donated to DePauw and managed by Chicago Title and Trust Co. was, importantly, the word of Rector himself. He had not only the intent but also the means to carry it out.

In explaining to Longden his $50,000 gift, Rector said "it is merely a further addition to the Scholarship Fund, which everyone has assumed to already be adequate for its intended purpose, and which I have always intended to make good no matter how much might be required to be added to it." And if the Fund proved to be too small to finance the great increase in scholarship students which was then occurring, he said, "I can further assure you that if the present addition is not sufficient there is more for the same purpose where that came from!"[4]

With such largess and active involvement by the program donor, his demonstrated business skill, and his interest in keeping control over the Foundation financing, it is small wonder that during his lifetime Rector's views on the handling of Foundation moneys prevailed with little if any serious critique.

Rector had shown in amassing his fortune that he was an astute businessman. As donor of the Foundation holdings, he was familiar with them. When he felt the time was right for changing the portfolio, he would do so.

For example, in his 1924-25 report on the Foundation, Longden noted that its financial condition had prospered with an increase in stock value and its sale at a high price, for a gain of about a quarter million dollars. With Rector's additional $50,000 out of his own pocket during that period the overall increase came to a sizeable $300,000.

The Foundation account had large holdings of Burroughs Adding Machine Co. stock which Rector had received over his years of service for the company. Rector also had further sizable holdings of the stock in his own name.

Rector's correspondence of the time[5] indicated he believed that the market for Burroughs had slowed and that he was coordinating disposal of the Foundation's holdings and those of his own to help gain the most advantageous price. Other securities offered better returns. In February 1925 he received $311,941.95 from sales of 4000 shares of Burroughs stock from the Foundation account and had deposited the funds in the Harris Trust & Savings Bank. He directed the Bank to buy $300,000 of Liberty Bonds with good yield pending permanent reinvestment of the money.

Rector's active involvement in funding matters was not at all restricted to the scholarship program. For example minutes of Trustee meetings show that in January 1920 he subscribed $10,000 for a campaign getting underway to raise $100,000 for an endowment fund for retiring professors. In June of that year Rector proposed to the Board a recommendation by President Grose, which was adopted, for a campaign to raise $1 million for further endowment for various University purposes. At a Budget Committee meeting a year later Rector was elected chairman in the absence of the regular chairman. At a January 1922 meeting he gained approval for a $500,000 earmarking from the endowment campaign for buildings. He donated the amount himself.[6]

TRUSTEES TAKE OVER FUND MANAGEMENT

Rector's passing left a void in management of his endowment which the trustees moved to fill following his memorial service held October 16, 1925. The Board's Executive Committee met in Indianapolis on October 26 at the office

Henry H. Hornbrook

of its Secretary, Henry H. Hornbrook. Hornbrook was instructed to get the Harris Trust and Savings bank to transfer over to the University a total of $31,067.31 in cash and $340,000 in bonds that Rector had placed in the bank under his name.

A meeting of the Investing Committee was set for October 31 in Greencastle. The Investment Committee appointed a subcommittee "to confer with President West [of the

Board] and the Chicago Title and Trust Company with regard to the future custody and handling of the endowment funds of the Rector Scholarship Foundation."

The subcommittee met with Chicago Title and Trust officials in their office on November 20. The officials told the DePauw delegation that their firm had a capital of $12 million, a surplus of $11 million, an income large enough to pay 16% dividends a year, and that it did not do banking or accept deposits. It intended to set up a $2 million reserve fund for the security of clients whose trusts it was handling, to cover losses for which the company would not be legally liable.

With this background, the subcommittee recommended that DePauw contract with Chicago Title and Trust Co. to invest the Rector Foundation funds for the University. Safeguard provisions in the recommended contract would include commitments by the company to: (1) use the reserve fund to cover errors of judgment by the company in making its investments for DePauw; and (2) repurchase upon DePauw's request any loan or security investments it had made for DePauw. This followed the pattern of safeguards that were in place for the University endowment handled by Union Trust in Indianapolis. The subcommittee concluded that this arrangement would be as safe for the University as would be the alternative of the Investment Committee making the investments itself. At a November 24 meeting in the Union Trust office in Indianapolis the Investment Committee unanimously approved the recommendation.

As for the bonds with Harris Trust & Savings Bank in Chicago that were now in DePauw's name, the Investing Committee at its November 24 meeting empowered their sale "whenever the bond market was favorable, the proceeds to be invested in 6% real estate mortgages."[7]

FOUNDATION ASSETS REINVESTED

At a January 27, 1926, meeting the trustees gave the Investing Committee "full power to enter into a contract with the Chicago Title and Trust Company to invest the Rector funds." Trustee Maurice J. Flynn of Chicago was appointed DePauw's agent to receive from Chicago Title and Trust, the executor of Rector's estate, 10,000 shares of Burroughs Adding Machine Company stock, and authorized to sell that stock for not less than $85 a share. A sale at that price would have brought in at least $850,000, but in the actual marketing by Chicago Title and Trust the amount was subsequently reported as $667,492.79.

As of the January 1927 meeting the status of Rector Scholarship Foundation funding was listed as follows:

Amount in Foundation
as of June 30, 1926................................... $1,280,349.12
Additions during the year from sale of
Burroughs stock by Chicago Title and
Trust from Edward Rector Estate............... $667,492.79
$1,947,841.91

16,937.5 shares of Kellogg Switchboard
and Supply Co. —
5 shares Bedford Athletic Co. —
Midlothian Country Club (probable value)............ $100.00
Union League Club (probable value) $1,000.00
Annual income from the entire fund was reported at about
$123,000 a year.

The Kellogg shares bequeathed to DePauw under the Rector will were worth about $14 a share on the market at the time. They were to be sold and the proceeds - about $237,000 at that price - were to be turned over to Chicago Title and Trust for investment. This plus the Burroughs stock from the Rector Estate brought in about $905,000 from the will, thereby making the total Rector donation approximately $2.2 million.

Marketing the Kellogg shares posed a problem. According to Board minutes in January and May 1928, the president of Chicago Title and Trust, Harrison Riley, in consultation with West and Lucy Rector, believed the Kellogg holding should be reduced because "Kellogg had not been in a prosperous condition." Riley started disposing of the stock gradually with a 7,000-share sell-off at $12 a share ($84,000), followed by further sales reducing the Kellogg holding to below 6,000 shares.

Overall, by 1930 most reinvestment of the Rector-donated assets had taken place. The University's then acting treasurer, Harold E. Robbins, reported that as of May 31 DePauw's investments exclusive of annuity funds totaled $5,250,441.68, of which $2,207,307.63 was endowment of the Rector Foundation and expendable only for scholarships.

Harold E. Robbins

Of the $5.25 million overall a total $4,927,366.88, or 93.8 percent, was invested in real estate mortgages in Indianapolis and Chicago. The real estate holdings in Chicago totaled $2,306,550. Stocks and bonds accounted for $77,017.50 of the portfolio and real estate in Greencastle for $34,400.[8]

RECTOR SCHOLARSHIP
EXPANSION CONTINUES

Undeterred by the somewhat reduced proceeds from the Kellogg security sales below earlier expectations and prospective corresponding diminution of Foundation income, Longden continued to pursue his expansionist vision for the scholarship program. He told the trustees at their January 1929 gathering that 550 Rector Scholars were on campus at the time and the number probably would rise to 600 the next year in view of what he regarded as the revenue "surplus."[9] (From Longden's operational standpoint a "surplus" existed when Foundation income exceeded outlays for the Scholarships. No system was then in place for saving a portion of the proceeds for reinvestment in the endowment to prevent its future deterioration in purchasing power due to inflation and rising tuition costs.)

Furthermore, as noted in the previous Chapter, Longden hoped to broaden the Foundation program by creating a new category of Rector Scholarships – a half dozen traveling fellowships for postgraduate studies, at about $1,000 a year each.[10] By mid-1929 he had the new program in place at $1,200 per traveling fellow.

Robbins in 1930 reported that the University was paying its bills promptly and was taking advantage of all cash discount offers. The number of new Rector scholars continued to move upward, reaching new highs of 235 for the 1930-31 school year and 271 in 1931-2.

In 1931, without the cash in hand, the school issued $250,000 in notes for capital improvements based on expectations of payments through donations.

A WARNING OF ENDOWMENT
PORTFOLIO PROBLEMS

Meanwhile a warning of portfolio problems from over-investment in real estate came from outside reviewers. A Methodist Educational Survey of 1930-31 severely criticized DePauw's "lack of adequate diversification in the trust fund investments" and also said the school should not be borrowing from endowment funds to pay building debts or for any other purpose.[11]

The Survey said: "The principle of diversification is generally recognized today by authorities as the most fundamental safeguard for the capital of the fund as well as the best means of obtaining a steady flow of income at a

G. Bromley Oxnam

satisfactory rate. The extent to which this fundamental principle has been ignored at DePauw University is startling."[12]

G. Bromley Oxnam, who succeeded Murlin as DePauw's president in 1928, took note of the Methodist survey in his report to trustees at their June 1931 meeting but defended the school's policy. Oxnam said DePauw "to date" had not suffered loss in current income from its endowment funds, while institutions with common stocks in their portfolios were facing serious shrinkages in income and values. "At the present moment," he said, "our policy has proved to be wise and the University ought to congratulate itself upon its present condition when compared with institutions of similar rank."[13]

THE GREAT DEPRESSION HITS DEPAUW

The Great Depression, however, was spreading through all sectors of the economy and it soon attacked the real estate loans portfolio on which rested the great bulk of DePauw's endowment. While mortgages could still be carried for a time at face value on the books, payments were deteriorating and in some cases amounts due became uncollectible. Meanwhile other income sources for the school such as donors and tuition payments were slowing down.

The financial crisis for DePauw was full-blown when the trustees came to grips with it in 1932. A new heating plant was needed to get the school through the next winter, but the $30,000-$40,000 required for its construction was nowhere apparent. Problems with an expected major donation to help pay for the $250,000 borrowing had arisen. Endowment income was down significantly and the number of tuition-paying students was dropping.

Oxnam and the trustees began energetic measures for DePauw's financial rescue by cutting expenses and making attempts to increase revenue. Aggressive financial reorganization and retrenchment steps included shrinking faculty size and salaries. By the end of the 1932-3 year, salaries had been cut three times for a total reduction of 46 percent.[14] The trustees authorized $250,000 worth of "plant improvement bonds" to cope with facility needs. Tuition was raised by more than 40 percent from $175 to $250 in 1934.

Student enrollment was kept up by granting more Rector Scholarships than could be paid for by income from the deteriorating Rector endowment. And in his report to the trustees meeting of Jan. 17, 1933, Oxnam again referred to the Methodist Survey. This time he called for a plan for "investing future maturities and other endowment gifts upon a broader basis of diversification."[15]

IMPORTANCE OF RECTOR ENDOWMENT
TO DEPAUW'S SURVIVAL

It is difficult to overstate the importance of the role of the Rector endowment in DePauw's struggle for financial survival during the depths of the Depression. The depreciation of funds for a single scholarship or several of them would not be a focus of attention for the school's managers. But the Rector program was so large a part of the school operation that misfortunes to the Foundation endowment affected far more than the scholarship program itself.

Of the school's total $5.25 million in endowment, $2.2 million, or about 40 percent, was in Rector funding. A substantial portion of the school's income came from men's tuition. Rector Scholarships paid for the tuition of a significant portion of the male student body. Thus the Foundation disbursements, while spent for academic scholarships in the first instance, figured importantly in what the University management deemed to be available for expenditure generally.

The Rector Foundation income decline in effect reduced University funding availability for other purposes. In the 1932-33 school budget, already severely tightened, a projected "surplus" of $22,023.26 had been proposed to be used to meet payment due on the $250,000 "plant improvement" bond issue. However the "surplus" was based on expectation that the Rector Foundation would be paying $33,845.75 in student fees the first semester. As of mid-year the amount was still unpaid. The trustees were told in December 1932 that defaults in interest payments due under the Rector portfolio, lowering the amount available for scholarships, "had made it impossible for the University to meet its current obligations."

Meanwhile the Rector program was being used to offset a decline in tuition-paying non-scholarship students. In the 1932-33 year, while the number of tuition-paying students dropped by 33 from the previous year, the number of freshman Rector Scholars was increased by a dozen to a record 283, for an all-time high of 700 Rectors on campus. Thus for that year in a total school enrollment of 1,639, nearly 43 percent of the student body, including the bulk of all men students, were there through the Rector program. As DePauw historian George Manhart points out, "in order to keep up student attendance more Rector scholarships were granted than could be paid for from the income of the Rector investments."[16]

Additionally, the University was borrowing from various sources to make ends meet, including from its endowments. How much may have been moved out of the Rector ledger, or into it from other school funds, was not identified clearly at the time amid what could be termed the "chaotic" bookkeeping conditions of the school's business office (see Oxnam quote below). Sometime subsequently an amount of $312,000 was stated to be a University IOU to the Foundation.

In sum, while the Rector endowment book value remained at around $2 million during the Depression, the true market worth fell significantly with the plunge in the Chicago real estate market and so did income. Exact amounts are not clear from trustee minutes at the time, partly because of shifting mortgage values and various audits and appraisals turning up differing figures.

Rector Foundation income, the most important element for the school's operational planners, dropped by about 60 percent, probably to around $40,000-$50,000 a year, due to malperformance of the assets. Before the crash the mortgages had been paying 6 percent and more, bringing in more than $120,000 annually. After, the Foundation was no longer paying its own way at the level of scholarships its administrators were granting or wished to grant.

DIFFICULTIES WITH THE
ENDOWMENT MANAGERS

With regard to the Rector endowment, its income was shrinking and the trustees sought to protect the principal. Chicago Title and Trust in 1932 wanted the University to join in foreclosure of mortgages in the Rector portfolio that were in default. This was unacceptable to the University; it asked the Chicago firm to repurchase the mortgages under DePauw's interpretation of the endowment management contract negotiated after Rector's death, providing for the broker's reacquisition of investments upon the University's request. The amount involved was large – according to year-end figures, probably more than one-third of the endowment assets were in foreclosure or default.

At a March 29, 1932 committee meeting on urgent financing issues, the trustees decided first to try to work out the dispute with Chicago Title and Trust in "friendly cooperation" rather than immediately insisting on the DePauw position. A meeting of the Investment Committee with Chicago Title and Trust officers was set for April 1. The meeting brought no solution. The company interpreted the contract to require what it regarded as a reasonable time, six months or less, for notice from the University calling for a repurchase. The committee said the contract provided for repurchase on demand if and whenever the University notifies that a particular investment is unsatisfactory.

After further fruitless exchanges with Chicago Title and Trust, Hornbrook finally concluded that the safest course was to negotiate a supplemental contract with the company that would skirt the safeguard controversy and proceed with management of a reduced portfolio. Under the supplemental agreement Chicago Title and Trust would proceed with mortgage foreclosures, without prejudice to the University's rights on investment repurchasing.

The Investment Committee approved the supplemental agreement at an August 5 meeting. On September 12 it ordered disposition of $40,000 in uninvested Rector money held by Chicago Title and Trust in a manner far removed from Chicago real estate: the DePauw Treasurer was to buy Government Liberty Bonds, which would be deposited in a vault in Indianapolis in the presence of at least two members of the committee.

A comparable situation arose in 1932 with Union Trust Co. of Indianapolis on its custody of the DePauw endowment. Union Trust also had invested in real estate, as per instructions, and it too had a repurchase clause in its management contract with the University. However the discussions between the Greencastle school and its longtime investments agent in Indianapolis were far more amenable than those with Chicago Title & Trust going on at the same time, and the delinquencies in the $2.6 million Union Trust DePauw real estate portfolio, at slightly over $180,000, were far less than the nearly $600,000 in delinquencies subsequently found in the Chicago Rector account of $2,275,000.

Union Trust now offered DePauw officials what was in effect

a "best efforts" approach on the outstanding portfolio, subject to DePauw review on any item. The University by early June 1932 concluded a new agreement with the Indianapolis firm that worked out relatively satisfactorily from the school's standpoint during the ensuing period of endowment management under difficult economic conditions. Union Trust also helped DePauw by such means as lending money and providing collateral.

As of the end of 1932 DePauw's books listed the Rector scholarship endowment fund as totaling $2,206,720.50. However of this amount, $305,194.49 consisted of mortgages in foreclosure and $570,095.00 of mortgages against which there were principal and/or interest defaults.

All told, $875,289.49 of the $2.2 million Rector endowment – almost 40 percent of the total – was in non- or poorly-performing assets. Furthermore University trustees familiar with the Chicago real estate mortgage situation believed that "the number and amount of mortgages in default could not improve within a period of from 12 months to 3 years but on the contrary might be reasonably expected to become worse."[17]

DEPAUW INVESTMENTS' "FATAL LACK OF DIVERSITY"

By the spring of 1932 the trustees also were evidencing serious concern about what one of their leading members, Kenneth C. Hogate '18, a top *Wall Street Journal* executive, termed a fundamental weakness in DePauw's investment policy: namely, that practically all the funds were in real estate loans. A similar criticism had come from the 1930-31 Methodist Educational Survey.

Kenneth C. Hogate

Hogate, a New Yorker, brought to an April 1932 meeting an executive from the Farmers Trust Co. of New York, a firm handling trusts similar to DePauw's. The executive, Carl Montgomery, spoke on diversification of investments for such trusts.[18]

An even more definitive critique came from a special committee set up by the trustees to examine the University's investment policy. The special committee presented its findings the following March 16, 1933. The committee chairman, Arthur R. Baxter, a trustee from Indianapolis, told the board's Executive Committee that he was "alarmed" by "the very apparent lack of any planning in the past, and, therefore, the result which now confronts us." He had two particular criticisms:

> *Lack of diversification.* "There is almost a total absence of any diversity in this investment. Substantially the entire fund is invested in real estate mortgages. This is most unsound and I am amazed that any fund of five million dollars would be invested in a single class of securities. The very first principle of investing trust funds is diversity, and this principle has been violated, as to this fund, more flagrantly than any fund of which I have any knowledge."

Baxter said there was "a fatal lack of diversity" even within the real estate mortgages in the DePauw endowments, since almost the entire amount was invested in only two cities, Chicago and Indianapolis. He also cited a lack of diversity in maturities of the loans and in the amounts loaned on single pieces of property, especially in Chicago, site of the Rector fund investments.

> *High delinquency rate.* Baxter said that of a $2,275,000 portfolio in Chicago at that time $474,000 was under foreclosure, $70,500 was delinquent in principal, $9,800 was delinquent in interest and $26,800 was delinquent interest on the items under foreclosure, for a total delinquency of nearly $600,000. Of the $2.6 million invested in the Indianapolis area, $163,000 was delinquent on principal and $18,500 was delinquent interest. "To collect any considerable portion of this delinquency is, of itself, a

major problem, and especially so when it can be quite positively assumed that this delinquency will shortly be considerably increased," he said. "Indeed, in view of the sentiment which is now sweeping the country in favor of a drastic reduction of real estate mortgages, the particular class of investments now held by DePauw are in peculiar jeopardy."

Baxter proposed an investment policy based on diversification and subject to periodic review. He suggested that 50 percent of the total be invested in high grade bonds, 5 percent in highest grade preferred stocks, 5 percent in highest grade blue chip common stocks, 20 percent in real estate mortgages, and 10 percent miscellaneous. For execution of investment policy, he proposed using a supervisory or consultant firm which would make recommendations on securities but have no financial interest in them, with final decisions on the recommendations to be made by the trustees' Finance Committee.

After hearing Baxter, the Executive Committee approved his suggestion in principle and a policy was subsequently put in place for endowment portfolio readjustment as rapidly as possible. Real estate should comprise no more than 20 percent of the endowment holdings, and no more than 15 percent should be in high grade preferred and common stocks. The remainder was to be in high grade bonds.[19] The Committee ordered the hiring of a full-time employee to look after the mortgage delinquencies and work with the Chicago and Indianapolis custodians.

RECTOR PROGRAM ENLISTED IN DEPAUW'S FINANCIAL RECOVERY

A further use of the Rector scholarship program to aid in DePauw's finances was included by Oxnam in a budget-balancing package he presented to trustees at the start of the 1935-36 school year. It involved a cut in the issuance of Rector awards and a revision in the payments schedule for the Scholars.

G. Herbert Smith

The scaling back of the Foundation outlays was formulated just as a changing of the guard in management of the Rector Scholarship Foundation was underway. The distinguished Professor Longden was retiring in 1935 after more than a half century of service to his *alma mater*, including directorship of the Foundation since its inception in 1919 and vice presidency of the University since 1922. He was to be succeeded as Foundation director by G. Herbert Smith, himself a Rector Scholar and 1927 graduate, who had joined the staff in 1932 as dean of freshmen and served under Longden at the Foundation.

In presenting his further financial rescue plan to the Budget Committee on Sept. 30, 1935, Oxnam acknowledged that the University had had a "chaotic, I should say, disastrous situation" in its business office, and had run an operating deficit in 1934-35 now found to be $76,000. But he said the school's financial management system was being reorganized, various means for savings had been found and some increases in income were in prospect, cutting the deficit for the coming year to a projected $27,000. He promised a balanced budget within another 12 months.

A major element needed for success of Oxnam's proposal was a reduction and revision in the Rector program proposed by Smith, the new Foundation director. Savings from Smith's plan were to come to $10,000 in the year immediately ahead and to $40,000 within three years, which along with an increase in student fees would put the DePauw budget in the black.

The idea underlying the Smith plan was to cut back Rector scholarships to the number the fund could support on a sustained basis, and to pay out the scholarships on a graduated scale so that the scholars would initially pay part of the tuition themselves. In cutting the number of Rector scholars, Smith proposed reducing the on-campus total for 1935-36 to 350, compared with the 700 scholars on campus three years earlier.

"Even now," Smith said in a Jan. 7, 1936 speech describing his scheme, "the present income from the endowment will not pay the tuition of all the [382] Rector Scholars who are on the campus."[20] Smith said the size of the Rector reduction would be offset by adding an equal number of paying students. Under this scenario the University's income would rise by $250 for each additional paying student, without having to hire more faculty.

As for pay-outs to Rector Scholars, Smith's plan revamped the Rector Scholarship payment schedule in a way to provide a substantial financial boost for the University in the immediate years ahead. It would do this by installing a graduated payments scale. The concept of a graduated payment scale for Rector Scholarships already had been advanced in earlier proposals addressing the problem of failure of scholars to complete their college terms.

DePauw's tuition fee at the time was $125 a semester, $250 a year. Under Smith's scheme, incoming Scholars would pay $50 in cash in each of their freshman semesters, and the Scholarship would cover the remaining $75 per semester. Sophomores would pay $25 per semester, with the Scholarship picking up $100. Juniors would receive full tuition free. For seniors, the Scholarship would pay full tuition plus $50 in cash the first semester, and full tuition for the final semester plus $100 in cash upon graduation, as payback for their cash outlays as underclassmen.

Smith expected quick financial benefit for DePauw. Under the scheme, if 100 Rectors entered as freshmen in the next school year (1936-37), they would pay $10,000 in cash. The following two years there would be $15,000 additional income a year, for a total of $40,000 in the three years.

Thereafter $15,000 would be paid out to graduating seniors each year, provided all 100 earned their diplomas. But in practice, there were likely to be many drop-outs along the way. In the meantime, University officials were expecting better financial times ahead.

FINANCES START FIRMING UP
AFTER MID-THIRTIES

By the mid-30s signs of an improvement in DePauw's financial situation began to appear. The Rector corpus hemorrhaging had stopped, though just how much its devalued real estate holdings would bring in future sales would not be known for some years.

The principal of the Rector fund continued to be carried on the books at about $2 million, as it had been after the donor's death. As of June 30, 1936, the total was recorded at $2,192,064.49, but of course this did not reflect deteriorated values in the actual marketplace. Income from the endowment was perhaps around one half of what it had been a decade earlier, and the cost of tuition it could pay for was up.

The Rector scholarship program would never again be as large a component of the University percentage-wise as it had in the past, although this was not just because of or even primarily because of the Depression hardship. Other factors were coming into play which would greatly alter the student aid scenario at DePauw.

Yet battered as it was from the financial crisis, the Rector program was not coming to an end. DePauw was still able to say in 1937, "The advantage of being able to select annually, one hundred outstanding high school boys who have ranked in the upper ten percent of their graduating class in scholarship is a unique privilege not enjoyed by any other similar college in the United States."[21] It remained, as noted in a *New York Times* article early in World War II, "the largest singly endowed foundation for one institution granting scholarships in the United States."[22]

A trustees committee in 1944, in researching Foundation and University payments for Rector scholars since the program began in 1919, said the Foundation "has been a life saver in many ways."[23] It still would be a significant contributor to DePauw in ensuing years.

***

Chapter 9

FUNDING IN THE POST-CRISIS YEARS

*"Going into the 21st century, the Rector fund was still
the second largest scholarship endowment at DePauw."*

As DePauw's finances showed signs of post-depression
improvement in the mid-1930s, so did its management
practices in handling its endowments. President G.
Bromley Oxnam set up a new position of Comptroller in his
reorganization of the school's business operations. The new
comptroller, Ralph E. Schenck, reported to the trustees in the
fall of 1936 that the status of Rector Foundation moneys was
becoming easier to track because of the reforms.

Schenck said that under the new setup "all material on a
subject is filed in one office and in one place in that office." He
said a history of all fund accounts was carried forward "so that the
benefits to, and the obligations of the University in connection
with each fund have now, in the majority of cases, been definitely
established."

Schenck further declared it to be "very essential" that the
University comply strictly with the terms of each gift, a result
which he said would be assured "eventually." He also stressed
care in maintaining principal funds separate from income and in
expending all money received "only for the purpose for which it
was provided."[1]

As of June 30, 1936, the book value of the Rector
endowment stood at $2,192,064.49, an amount similar to earlier
years, although the real market value at the time was far less

due to the lower appraisals of the real estate holdings. A comptroller's table on "Diversification of Investments as of December 31, 1936" shows that of the total $5.5 million in University endowment assets 68.1 percent, or slightly more than two-thirds, was still in real estate and mortgage loans in Chicago and Indianapolis. Schenck's accounting placed the University's past borrowing from the Rector fund,

Ralph E. Schenck

under a heading of "Rector Loan to DePauw University," at $312,000, an amount that the trustees resolved to reduce as monies became available to do so.[2]

DISPUTE EASED WITH CHICAGO TITLE AND TRUST

Differences had continued between DePauw and Chicago Title and Trust over its responsibility in handling the Rector account notwithstanding the attempted compromise in 1932. In January 1935 the DePauw Board of Trustees urgently sought the opinion of a Chicago attorney on the University's rights under the original and supplemental contracts with the Chicago firm. A year later it called for vigorous prosecution of its claim against Chicago Title and Trust for non-fulfillment of contract and it reserved a right to review for trustee approval any proposed settlement that might be reached by negotiators. The school paid more than $6,000 out of Foundation funds to the law firm of Deneen & Massena that year to pursue the suit.

Then in 1936 a deal was reached in which Chicago Title and Trust agreed to pay DePauw $70,000 a year over five years while proceeding with a gradual disposal of the real estate. The income contract with the Chicago company, signed July 9, 1936, was retroactive to May 1, with the payout equal to about 3.5 percent on the original value of the Rector investments.[3]

The Chicago firm's payments immediately boosted Foundation income above pre-contract levels. In a report on the last half of 1936, Schenck said the Rector income for the year was now projected at only $9,000 below the outlays for tuition of enrolled Rector Scholars compared with a deficiency of $53,000 for the previous year. But continuing to describe the situation as "serious" in view of diminished yields from investments, Schenck urged that the number of Rector Scholars be held to what Foundation income could pay for and that the number of paying students be maximized.[4]

Chicago Title and Trust continued to pay into the Rector fund over the next five years under the contract and to dispose of real estate. In 1940 the trustees agreed to a settlement and liquidation agreement with the company, and with the U.S. war effort gearing up, the real estate market was improving markedly.

By January 1942 University president Clyde E. Wildman was giving a report to trustees which contrasted in tone with the school's earlier contentious dealings with the Chicago firm. "The arrangement with the Chicago Title and Trust Company is working nicely," Wildman said. "Since July 27, 1940, twenty-five properties in Chicago with a book value of $392,498.28 have been sold. The loss of principal taken on those properties was $111,810.87. So far such losses are covered by the $250,000 in cash which we received from the Chicago Title and Trust Company."[5]

By 1946, the real estate issue was largely resolved. Wildman reported to the Board on June 15 that the last piece of Chicago real estate owned by DePauw had been sold. "There was a time when it was feared that the University would lose as much as half a million of Rector assets in Chicago," he said.

But improved property prices cut the paper loss down to $344,082.83, the president said. And with Chicago Title and

Trust contributing $250,720.88 from its reserve fund for such contingencies, he reported the total cumulative net loss from the Rector real estate portfolio over the years reduced the principal in the end by only $93,361.95.[6] The Rector account as of June 30, 1946, shows a reduction of $96,906.58 "for losses sustained."[7]

In sum, when all was done by 1946, DePauw had suffered a paper loss of about $340,000 on its Chicago holdings under the Rector endowment, but Chicago Title and Trust's payments of $250,000 out of its reserve fund cushioned the blow so that the actual drawdown on the endowment principal in the end was only about $90,000. The trustees formally approved a write-off of this amount. The Foundation principal on the books was reduced to $2,087,240.10 as of June 30, 1946.

RECTOR PROGRAM MOVES AWAY FROM DEFICIT

Meanwhile the Rector program began shifting from a "deficit" to a "surplus" status from the standpoint of DePauw's bookkeepers after 1936. While Schenck and G. Herbert Smith both noted that year that the income from the Foundation was below the amount needed for the Scholars' tuitions, the balance soon began to tilt the other way with the establishment of new policies and conditions. A goal now was to keep the Rector expenditures within income.

One step toward financial solvency for the Foundation's operating budget took hold in the 1936-37 school year, when Smith's revised Rector scholarship payment schedule took effect. Under the new system the Scholarship pay-out for incoming freshmen Rectors was only 40 percent of tuition the first year, as noted in the previous chapter, compared with full tuition previously. Another step was reducing the number of Rector Scholars on campus by replacing graduating upper classmen Scholars with fewer Rector Scholars in incoming freshmen classes.

In the 1936-37 school year, the Foundation awarded 102 freshman Rector Scholarships, the same level as the previous year, but the new class of Scholars was paying $100 of the $250 first-year tuition cost compared with no student contributions by the prior classes. The new students also paid $50 of the cost when they became sophomores. The new Rector awards dropped to 95 each year for the following two years, to 80 in 1939-40, and to 69 in 1940-41. Over this five-year period tuition payments by Rector Scholars came to $62,750, while $367,800 came from Foundation income.[8]

By October 1940 Wildman noted to trustees that the gender ratio on campus, then 803 men and 722 women, had

reflected a decline of men mainly due to the decrease in the number of Rector Scholars. "There are actually more paying men students this year than there were last year," he said. "We must live within the income from the Rector Scholarship Foundation."[9]

The shift downwards in Rector program levels to stay within Foundation income reduced the program's impact on financing of the student body generally. As of

Clyde E. Wildman

April 30, 1940, the University's income from the Foundation was $67,741, about 29 percent of the $235,337 realized from student tuition.[10] Back during the depression in 1932-33, nearly 43 percent of the total student body, including most of the men students, were there as Rector Scholars.

The advent of World War II rapidly accelerated the decline in males on DePauw's campus and for the last two years of the conflict, the Rector program was basically in stand-by. The 1942-43 school year began with the number of Rector Scholars in school down to 243 and due to drop significantly.[11] A year later the campus total was only 54.

A corollary to the departure of DePauw's men for service in the armed forces therefore was a great drop in Rector Scholarship

Foundation expenditures. Since its assets were still producing a revenue stream, the Foundation now had more income than it could spend on scholarships. Wildman suggested setting aside part of this "surplus" for postwar use, and for "granting a few Rector scholarships to needy students from foreign countries such as Norway, Greece, Poland, Russia, China, and the British Empire." Such awards to non-Americans, he said, would "make the Rector name known and loved around the world."[12]

RECTOR FOUNDATION, DEPAUW PAY OFF DEBTS TO EACH OTHER

The Rector endowment book value continued to be listed at approximately $2.2 million in the years after the 1936 Oxnam financial reform began its more accurate accounting. This total included $312,000 shown as having been borrowed from the Rector fund. The trustees in 1936 adopted a policy of reducing the University's IOU to the scholarship fund as moneys became available to do so.[13] In 1937 the trustees voted to apply at least $5,000 a year, and more if possible, to reducing the Rector loan.[14] Various further amounts were applied to the debt reduction in ensuing years.

Meanwhile the Foundation's status as a deficit operation was changing to a surplus as it reduced program size to keep within income. As noted above, with World War II sweeping the men into military service it became apparent that a sizeable portion of the Rector income could not be spent for scholarships at DePauw during the war.

This situation set the scene for a new twist in the Foundation's financial relations with the University. In 1943 the school's auditors went back to the Rector program's beginnings in 1919 to determine in what years the Foundation payments had failed to cover the tuition costs granted to the Rector scholars. By scoring the underpayments as "indebtedness" of the Foundation to current operating expenses of the University, the auditors concluded that by 1943 the Foundation had accumulated a debt to DePauw totaling $305,645.63, an amount roughly equal to what the University had been said to owe the Foundation.[15]

Wildman dealt with the anomalous picture indicated by this bookkeeping by moving to "improve … our interfund situation … as rapidly as possible". He proposed applying the Foundation's operating "surpluses" to reduce the University's debt to the Rector fund. As the school president explained in a November 1943 report to trustees:[16]

- When he took office in 1936, he found that DePauw's indebtedness to the Foundation was $339,001.76 including the $312,000 listed that year plus $27,001.76 in a loan before 1935. University payments had reduced this debt to $271,193.81 by June 30, 1943.
- The Foundation's "operating profit" for the 1942-43 year was $11,383.18, so this was applied to reducing the Rector loan further. An anticipated Foundation operating "surplus" for 1943-44 of $37,145.93 also would be applied to loan reduction.

The questions of how much "indebtedness" the Foundation had accumulated, and whether it was appropriate to use Rector Foundation "surplus income" to pay this off, were dealt with in a special report issued the following year by the trustee's Committee on Investment and Real Estate chaired by Frank Evans.[17] Evans said the committee undertook thorough research including all correspondence, audits and annual reports from the Foundation's beginning in 1919 to the present time. Tallying all the "surplus" years of Foundation operation and all the "deficits" when Rector Scholar tuition totals exceeded Foundation payments to the University, the report concluded that there had been a deficit every year from 1930-31 on, amounting to a cumulative deficit since 1919 of $285,474.69 as of June 30, 1943.

The research also included a study of Rector's will, discussions with persons familiar with the Foundation's beginnings, and consultation with legal counsel as well as examination of the files. Evans said it was determined that Rector did not expect the scholarship fund "to ever become a liability or a charge upon the other funds of the University." Rector's intent, he said, clearly was that he "wanted this Foundation to pay entirely for all the scholarships granted under it and that he did not mean nor wish that the Foundation should in any way be a burden upon the current income of the institution or the Rector Scholars who were the beneficiaries."

Accordingly, Evans moved that all "surplus income" from the Foundation in the current and future years be applied against the debt owed to the Foundation until the debt is liquidated. The trustees unanimously adopted the motion, one of them emphasizing that the number of Rector Scholarship awards was not being reduced.[18]

The debt was eliminated in due course without affecting the Rector fund principal, since the $312,000 "loan" had been carried as an asset in the fund books on the assumption that it would be repaid. As of June 30, 1946, the Rector fund balance remained at about $2.1 million, close to its bookkeeping balance 10 years earlier, and it continued at that level until 1950.

A FINAL RECTOR DONATION

The final Rector donation to the historic program came from Lucy Rector following her death in 1949 at age 94. Edward Rector's wife had been a staunch and vigorous supporter of the scholarships since their inception. Under her husband's will she had been receiving $10,000 a year from his estate.

From her estate came approximately $137,000 in 1950. This raised the Rector scholarship fund principal to $2,224,374.58.[19]

RECTOR FUND STARTS LONG-TERM GROWTH[20]

S tarting in 1952, the Rector Scholarship endowment began a long-term growth, at first slowly, then at an increasing pace in the latter part of the century. In part this was because the school adopted a more conservative fund management policy under which gifts to the Rector program were added to the principal rather than being used for ongoing expenses. This was how the Edward Rector and the Lucy Rector donations originally had been recorded, and the practice was now extended to the non-Rector donors to the fund. With the policy of keeping spending within the endowment's income remaining in place, the corpus expanded commensurately with the additional gifts as did the income therefrom.

These gifts from Rector alumni and others, mostly individuals, kept coming in over the years. Records show more than 300 gifts from the 1950s until the year 2000. The donations ranged from $10 upward.

The largest came from Robert L. Edwards, a 1933 Rector Scholar graduate, and his wife Jane, who graduated from DePauw in 1931. Robert gave $1.84 million over a 15-year span 1983-98. Jane gave $1.86 million in 1998. Each of these gifts exceeded Rector's original donation of about $1 million to start the scholarship program in 1919, and the combined total of $3.7 million from the Edwards exceeded by $1 million Rector's overall endowment

Robert L. and Jane (Isackson) Edwards

for the scholarship program including the funds from his will.

All told the private contributions totaled more than $4 million by the end of the century and continued to increase thereafter. Of course the post-Rector donations to the program, while significant in dollar terms, came nowhere near that of the original endowment in purchasing power because of ever-rising tuition costs. Nonetheless they made an important contribution to the program's continuing strength in the latter part of the century.

A second and larger reason for the scholarship program's longterm financial growth was DePauw's adoption in the early 1980s of a value maintenance and growth system for its endowments that had been developed for institutions of higher learning.[21] This revised system contrasted with the school's original practice of spending virtually the entire income from the Rector fund on scholarships without retaining a portion of the proceeds for reinvestment to maintain the future strength of the endowment.

Under the new system the assets of all endowments University-wide are handled in a single investments pool managed as a whole with a diverse portfolio. The investment strategy views the endowment in terms of "total return." This includes growth from reinvested interest, dividends, and asset appreciation that historically tends to grow over the years. The trustees annually set a figure for spending from the pool, expressing it in terms of a percentage of the assets. They normally try to set the amount sufficiently below the anticipated total return so that what is retained will sustain the pool's growth at least at a pace keeping up with inflation.

Each endowment owns shares in the pool based on the size of its investment in the pool. Distributions from the pool to its members are made each year according to a percentage of the rolling value of the pool's assets averaged over several immediately preceding years. (The rolling average is used to smooth out variations in payment amounts to program managers so they will not have to face large budget changes from one year to the next.)

RECTOR FUND IMPORTANCE CONTINUES
INTO 21st CENTURY

U nder the revised system for fund maintenance, and including gifts, the Rector endowment account grew from $2.5 million in mid-1982 to $3.3 million a year later, to $4.7 million in mid-1985, to $7.6 million by 1990, and to $10.6 million in mid-1995. By the end of the millennium the Rector account stood at $24 million,[22] approaching nine times the dollar total donated for the historic program by its founder three-quarters of a century earlier.

The fund would have been far greater by 2000 had a reinvestment policy been instituted years earlier. Even so, it is doubtful that the program could have continued indefinitely to finance 100 or more full scholarships annually as it did during its inaugural period. Tuition costs had multiplied at DePauw as they had elsewhere across the land. By the turn of the century DePauw's tuition had climbed to about $20,000 a year, some 267 times higher than the $75 in 1919.

While the number of scholarships the Rector fund could grant annually was now far less than its donor originally envisioned, going into the 21st century it was still the second largest scholarship endowment at DePauw and big enough for a major role in bringing academically gifted scholars to the University in future years.

***

Chapter 10

ADMINISTRATIVE REFORMS, READJUSTMENTS AND A REVIVAL

"Rector Scholarships will again be the preeminent academic scholarships at DePauw."
— Madeleine R. Eagon, Vice President for Admission and Financial Aid, 2005

G. Herbert Smith was well groomed to succeed Longden as director of the Rector Scholarship Foundation following Longden's retirement in 1935. Smith himself had been a Rector Scholar, graduating from DePauw in 1927. After earning a master's degree at the University of Illinois and engaging in administrative duties there, he returned to DePauw in 1932 to become Dean of Freshmen. Longden took him on also as an assistant to the Foundation director.

Smith stepped into the directorship role with a range of recommendations, combining administrative reform and financial savings while at the same time continuing what he said was Rector's vision for the program. Like his predecessor, he regarded the Foundation and the University as inextricably intertwined. As he said in outlining his recommendations in January 1936, "I am thinking of the Foundation as part of DePauw University, fully realizing that the interests of the Foundation are inseparably bound to the best interests of DePauw."[1]

Smith's portrayal of Rector's objectives went beyond Longden's description in the matter of qualifications for scholarship selection. Longden had said it was Rector's

G. Herbert Smith

intent "that the chief, invariable and constant requirement should be scholarship ..."[2] Smith said "it would appear that in addition to scholarship and character, these men must have qualities of leadership and personality which will enable them to compete with the mass of college men. ... Scholarships in the future should be granted on the basis of character, scholarship, leadership and personality."

The new Foundation director said he came to this conclusion because of changing times since the scholarship program was inaugurated in 1919. A college education used to be for the few and graduates could get satisfactory jobs upon graduation because they were among a select group, he said. But the supply of graduates had expanded so much over the past decade, he said, that employers now were looking beyond scholastic attainment in their hiring. The difficulties for job-seeking graduates were exacerbated by the Depression.

Smith referred at the same time to the findings of the 1919-32 study that only 43 percent of Rector Scholars entering DePauw had graduated. He concluded that a closer examination of the "true character" of each applicant was needed.

To achieve this, Smith proposed a personal interview with the applicant by the Foundation director where feasible before awarding a scholarship. He quoted Rector's own correspondence from earlier years voicing concern over drop-outs and suggesting more rigid screening in determining applicants' scholastic standing.

"It is, of course, very much better to refuse scholarships to applicants not entitled to them on the basis of scholarship, than to have them come to DePauw and forfeit their scholarships," Rector had said to Longden in a February 1920 letter.

Following is Smith's table for Rector Scholars 1919-37:

Year	Number Entering	Total in College	Tuition Paid to DePauw
1919-20	58	58	8,700
1920-21	102	155	23,250
1921-22	145	242	36,300
1922-23	151	319	47,850
1923-24	156	411	61,650
1924-25	189	477	71,550
1925-26	215	516	118,660
1926-27	200	535	107,000
1927-28	198	540	108,000
1928-29	209	550	110,000
1929-30	203	535	107,000
1930-31	235	561	112,200
1931-32	271	620	124,000
1932-33	283	700	140,000
1933-34	84	513	102,600
1934-35	130	464	116,000
1935-36	102	387	96,750
1936-37	102	346	86,500
Total	3,033[3]		$1,578,030

With the drop in Foundation income ensuing from the Depression, Smith said only a limited number of scholarships could be granted. He anticipated 300 or 400 hundred applicants for the next school year from the high 10 percent of their classes, of whom no more than 100 could be chosen. "We are now in an excellent position to try to put Mr. Rector's desire into operation," he said.

As for the 25 percent voluntary withdrawal rate among Rectors in 1919-32, Smith believed his proposal for a graduated scholarship pay-out rate would encourage Scholars to remain at DePauw the full four years because the award's peak value would come at the end. As a senior, the Scholar would not only enjoy full tuition free but also would receive cash disbursements of $50 the first semester and $100 the second.

While Smith's revision in scholarship payment scales was projected to save the Foundation $40,000 over the next three years, it is not clear that it accomplished much to keep the Scholars on campus until graduation. A 1937 survey after 3,100 Rectors matriculated found that 248 lost their scholarships before graduation and 1,488 did not graduate for other reasons. The total of 1,364 who did graduate was thus almost identical to the 43 percent reported in the 1919-32 survey.

Notwithstanding the sharp cutback in Rector Foundation finances, the number of new scholars entering DePauw each year continued to top one hundred annually in the period between the depression and World War II, although the totals were considerably below the previous peak. By 1936-37, according to Smith's count, more than 3,000 Rector Scholars had come to the Greencastle school since the program began in 1919. Tuition for the school from their attendance had totaled $1.58 million.

LOCATIONS OF SCHOLARS AND ALUMNI

While the Scholars came from around the nation and, in a few instances, from abroad, the great majority continued to be from Indiana and neighboring states. The 346 on campus in 1936-37 were from 23 states. Of the total, 179 were from Indiana, 62 from Illinois and 39 from Ohio.

Starting in 1935-36 an experiment was tried in exchanging a few Rector Scholars with foreign students for a year abroad. The Foundation granted tuition to the foreign student to come to DePauw, in exchange for tuition for the Rector Scholar at an overseas institution. The exchanges proved successful and were continued in succeeding years.

With the increasing number of Rector graduates came a growth in Rector alumni associations in some of the larger cities.

The organizations were keyed to keeping alive friendships made on campus and "the Rector spirit." The first Rector alumni group was formed November 29, 1927, at the Union League Club of Chicago, a club of which Rector had been a member. Over the next decade Rector alumni clubs were founded in Indianapolis, Detroit, Philadelphia and Washington, D.C.[4]

THE RECTOR RECORD[5]

When the newsletter *The Rector Record* was launched in 1926 it was originally conceived as a regular quarterly publication, but it never achieved that status. Volume I, datelined Greencastle, Ind., January, 1927, was published under the editorship of Coen G. Pierson, the DePauw history

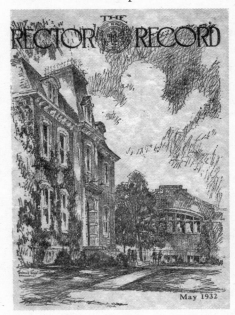

May 1932

professor graduated from the original Rector class. The *Record*'s six printed pages included class notes, reports of Rector Foundation activities and assorted literary contributions. Two more issues were published that year, in May and December.

The next issue came out in March 1928 with four pages as Volume II, No. 1. It carried no masthead. A lead editorial was signed "H.B.L.", Henry Longden's initials. There were two more issues that year.

In 1929 a six-page issue appeared in May, said to be entirely student-produced, under the editorship of Albert R. Crews. In November of that year an issue was published under the editorship of Russell Alexander, who remained in that capacity for the limited duration of remaining issues – one in April 1930 and one in January 1931. Alexander also put out a 27-page *Rector Record* booklet in May 1932 that listed activities of Rector Scholars.

The next *Rector Record* in the DePauw library files was dated October 1951, a four-page typewritten document signed by Farber as Foundation director. It was listed as the periodical's third edition. A fourth edition, about the same length, by Farber, was dated Spring 1952.

The next and final *Rector Record* appears to be a short issue dated Fall 1957 with an item "from the Secretary's Desk", written by then Foundation director John Wittich. Wittich said that the *Record* had not been needed as much as previously because other DePauw publications were keeping all DePauw friends pretty well informed. However, he said many Rector alumni had written to ask what happened to the *Record* and that at the last Alumni Weekend the Rector Executive Committee had directed that the *Record* be published annually. There is no evidence in the DePauw archives that this was done.

RECTOR MEMORIAL LIBRARY

Another of the Rector alumni activities, announced June 13, 1937, was to create a "Rector Memorial Library".[6] The idea was to have a collection of books contributed by alumni in honor of the great benefactor. The volumes would be located in a special section of the DePauw library.

Lists of books needed by the library were submitted by

the school librarian.[7] An alumnus could give a book or a cash donation. The donor could inscribe his name on a bookplate pasted inside the book front cover.

Rector Scholars were solicited for donations to the library and a substantial number gave. At that time in the late 1930s, a $5 contribution was considered equivalent to the cost of one book.[8]

In the early 1960s funding for the book program was established as a Rector Memorial Library endowment. As of the end of the century the endowment principal stood at around $6,000. More than two thousand books had been donated, though they were distributed throughout the library collection and not held in a separate section.[9]

WORLD WAR II IMPACT
ON RECTOR SCHOLARSHIPS

America's entry into World War II had the effect of all but suspending the Rector program. By 1942 the number of Rector Scholars on campus had shrunk to 243, and by the end of the 1943 spring semester and thereafter the great bulk of the male student body had entered the armed forces. By the end of the war, 600 Rector scholars had gone on active duty, of whom 45 died.[10] Among those most distinguished in combat was David M. Shoup, who won a Medal of Honor and later became commandant of the U. S. Marine Corps.

Smith in August 1942 advanced a proposal intended to help keep DePauw afloat for the duration of the war and the Rector program in continuing active operation. He would do this by linking Rector Scholarships with the Army Air Corps: Rector applicants would have to pass air corps physical and mental requirements, in addition to the Rector Scholarship criteria. They would then enter DePauw and the Air Corps reserve at the same time. Presumably the students would stay on campus for course work before being called to active duty.[11]

Smith's plan was put forward by DePauw but not accepted

by the Army. Instead, the armed forces established national programs that they instituted at various colleges, including DePauw.

At DePauw, the U.S. Navy established V-5 and V-12 training courses in which students – some from DePauw and others from elsewhere – were housed in school buildings and instructed by DePauw professors. V-5, preliminary training for naval aviation cadets, began January 7, 1943, with instruction for approximately 200 men a month. V-12, for naval officer candidates, began July 1 of that year with enrollment of 400 seamen for course work under college staff. Meanwhile civilian enrollment at DePauw dropped to 1,174 by the winter semester of 1945 and of these only 232 were men.[12]

Smith had left DePauw in 1942 to become president of Willamette University. Succeeding him as Rector Foundation administrator on an interim basis, with the title of Secretary, was Dean of the University Edward R. Bartlett.[13] Following Bartlett in 1946 in this Rector administrative leadership role was Robert H. Farber, with the title of Director of the Rector Scholarship Foundation.

Farber, also a former Rector scholar, had assisted Smith at the Foundation from 1935 until he was drafted into the Army

Naval aviation cadets trained at DePauw under the V-5 program during World War II.

in September 1940. Farber served five years in the military including overseas combat duty. Upon returning to Greencastle he resumed an outstanding DePauw career with many years as university dean, vice president and acting president.

WARTIME AND IMMEDIATE POSTWAR ADJUSTMENTS

The war brought on a spate of new rulings concerning Rector Scholars, devised to meet exigencies arising during the conflict and the immediate postwar period. Bartlett, and then Farber, issued a number of policy directives on the scholarships as the situation advanced.

Starting with the 1942-43 school year, Rector Scholars for the first time were allowed to use their scholarships for summer school, so as to accelerate their graduation if possible before going into active duty.

Due to the pressure of accelerated course work, grade minimums for Rector Scholars were lowered from a general average of 1.33 to 1.25 for each semester for those in the second, third and fourth college years. The freshman requirement remained at 1.00, a C average. Scholars who were drafted had their scholarships reserved for them when they returned to DePauw after military service. Scholars who volunteered from campus to go into the armed forces were to be given "first consideration" for continuance of their scholarships should they return to DePauw.[14]

A sea change in the college scholarship scene took place with enactment of the national "GI bill" providing for federal funding for education of veterans after World II. The GI bill paid not only for tuition but also for fees and books, plus a monthly allowance in cash. Returning servicemen who had uncompleted Rector Scholarships, and veterans entering as freshmen, had the option of the Rector terms, in essence full-tuition payment, or the GI bill with its more extensive benefits.

With its limited funding, the Foundation priority was new scholarship awards for freshmen. One encouragement to get veterans to use the federal option was to continue them on the rolls as honorary "Rector Scholars" even though they used the GI bill. This policy also helped keep up the total numbers of Rector Scholars recorded as being in the student body.

The Scholarship program soon headed back to a more normal operation after the war. By the fall of 1946 there were 203 Rector Scholars on campus, including 67 freshmen and returning veterans. A significant number of veterans did not choose to use GI bill benefits while completing their DePauw studies because GI bill benefits not used at the undergraduate level could be drawn on for graduate work.[15]

The lowered academic minimums for Rector Scholars were soon revised upwards to a 1.5 average each semester for upperclassmen and a 1.25 average for the freshman year. In performance, their grades compared favorably with pre-war Rector Scholars, with an average in 1945-46 of better than B.[16]

MEANS CRITERIA INTRODUCED FOR RECTOR SCHOLARSHIPS

As of 1946-47, the first postwar year, the *DePauw University Bulletin* listed the "Edward Rector Scholarship Foundation" first among the school's available scholarships. After noting that aid available "differs according to the desire of the donors," it said "Mr. Rector's purpose, by means of the Foundation, was to bring a number of outstanding men students to the DePauw University campus each year ... Rector scholarships are awarded entirely on the basis of merit to young men of character who have excelled in scholarship while in high school. Since the scholarship is based on attainment, it is no little honor to be selected; therefore it is sought regardless of financial need. ... Too much stress cannot be placed on the honor of holding this scholarship."

This statement of Rector's intent was almost verbatim as had been repeatedly expressed by the Foundation since Rector's original pronouncements. Henry Longden's valedictory treatise on the Foundation in 1934 used a cover quote from Rector: "The Edward Rector Scholarship Foundation is intended to be exactly what its name implies, a Foundation for *Scholarship* ..." (emphasis added by Longden)[17]

While Longden's successor as Foundation director, G. Herbert Smith, had instituted a substantial change in the method of Scholarship payments by graduating the payments from freshmen through senior years, the total amount continued to be full tuition "regardless of financial need." However the then-University president, Clyde Wildman, began to push the idea of allotting the Scholarships according to ability of the student to pay. In discussing proposed tuition and fee increases with the trustees in June 1940, Wildman "stated that we shall soon have to alter the basis upon which the Rector Scholarships are awarded by having a graduated scale based upon the need of the recipient, thus enabling each Scholar to receive just what he needs." [18]

Wildman and his financial aid advisers continued to favor this revision, which they deemed of increasing urgency as schooling costs continued to rise and Foundation income was not growing commensurately. However it was a controversial issue. Longden was particularly opposed. While he was long retired, Longden still lived in Greencastle, remained actively interested in the Rector program and was listed as a member of the University Corporation Committee overseeing the Foundation.

Longden was not shy about expressing his views to school authorities.[19] He felt that introducing a student's financial need when considering a Rector award would dilute the standing of the Scholarship, lowering its esteem in the eyes of others compared with an award "entirely on the basis of merit" as it had been from the beginning.

Longden could note that Rector himself emphasized scholarship, and on the question of whether his program was intended primarily to benefit young men without means to secure a college education, Rector said "the answer is 'No, the scholarships are awarded upon the basis of scholarship and character, and nothing else.'"[20] As Longden's treatise pointed out, Rector's approach for needy scholars was to establish a separate loan fund which they could draw on.

Wildman eventually put the Rector scholarship payments revision before the trustees in February of 1948.[21] He presented a statement by Farber as Foundation director which said Rector's original proposal and his will show clearly that Rector's objectives included: "financial aid to young people who could not otherwise afford to attend DePauw University," and "higher scholastic standards by bringing one hundred of the brightest high school seniors to DePauw each year, making an annual total of between three and four hundred scholars on the campus ...."

(Rector's exact words in his original June 6, 1919, statement of objectives were to "afford an opportunity to some of the young people of the State to secure a college education, of the kind that can be had at DePauw, who might not otherwise be able to do so. Another is to bring into the University, in each Freshman class, a hundred of the brightest High School students of the State. ...."[22]

(In the same statement, Rector proposed to establish out of the scholarship fund a loan fund so that "no student who might be awarded a scholarship would be unable to take advantage of it for lack of financial means to do so." The loan fund was established but eventually fell out of use.

(Rector also knew early on that for many if not most Rector Scholars, the scholarship was what enabled their college education: of the 48 in the first class of Rector Scholars, a subsequent survey showed only six could have attended college without such help.[23])

Farber noted that tuition, $75 a year in 1919, had climbed to $350 by 1947-48 while income from the Foundation that year was $61,943.79 – enough for only 40-50 new scholars each year, one half of the Rector goal. He proposed to meet Rector's objectives by being able to award the stipends at less than full tuition, depending on the Scholar's financial need. He also mentioned the possibility of an option for a non-paying honorary Rector scholarship for those who qualified as Rector Scholars on a merit basis but did not need funding assistance. He emphasized that whether the stipend was need-based or not, the scholastic requirements for a Rector scholarship would remain as high.

The trustees approved the Rector Scholar payments revision following clearance from legal counsel. In 1948-49, the first year of needs-based Rector scholarship operation, there were 214 Rector scholars on campus, of whom 187 received full-tuition payments, 14 one-half stipend, 10 one-fourth stipend, and three were honorary. Their overall grade average for the year was a high 2.12 (2=B).[24]

PROGRAM CHANGES AND PROMOTIONS FROM THE 1950S ON

While the Rector program remained important in DePauw's student aid scene after World War II through the end of the 20th century, its comparative preeminence eroded as other endowment fundings multiplied, the University's scale of financial operations grew and administrative layering increased. Also diminishing were special Rector campus and alumni activities that had taken place in earlier years, despite many efforts by the program managers to keep these manifestations of the "Rector spirit" alive.

Succeeding Farber as director of the Edward Rector Scholarship Foundation in 1952 was John J. Wittich, also a former Rector Scholar and DePauw graduate. Wittich's broader responsibility was as director (later dean) of admissions.[25] He had been serving as a Foundation associate director under Farber. Wittich also had an outstanding career, going on to the presidency of MacMurray College after leaving DePauw.

John J. Wittich

In his first annual report submitted in June 1953 Wittich addressed the perennial issue of how best to select Rector Scholars. He proposed that an annual competition for the scholarships be held on campus at Greencastle rather than being distributed in mailings to high schools. He said this would simplify the handling of tests and ensure greater validity for test results. And since "the Rector Scholar Association does little else as a group than meet to eat and to elect new officers," he proposed to give the association a purpose by having it supervise the scholarship weekend.[26]

Results of the 1954 on-campus-testing experiment were mixed. While the testing process was more efficient, the number of competitors was slightly reduced as was the percentage of acceptances of awards made. However, it was assumed that the on-site event encouraged enrollment at DePauw anyway because even students who did not receive Rector awards would be favorably influenced in their view of the University just from visiting there. Past campus visits by prospective students were known to have such a result.[27]

Other promotions continued or advanced under Wittich's stewardship included an orientation meeting in September for freshman Rector Scholars, at which the director would outline the purposes and requirements of the program; a meeting of the scholars with Mrs. Grafton (Hazel Day) Longden, a 1915 DePauw graduate and daughter-in-law of Henry Longden, who would relate the Rector story; a yearly Rector Scholar Dinner for the undergraduate scholars intended to engender a unifying Rector spirit; alumni dinner gatherings; and mailings of Scholarship competition announcements, Rector newsletters, a directory of Rector Scholars, and a 25th Anniversary Booklet on the program.[28]

Wittich reported in 1958 that in a typical year DePauw was granting about $104,000 in scholarships from the Rector Foundation, $21,000 from other endowed funds, and $35,000 from the general budget. A survey of freshman scholarships awarded as of June 2, 1958, produced interesting results. It showed that 32 percent of those offered Rector Scholarships declined them. The highest rate of refusals applied to offers of payments less than full tuition. The highest rate of acceptances was for full tuition and for the honorary Scholarships.[29] An even greater refusal rate – 40 percent – was found for DePauw's non-Rector scholarship offers.

Wittich felt that the Rector full-tuition award program had been "emasculated" by the allotment of lesser amounts on the basis of need, but he recognized the pressures at the time to provide assistance to students without other means.[30] Also, he recommended that the school initially offer more scholarships than it planned to award – "able candidates are lost when scholarship funds are withheld from them in May, only to be offered to less able candidates in August."

RECTOR ACTIVITIES DECLINE

Wittich left in 1961 and was succeeded by his assistant, Louis J. Fontaine, as acting director of the Foundation. The trustees followed through in 1962 by officially appointing Fontaine as director of the Foundation, as well as to the broader post of director of admissions.

Fontaine, a 1954 DePauw graduate, held the position of Rector Foundation director until 1980, making him the longest-serving official in that post in the history of the program. Longden was its chief operating officer from its founding in 1919 until his retirement in 1935, a span of about 16 years. Fontaine's tenure covered about 18 years, and he was the last to hold the title of

Director of the Foundation. The University dropped the title thereafter.

Far-reaching changes in the student financing scene were occurring over this time and they were diminishing the Rector program's relative role at DePauw. Tuition costs were rising faster than the Rector endowment income, reducing the Foundation's capabilities in awarding scholarships. Other sources of student aid were multiplying.

Louis J. Fontaine

Federal, state and local governments were increasingly offering student assistance programs of one kind or another. New private endowments were being established, accompanied by various conditions.

One example of new private assistance for DePauw students that affected the Rector program was a fund set up by Rolland Malpas, a well-to-do Indiana businessman. It was intended for needy young men born in Indiana of American parents who graduated in the top ranks of Indiana high schools and were well-rounded in their activities. A Malpas scholarship could pay for tuition, fees, books, room and board. The fund was not part of DePauw's endowment and its scholarships were not awarded by DePauw, but by trustees of the Malpas scholarship fund from a candidate list submitted to them by DePauw. Fontaine found that Malpas outmatched what he could offer from the Rector Foundation.

Another Indiana-oriented student aid scholarship was established by Edgar Prevo, a Greencastle businessman, for tuition at DePauw. The scholarship had to go to a student from Putnam County.

Still another scholarship measure, developed later on a larger scale, was a state-wide program for Indiana communities funded by the Indianapolis-based Eli Lilly Foundation. It provided funds for communities in most of the state's 92 counties to pay for at least one scholarship for full tuition, fees and books at an Indiana college. It was left to each community to set the criteria for its scholar selection.

In sum, the Rector awards were losing their previous dominance as well as their distinction amid the expanding array of scholarships available for DePauw students. The University itself was using some of its greatly expanding operations budget for student aid. The school's scholarship awarding procedure was evolving into a molding of assistance packages to match the interests and needs of those coming to DePauw.

An important factor was the desire to keep up with competition from other schools likewise seeking the best scholars. A senior DePauw financial officer at the time recalled pressure to raise tuition rates because "prospective students often equate quality with cost." But he said "with every increase in tuition we do, of course, provide more scholarship funds to assist the really needy."[31]

Changing student attitudes also affected participation in Rector program activities. Fontaine wanted to maintain and strengthen student participation, but found that students in the 1960s were in a rebellious, anti-authoritarian mood and not as heedful of traditions as their predecessors.[32]

As one example of increasing difficulties for Rector promotions, Fontaine cited the annual dinner for Scholars. The dinners had been a yearly feature on campus since early in the scholarship program. One of Wittich's initiatives had been to promote this dinner, but attendance by the Scholars was dwindling; some Scholars who did come were poorly dressed, and they treated the proceedings with little respect. Fontaine decided to end the dinners, which he did without administration objection, and they were never resumed in the 20th Century.

Wittich's proposal to oversubscribe Rector awards to offset refusals by candidates was not adopted as a formal policy, although Fontaine did some oversubscribing in practice.[33]

Starting in the 1970s the Rector Scholarships were no longer named first in the *DePauw Bulletin*'s listings of available awards, but rather were named alphabetically among many others, placing the Rector awards far down the list.

Fontaine continued to be concerned about what he saw as the "fading away" of the Rector program but found a lack of enthusiasm for several proposals he made to reverse the trend. One of them would have produced a 50th anniversary yearbook on the Rector program including thumbnail sketches of outstanding graduates. Another would have taken the Rector funds out of the University investment pool and put the Foundation under management by Rector Scholar alumni, who would pick the Scholars and also invest the assets to achieve better financial growth. However University President William E. Kerstetter "very politely said 'no'," Fontaine recalled.

Meanwhile the bureaucratic apparatus for student admissions was growing exponentially. When Fontaine first joined the staff in 1957 the Rector Scholar selection was still conducted much as it had been since the beginning: a committee composed basically of the University president, the Foundation director, the dean, and the comptroller met twice a year to go over applicant material prepared by the Foundation and in a space of about three hours would determine the Rector scholar awards.

The Foundation staff earlier had a Director and two assistants. By the time he left 23 years later Fontaine recalled there being a full-time director of admissions, a full-time director of financial aid, five assistant professional administrators, and a clerical staff of 13.

Fontaine left in 1980 and was succeeded as director of admissions by David C. Murray. The title of Director of the Edward Rector Scholarship Foundation, which Fontaine also held, was dropped, and there was no further reference to the Foundation in the official *DePauw Bulletin* listings thereafter.

WOMEN INCLUDED IN RECTOR PROGRAM

In establishing his Scholarship program in 1919 Rector said it was limited to men because women at DePauw then largely outnumbered men, and the women needed more living quarters. So the Scholarships were for the men, while for the women he had built the handsome Rector Hall and willed funds for Lucy Rowland Hall. But were it not for these constraints, he said he would rather base the awards on merit alone.

Rector's one gender-neutral exception to the males-only policy, providing eligibility for Scholarships for any students, male or female, winning top honors in their class, had promptly produced results: The first Rector Scholar graduates were women who were enrolled prior to the entry of the first Rector men in 1919 and earned Rector Scholarships by scoring first in their classes. Edith Richards was mentioned earlier. Grace H. Ruthenburg graduated as a Rector Scholar in 1921 as did Gladys M. Amerine in 1922, and three women were among 52 Rector graduates when the original Rector class graduated in 1923.[34]

Over the years the University received many requests from or on behalf of women seeking Rector Scholarships, some from prominent alumni or friends. There was then a great sparsity of scholarships for women at DePauw.[35] Longden, as the Rector Scholarship Foundation director, stood steadfast against awards for women except when they led in their college class grades. That had been Edward Rector's original criterion, although Longden too had said he would have liked another donor to establish a comparable program for females.

Wittich, with his years of experience as admissions director, said that DePauw needed an emphasis on scholarships for gifted men. He said it was comparatively easy to attract good women students, but not men. One reason for this, he said, is that women mature earlier than males. Thus under a gender-neutral academic awards program for incoming highschoolers he said more women than men would qualify, running counter to DePauw's quest for higher academic quality males.[36]

The Rector program's males-only limitation was finally removed with little ado in 1982 under the administration of University president Richard F. Rosser. Rosser told the trustees at an April 1982 meeting:

"In researching the history of the Rector Endowment, we have discovered that there was nothing in Mr. Rector's original intention which precluded Rector awards for women! Not only was the decision to use Rector funds for male students only an administrative one, but the basis of Rector awards changed significantly at various times in order to reflect the needs of the college for particular kinds of students. Hence, beginning next year we would like to be able to award Rector Scholarships for women — a change that will permit us to use Rector funds more prudently and efficiently."[37]

A NEW LIFE FOR RECTOR'S VISION

Succeeding Murray in 1996 as dean of admissions and financial aid was Madeleine R. Eagon, who subsequently became a vice president for admissions and financial aid. Competition among colleges for "the best and the brightest" new students at the time was strong and intensifying, and a number of other institutions had deeper financial resources than DePauw. The acquisition of a high caliber student body was good for a school not only for attracting future enrollments but also for retaining a strong faculty because professors prefer to teach where students are high quality.

With the arrival of the enormous Holton gift for scholarships in 1999 that will be related in the next chapter, Eagon saw an opportunity to make best use of DePauw's scholarship resources by revitalizing the Rector program and marketing it in tandem with the Holton Scholarship program to attract more of the nation's top students.[38] The Rector emphasis was on scholastic

Madeleine R. Eagon

excellence. The Holton emphasis was on overall quality and leadership.

"Rector Scholarships will again be the preeminent academic scholarships at DePauw," Eagon said. "We will award full tuition and room-and-board Rector Scholarships to the academic and intellectual superstars."[39]

Under the Eagon proposal, which the trustees approved for the next four years,[40] the top 25 high-achieving students in the incoming student pool each year would receive Rector Scholarships, based on academic merit. The scholarships of the highest 10 would cover both tuition and room and board. The highest in the academic pool could get full tuition awards known as Presidential Rector Scholarships, in 2000 about $20,000 a year, *plus* room and board. The second tier would receive a tuition stipend of $11,000 annually

The system for Rector recruitment involved screening of all applicants for admission to DePauw for the best academic records and test scores, plus consideration of special talents and leadership abilities. There was no means test. Those with the high academic qualifications worthy of Rector awards were advised they could be offered a Rector Scholarship upon enrollment, whether or not they had applied for that particular award.

Further steps were taken to impress the potential enrollees with campus visits because recruiters have long known that a campus visit greatly improves the likelihood of the candidate choosing that school. The prospective Rectors were invited to Greencastle for an honors weekend in the spring with special treatment including meeting with outstanding professors, dining with the University president at his home and staying with Rector Scholars on campus. Expenses for the visit were paid out of the school's admissions budget, not the Rector endowment itself which was reserved for scholarship payments.

The Rector and Holton programs were to be regarded

as complementary rather than competitive. While the Holton scholars had to be very good students, they did not have to be among the academic elite (top test scores) of their high school class, as did the Rector scholars. The Holton emphasis was on the candidates' potential to be leaders in college and thereafter. There would be 50 Holton scholarships awarded annually, 10 full tuition and 40 partial tuition.

With its revived status, the Rector program by 2000 was once again a top drawing card for DePauw in student academic excellence. It returned to a front listing in the University *Catalogue* description of grants and scholarships. DePauw's recruiters were telling high-ranking high school students that the Rector scholarship was the premier merit scholarship.

A RETURN TO ITS ROOTS

Thus with the start of the 21st century the Rector program was returned to its roots in a significant way: Edward Rector's emphasis on having academically excellent students at DePauw was again stressed. Major differences from the original included the lowering in numbers of new scholarships, due to the decline over time in the endowment's relative tuition financing ability, and full eligibility for women.

Another difference in 2000 was the absence of geographical concentration on Indiana. By the time of Rector's death in 1925 his scholarship awards were beginning to spread outside the state, and his will allowed such awards. By 2000 there were numerous other sources for funding Indiana students at DePauw. Rector was also proud of non-Indiana DePauw students who achieved distinction after graduation.[41] So it seems safe to speculate that Rector might in time have favored awards regardless of high school location provided the students met top academic criteria.

A massive change had occurred in the scholarship scene between 1919 and the turn of the century. In the early years there was a comparatively large population of academically capable high school students, in Indiana and elsewhere, unable to afford a college education, compared with limited scholarships available. Over the decades the balance shifted with a proliferation of financial aid for higher education. Students could now do more picking and choosing, and the colleges faced stiff competition in attracting the best.

The Rector program proved valuable to DePauw in both scenarios, and the recurrence of basic Rector themes for his scholarship program by successive generations of DePauw administrations speaks to their respect for the great benefactor's original vision. Longden extolled and expanded on Rector's views throughout his long tenure as Rector Scholarship Foundation director. DePauw president Clyde Wildman told trustees two decades after its 1919 founding that "twenty years of experience with this Foundation have proved the great wisdom of Mr. Rector in creating the Foundation."[42] Eagon, an author of the program's 2000 revival, said "Edward Rector was incredibly forward looking – it was a brilliant idea."[43]

***

Chapter 11

THE GREAT HOLTON GIFT[1]

Both Rector and Holton "wanted to help bring high quality young people to college for the future good of society, and they were utterly generous in using their fortunes to this end."

On May 16, 1997, DePauw proudly announced "the largest gift in its history," a donation of "more than $30 million" that came from a joint charitable trust set up by the recently deceased Philip Forbes Holton and his wife, Ruth Clark Holton. The Holtons had been members, but not graduates, of DePauw's 1929 class. Philip Holton had been a Rector Scholar.

The University put the money into a Ruth Clark and Philip Forbes Holton Memorial Fund that it made part of the school's permanent endowment. Proceeds were to be spent in accord with the Holtons' wishes: namely, for scholarships for DePauw students "of high character with academic and leadership potential." Preference would be given to students from Indiana, Illinois, Michigan and Ohio, as desired by the Holtons, who believed that "Midwest values were distinctive."

University president Robert G. Bottoms drew a comparison with the original Rector gift. "In 1919 Edward Rector made a historic gift for scholarships that has shaped this University and helped educate thousands of leaders for our country," he said. "I believe the gift of the Holtons will create the same impact for DePauw in the 21st century that Mr. Rector's gift did in this one."

Philip Forbes Holton and his wife, Ruth Clark Holton, made "a historic gift for scholarships."

The new Holton scholarship program was still in its infancy when another bombshell announcement came on August 19, 1999: the Holtons also had bequeathed generously to the program from their estate, and this added another $98.4 million to the previous amounts from their trusts. In sum, the total for the Holton Memorial Fund for scholarships was now $128 million.

"The total of $128 million," the University's new announcement said, "makes it the seventh largest single gift to a college or university and the largest single gift ever given to a private liberal arts university in the history of higher education."

The endowment was expected to generate about $6.25 million a year. Bottoms said this would pay for about 75 Holton scholarships a year, bringing the total of Holton scholars on the DePauw campus to 250-300 at any one time.

The Holton philanthropy for DePauw warrants a chapter in this book not only because of its extraordinary size, dwarfing all other donations to DePauw since those from Rector, but also because of its comparisons and contrasts with the historic Rector scholarship program begun 80 years earlier. One interface is noted in the previous chapter with the tandem marketing of the Rector and Holton programs. Other cross-references have come in remarks by Bottoms and others.

HOLTON BACKGROUNDS

Philip Holton was born in Pittsburgh, Pa., May 10, 1907. He and two siblings were raised in Hartford City, Indiana, by his mother's sister and brother-in-law, Elinora and Herman Krannert. Krannert was founder and first president of Inland Box Co., which later became Inland Container Corp. The Krannerts would later become major higher-education philanthropists themselves with major gifts to Purdue (School of Business) and the University of Illinois (museum and entertainment center).

Holton enrolled as a Rector Scholar at DePauw in 1925. He worked at his studies and achieved good grades. He joined the Beta Theta Pi fraternity. He played football. He picked up the nickname "Tuffy." While at school he also worked part time for Inland Box Company.

With his Rector Scholarship, Holton was able to finance his DePauw education in large part on his own, as had so many other young men. He later responded to an alumni questionnaire that 50 percent of his DePauw education was financed by the Rector Scholarship, 25 percent by summer work, and 25 percent by his work while attending school.

Ruth Clark was born Nov. 14, 1906, to a prominent family in Winchester, Ind. Her father, John Paul Clark, an Earlham graduate, was a well-to-do businessman who was twice mayor of Winchester, 1934-38 and 1943-47, and had been president of the Randolph County Council. An uncle, James E. Watson, also a Winchester native, was an 1886 DePauw graduate and U.S. Senator from Indiana 1916-33.[2]

Ruth also entered DePauw as a freshman in 1925. She took liberal arts courses and joined the Kappa Alpha Theta sorority. She met Phil Holton as a classmate on campus and they dated. Their romance blossomed.

In 1927 Phil left DePauw to enroll at the University of Illinois. Herman Krannert felt a degree in engineering was good preparation for a career in business, and DePauw did not offer an engineering degree.[3] When Phil transferred to Illinois University, Ruth left Greencastle too, to go home for two years and await Phil's completion of his college education. He graduated from the Urbana-Champaign institution *cum laude* in 1929.

Philip and Ruth married in Winchester in 1930. They subsequently had one child, Jane, in 1935. Jane died childless in 1974 at age 38.

PHIL HOLTON'S OUTSTANDING BUSINESS CAREER

After graduating from Illinois, Phil Holton went to work for Inland Box Company in Indianapolis full time. He had an outstanding career with the corrugated box company. He moved up the ranks to become president and chief executive officer in 1963. He became vice chair of the Board of Directors in 1970 before retiring in 1975.[4]

Other positions held by Holton during his years of business service included being president and board chairman of the Georgia Kraft Co., a container-board manufacturer co-owned by Inland; a trustee of the Institute of Paper Chemistry; and a director at the National Paperboard Association.

The Holtons' primary home was in Indianapolis. Holton was a member of St. Paul's Episcopal Church, a Republican, and a self-described conservative. They also had a retirement home in Naples, Fla., where the couple resided in later years. Holton died in Naples on April 30, 1995, at age 87.

A METICULOUS ESTATE PLANNER

Upon his retirement in 1975, Holton turned his attention to estate planning. He included DePauw among his planned beneficiaries as DePauw was clearly his favored *"alma mater"* notwithstanding his graduation from Illinois.

He had told others of his strong attachment to the Greencastle school and his high regard for its quality. Also, of course, it was where he and Ruth had met. She too liked DePauw. Philip Holton's brother, John P. Holton, graduated from DePauw in 1936.[5]

In a letter in 1975 to then President William E. Kerstetter, Holton confirmed his intentions to provide a gift to the University through a joint charitable remainder trust set up in the name of his wife and himself. He indicated his preference on use of the donation would be for scholarships for students with high character, academic, athletic and leadership qualifications, but details were not set at that time. He emphasized that the bequest must be kept confidential until after the death of both himself and his wife.

William E. Kerstetter

A meticulous man, Holton was one to keep close tabs on his assets. For DePauw, he would send to the University President early each year a handwritten letter reporting on the status of the trust fund.[6] Most of his estate was in Inland Container stock accumulated over his years with the company.

THE ESTATE VALUE GOES UP – AND UP

At the time of starting the trust in 1975, Holton valued it at about $1.5 million. The prospective donation was welcomed by University officials but not regarded then as extraordinarily large compared with various other donations.

As time went on Holton would continue each year to add to the trust more funds from his holdings. Inland Container merged with Time Inc., and the stock split several times. The book value rose, but Holton also would regularly caution in his communications with the DePauw leadership that the trust value depended on the market, and therefore its worth could go down as well as up. And he kept reemphasizing his desire for confidentiality.

Periodic discussions and letter exchanges took place between Holton and ensuing DePauw presidents. Richard F. Rosser (1977-

Richard F. Rosser

1986), who succeeded Kerstetter, tried to interest Holton in contributing to a physical education center. Holton made plain that he was not interested in "bricks and mortar." The center was subsequently built as the Lilly Center with input from other donors.

The value of the Holton trust kept rising during the 1980s due to a favorable stock market and more contributions from the Holtons. By 1985, Holton estimated the trust's market worth at $5,345,000, although the market was down at that particular time.

When Bottoms succeeded to the presidency in 1986 he realized that the Holton fund, whatever its eventual size, would be very, very substantial. He sounded out Holton about contributing in a fund-raising project for the library. Holton told Bottoms he need not solicit him for this project because "my plans are set."[7]

PURPOSE OF THE HOLTON GIFT DECIDED

With the value of the Holton fund continuing to climb, Bottoms later pressed again for directions from Holton on how the fund should be spent. In July 1987 the two, accompanied by their wives, had a seminal lunch-time meeting at Holton's Indianapolis home at which the donor set forth his views orally. By this time the fund was valued at about $10 million. Upon returning to Greencastle Bottoms drafted a letter encompassing the substance of Holton's views. Holton approved the letter with minor editing.

This letter exchange dated July 7 and July 10, 1987, became the policy charter of the Holton scholarship program that DePauw put into place after posthumous receipt of the Holton donation. The University regarded the terms as a binding commitment on the University. So did Holton before his death, as did his executor.

The principal points of the Bottoms-Holton letter exchange were that upon receipt of the donation DePauw would establish a Ruth Clark and Philip Forbes Holton Memorial Fund for scholarships. The scholarships would be offered "to outstanding young men and women in approximately equal numbers" who "exhibit the leadership characteristics so necessary in contemporary society."

In addition to academic excellence, the scholars must have shown in extracurricular activities in high school the ability to become leaders not only on campus but also in society after graduation. The recipients were to have demonstrated "high moral character through community and church involvement," and preference was to be given to students from Indiana, Illinois, Michigan and Ohio. Holton did not want the Fund to be operated by the school's financial aid office, because that would be administering it "like some government program."

THE GIFT VALUE SOARS FURTHER

As Holton continued to contribute to and evaluate his fund annually, the market kept going up. Not long before his death, he told his close friend and financial adviser, U.E. Uebelhoer, an associate at Inland Container, that he wanted to achieve a $20 million value for the trust. Meanwhile the value of the remainder of his estate was also climbing substantially. By the time of his death in April 1995 Holton knew his total estate was worth more than $100 million.

Two years after her husband died, on April 30, 1997, Ruth Holton died at age 90. She had been in ill health for years. The trust proceeds then went to DePauw. During the two years between the deaths of husband and wife the value of the stock in the trust had doubled to more than $30 million. Thus, upon receiving the funds, DePauw was proud to announce it had been given the largest donation in the University's history, and the creation of the Holton scholarship endowment.[8]

Then came an almost unbelievable happy surprise to the institution. Unbeknownst to University officials, the Holtons in 1985 had named DePauw as a residual beneficiary of one-half of their entire estate, in addition to the trust which had been established specifically with DePauw as recipient. Their estate

The Holton Memorial Quadrangle

assets likewise had been based on Inland Container and successor stock accumulated during Holton's working career. The Time stock had split several times. Time became Time-Warner. The value of the stock soared. Between the time of Phil Holton's death, when the Holton assets were in the $100 million range, and his wife's death two years later, the estate's worth doubled due to strong stock market performance, particularly in Time-Warner holdings.[9]

DePauw's share when the estate was distributed in 1999 turned out to be $98.4 million. This amount plus the $30 million trust put the Holton contribution total for the University at slightly above $128 million – four times greater than DePauw's previously-announced "largest gift in its history."

DEPAUW'S TWO GREAT SCHOLARSHIP PROGRAMS: COMPARE AND CONTRAST

DePauw's announcement of the Holton $128 million gift said:

"DePauw University President Robert G. Bottoms compares the impact of gift of Ruth and Philip Holton to a 1919 scholarship endowment of $2.5 million given by Edward Rector. Mr. Rector, a Chicago patent lawyer, wanted to provide full scholarships for exceptionally capable students. His initial purpose was to assure that each entering class had a sizeable contingent of the most outstanding students available. His endowed gift has made possible the education of some 4,000 Rector Scholars in the intervening 80 years. These graduates of DePauw are among some of the most accomplished individuals in this country and have been extremely loyal alumni. Philip Holton came to DePauw as a Rector Scholar."

Holton doubtless was favorably impressed by the Rector program as a means of bringing quality students to DePauw. His Scholarship enabled him to attend the school, and at the time he entered as a freshman in the fall of 1925, Rector had just died and the "Rector spirit" was in full swing on campus. All 18 men earning Phi Beta Kappa keys in 1925-6 were Rector Scholars. Perhaps more impressive for young Holton, a sports enthusiast and football player, all the captains of sports teams that year were Rectors as were 10 of the 15 lettermen on the football squad.

There are notable parallels between the two endowments:

- Both donors wanted bright students who had character, leadership abilities, and extracurricular interests, although Rector's strictest emphasis was on scholarship. Holton wanted good grades to be accompanied by demonstrated leadership in community and other activities. He would have included participation in sports as a criterion, until advised that federal law forbade athletic scholarships for Division III schools.

- Both donations were of such size that they would help lift the overall quality of the student body at the University. This was particularly true of the Rector program originally with its large impact on the male student body, instituted at a time when academic performance of the men had been comparatively poor.

- Both donors had Indiana backgrounds and they initially focused on high school students of the area – Holton for those from Indiana, Ohio, Michigan and Illinois, and Rector from Indiana's 92 counties, though the Rector awards later broadened to nationwide and in due course to students from foreign countries.

- Both were self-made men financially.

- Neither wanted to have the University managing his endowment funds during his lifetime.

- Neither proposed that his scholarship program be means-based, though both recognized that merit scholarships would aid needy gifted students in gaining a college education. Holton's Rector scholarship had helped him work his way through school. Rector in his youth had been too poor to go to college. While Rector's scholarships themselves were not needs-based, he augmented his program with a loan fund for his Scholars needing further financial assistance.

- Both donors had devoted wives who stayed in the background but appeared to be completely supportive of the philanthropies.

- Neither couple had living children to inherit their fortunes.

There also were differences between the great benefactors and their relationship to their scholarship programs. With the Holtons, their fund could go to DePauw only after their death. Philip Holton did not even know while he was alive how truly large the Holton Scholarship program would be. Holton seldom visited DePauw although he kept relationships with some old friends from student days there and he was pleased with periodic progress reports from DePauw officials and others on what was going on at the school.

The Holtons tended to be very private people, though gracious and cordial with their friends. They were a model of modesty about their donation during their lifetimes. Philip insisted that there be no announcement until after his death. He did not want to finance any buildings or have one named after him. DePauw's only physical memorial for the Holtons on campus after their death was the renaming for them of a small quadrangle outside the Roy O. West library.

Rector on the other hand established his scholarship program while he was still active in his career and he followed through in the six remaining years of his life with an intensity that has become legendary. He himself energetically shepherded the endeavor from Chicago and frequently on campus. Rector regarded each Scholar personally as one of "my boys". Concurrently Rector also was serving the University actively as a leading trustee.

While the Rectors were more gregarious in DePauw relationships than the Holtons, Edward Rector too sought to avoid aggrandizing himself personally. Some of his donations were anonymous. He also declined to have a physical structure named after him, although he financed a large women's residence hall that he named after his father, Isaac Rector, and another residence that he named after his wife, Lucy Rowland.

Rector originally limited his scholarship program mostly to men, for reasons described earlier, while providing other aid for women students. Holton from the start favored approximately equal distribution of scholarships between men and women.

Above all, it could be said of both donors: they wanted to help bring high quality young people to college for the future good of society, and they were utterly generous in using their fortunes to this end.

***

Chapter 12

AN INVESTMENT IN HUMANITY

"My investments in DePauw ... are investments in humanity, in the men and women who are to carry on the work of our country and the world when you and I are gone ... "
— Edward Rector

Edward Rector was keenly interested in the benefits of his philanthropy not only for the University and its students but also for humankind in the future. In a major address in 1923 about his contributions, Rector said:

> "I have been talking about my investments in DePauw, but they are not investments in DePauw University, they are investments in humanity, in the men and women who are to carry on the work of our country and the world when you and I are gone ... DePauw is merely the medium through which we may make such an investment for the future, and offers us the opportunity and the privilege."[1]

How well did Rector's scholarship program perform towards his lofty goal?

Three-and-one-half years after its 1919 launching, the philanthropist said the "experiment" thus far had proved to be "successful beyond our highest anticipations" in raising the schools' academic levels.[2] Unfortunately he died before a broader picture could emerge from the post-graduate careers of "my boys".

Two decades after the program's founding, University president Clyde Wildman told the trustees: "Its influence on the life of the University and on the men who have been Rector Scholars is beyond any possibility of estimate ..."[3]

Sixty years later University president Robert G. Bottoms reported that Rector's "endowed gift has made possible the education of some 4000 Rector Scholars in the intervening 80 years. These graduates of DePauw are among the most accomplished individuals in this country and have been extremely loyal alumni."[4]

Ninety years later, this chapter attempts to convey a sense of the program's societal benefits by recounting the achievements of some of its outstanding graduates and of Rector alumni generally.

Robert G. Bottoms

RECTOR ALUMNI GIVING TO DEPAUW

Before doing so, it should be noted also that Rector Scholars as a whole have contributed generously to an "investment in humanity" through their pocketbooks as well as through distinguished careers. University officials have found Rector Scholars, as a group, to be stronger donors to DePauw than any other sector in the graduate body.[5]

For example, in the school's sesquicentennial fund-raising campaign in the 1980s more than 18,000 alumni contributed $121 million. Twelve percent of the donors were former Rector Scholars, but their gifts accounted for 46 percent ($56 million) of the total.[6] Rector alumni have continued over the years to be a priority target for University officials engaged in fund-raising.

HOLTON MEMORIAL SCHOLARSHIP

O ne outstanding donor has already been mentioned in the previous chapter. **Philip F. Holton**, and his wife, **Ruth Clark Holton**, were students at DePauw in 1925-27. While they did not graduate from there, their attachment to DePauw remained intact for a lifetime and Holton was mindful of the Rector Scholarship that supported him financially at DePauw.

Holton's generosity toward DePauw, like Rector's, focused on educating high quality young people for the future good of society. At the time of their bequest, the Holtons' $128 million donation to DePauw in 1999 for a scholarship program was the largest gift in history to any private liberal arts college.[7]

GIFTS TO THE RECTOR SCHOLARSHIP FUND

A substantial number of Rector Scholars, as well as others, have given specifically to the **Rector Scholarship Fund** itself. Chapter 9 notes more than 300 such donations over the last half of the 20th century. Many Rector alumni felt they owed their DePauw education to Rector. Contributing to his fund was a way of saying "thank you" and of adding to the "investment in humanity."

The largest of these gifts came from **Robert L. Edwards**, a Rector Scholar, and his wife, **Jane**, late in the century. Robert gave $1.84 million to the Rector endowment and Jane $1.86 million – a total of $3.7 million, $1 million more than Rector's original overall contribution of $2.7 million, though of course the purchasing power of the original Rector dollars was far greater because of inflation over the years.

Edwards, from Newcastle, Ind., and his wife, then **Jane Isackson**, of St. Charles, Ill., a 1931 DePauw graduate, met at DePauw and married after his graduation in 1933. Edwards, a team swimmer and football player at school, loved sports and the outdoor life. Jane was active in theater and other extracurricular activities. Heeding the adage "go west, young man," Edwards headed to the Pacific northwest where he engaged in various businesses. He was particularly successful in real estate in the Seattle area, and in later years he engaged in breeding thoroughbred horses. The Edwards had children and their philanthropies also extended to other charities and institutions besides DePauw.[8] About his Rector gift, he said his scholarship had allowed him to stay at DePauw and he and his wife "want to reciprocate" what the college had done for them.[9]

There are other instances of philanthropies inspired at least in part by the Rector example although not involving Rector Scholars as such. **Jesse King** of St. Petersburg, Fla., who died in 2000 at age 86, kept among his personal papers a June 15, 1932, letter informing him that he had been awarded a Rector Scholarship. His executor wrote to the Rector Scholarship Foundation that while King was unable to enroll at DePauw mainly for economic reasons, "I thought you might like to know how much I believe the award of this scholarship meant to him during his life." Jesse and his wife **Lela King** established a Lela and Jesse King Scholarship Foundation providing college scholarships to local high school graduates in their area.[10]

Arthur E. Klauser wanted to get a Rector Scholarship upon enrolling at DePauw in 1941 but had to accept another scholarship because of a late timing in his application. Upon joining a fraternity he found Rector Scholars among his brothers whom he admired. Klauser graduated from another university after World War II military service but he retained his affinity for DePauw. His major donations to the University were inspired in part, he said, by the Rector example. He served as a

Arthur E. Klauser

lifetime trustee and among his gifts were valuable Japanese art objects put on DePauw museum display.[11]

ACHIEVEMENTS OF RECTOR GRADUATES

Any attempt to name specific Rector graduates for their contributions to society poses a painful problem in selection: if only some of the Scholars are listed, others must be left out; but to include all those with worthy careers, totaling literally thousands over the years, lies beyond the physical capability of a book of this size and probably beyond the tolerance of most readers.

Edward Rector himself spoke regretfully of this selection problem in talking of Scholars' achievements early in the program. "It is hardly fair to single out two or three and tell you of them," he said, "while saying nothing of a hundred others who are leaders on the DePauw campus now, and they will be leaders in after life wherever they go."[12]

This chapter seeks to present some representative segments of Rector alumni accomplishments by starting with the original Rector graduates; by drawing from the University's selections for Old Gold Goblet awards, DePauw's top honor for alumni; and by anonymous, but real, sampling from among other alumni who comprise the great body of Rector graduates.

First Graduating Class

John F. Cady, who was the "first Rector Scholar" – the first Rector selected in the original class of 1919 - graduated Phi Beta Kappa and went on to teaching, writing and research in the U.S. and abroad with a specialization in southeast Asia. While he never served on the DePauw faculty, Cady visited Greencastle frequently. He founded the Rector Alumni Association and was active in its direction for years. During his career Cady was a Fulbright Fellow, a Guggenheim Fellow and author of award-winning books. Following his retirement at Ohio University as a distinguished professor of history, DePauw awarded Cady an honorary doctorate.[13]

Rector's "high" man from the class of 1919 – **A. Dale Allen**, first listed in the class alphabetically – likewise served with distinction in education. After graduating from DePauw he taught at seven high schools in Indiana, earned masters and doctoral degrees from Indiana University, and for the last 15 years of his professional life held a professorship at Indiana University of Pennsylvania where he also served as an assistant dean. As one of seven children in a poor family, Allen, like so many other Rector alumni, credited his college education to "the generosity and encouragement of Edward and Lucy Rector."[14]

George W. Gore Jr., the one African-American member of the first Rector graduating class, went on to earn a master's degree from Harvard and a doctorate from Columbia. In his

George W. Gore Jr.

pioneering career he was a teacher of English and journalism, an author and a vigorous promoter of academic excellence. He served as president of the American Teachers Association and in 1937 founded the Alpha Kappa Mu national honor society for college upperclass students, whose purpose is to promote high scholarship. He served as president of Florida A&M University for 18 years until retiring in 1968 as president emeritus, after which he was an interim president of Fisk University.[15] (More than 10 other college presidencies were held by subsequent Rector alumni, including **G. Herbert Smith** and **John Wittich** named in Chapter 10 above.[16])

Of the substantial number of Rector scholars with distinguished teaching careers at DePauw itself, **Coen G. Pierson** was a favorite of Edward Rector from the class of 1919. Rector admired Pierson's devotion to education despite a lack of finances – "he led his class in scholarship from the beginning" – and predicted a bright future for his industrious student.[17] Pierson earned master's and doctoral degrees at the Universities of Illinois and Wisconsin, respectively. He returned to DePauw as a history professor, rising to department head in a 41-year DePauw faculty career. He was an early leader in the Rector Alumni Association. Among his many other contributions to the field of education was service as president of the Indiana History Teachers Association.[18]

Sam T. Hanna, from the original Rector class, became part of DePauw institutionally through an important component, the bookstore, and through active support as an alumnus. In 1930 he founded a bookstore in Greencastle which became known unofficially as "the downtown part of the xxx campus". He operated it until 1954, when the University decided to have its own bookstore, locating it in the college's Union Building. The school then hired Hanna as bookstore manager, a position he held until 1970, the year of his death.[19] As a devoted alumnus,

Sam T. Hanna (above right), from the original Rector class, and his son, Daniel H. Hanna, '47, grouped around G. Herbert Smith (center), a director of the Edward Rector Scholarship Foundation. Sam Hanna was longtime bookstore manager at DePauw. Dan was the first Rector Scholar to be the son of a Rector Scholar.

the jovial Hanna served twice as president of the DePauw Alumni Association. He also served as president of the Rector Alumni Association. His professional activities included presidency of the National Association of College Stores for seven years.[20] Hanna's son Daniel H. Hanna, '47, was the first Rector Scholar to be the son of a Rector Scholar. Dan Hanna served on DePauw's musical faculty.

Rector Recipients of Old Gold Goblets

The Old Gold Goblet, DePauw's top honor for alumni, has been awarded annually since 1941 for "eminence in life's work and service to *alma mater*." A substantial number of honorees have been Rector Scholars[21] and have come from a wide range of professions. The following profiles are largely from among Rector Scholars who received the top alumni award:

University Administration

Robert H. Farber was a Rector Scholar who returned to his *alma mater* for a lifelong career at DePauw that made him by reputation an institution in his own right, as had been the case with his early mentor, professor Henry B. Longden. After graduating in 1935, Farber signed on as a junior administrator with duties including assisting the director of the Edward Rector Scholarship Foundation. He earned a master's degree from the University of Chicago, his thesis dealing with the Rector Scholarship program, and a doctorate in education from Indiana University. After decorated overseas service in the U.S. Army during World War II, during which he rose to the rank of major, he returned to administrative duties at DePauw including directorship of the Rector Foundation.

In 1952 Farber was named dean, a post he held until his retirement 27 years later. He also held positions as vice president of the university and, in 1976-77, as acting president, but to many DePauwites he continued to be known as "Dean Farber."

(He subsequently joked that after 42 years at DePauw he was so often referred to as "dean" that many thought Dean was his first name.) Like Longden, Farber remained in Greencastle after retirement. He maintained an active interest in campus affairs well into the 21st century.[22]

Philanthropies and personal service to DePauw

Timothy H. Ubben and his wife, **Sharon Williams Ubben**, both graduated in 1958 from DePauw. Ubben was a Rector Scholar and while on campus was a leader in many student activities. He was president of the Union Board and first chairman of the Little 500 annual race, a festive athletic event that thereafter became a yearly tradition at DePauw. Ubben went on to earn an M.B.A. from Northwestern University in 1959, and in time became chairman

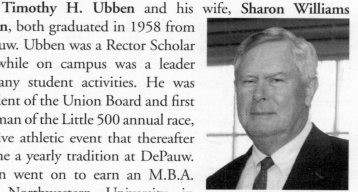

Timothy H. Ubben

and managing director of the Chicago-based Lincoln Capital Management Co., with over $50 billion in assets under its management.

Ubben continued to serve DePauw in alumni leadership roles. He was a president of the DePauw Alumni Association. For a record three times, he was chairman of the school's annual fund. In 1998 he became chairman of the Board of Trustees. The Ubbens' many philanthropies for DePauw included support for student scholarship funds and athletic capital projects. Probably their best-known donation was endowment for an annual lecture series on campus intended to enrich the learning environment at DePauw. The Timothy and Sharon Ubben Lecture Series has featured world notables ranging from Margaret Thatcher and Shimon Perez to Benazir Bhutto, Michail Gorbachev, Colin Powell and Tony Blair. The Ubbens have given substantially also to other causes and institutions, including the University of Illinois.

Business and Civic Affairs

John H. Filer attended DePauw as a Rector Scholar and after graduation in 1947 returned to his native New Haven to earn a Yale law degree. Active in politics as a young lawyer, he served in the state Senate in 1977 and 1978. In 1958 he joined Aetna Casualty and Insurance Company as an assistant counsel, rising to chairman and chief executive of the firm by 1972. Under his chairmanship until his retirement in 1984, Aetna's assets climbed from $11 billion to more than $40 billion, which the company said made it the largest shareholder-owned insurance organization in the nation.

Throughout his career Filer also contributed outstandingly in civic affairs. In the mid-1970s he headed a 60-man Commission on Private Philanthropy and Public Needs that won national praise. President Ford appointed him to the Task Force on Private Sector Initiatives. President Carter appointed him to the Commission on Military Compensation. Filer chaired the 40th anniversary campaign of the NAACP Legal and Educational Fund. Locally, he was instrumental in an Aetna-Hartford joint development of the Hartford Civic Center, and in bringing a National Hockey League, the Whalers, to Hartford.[23] Following retirement, one of his services was chairmanship of the Independent Sector, the nation's largest philanthropic coalition.[24] DePauw conferred an honorary degree on him in 1970.

Journalism

Bernard Kilgore, class of 1929, was judged by a media organization in the year 2000 to have been the "top business journalist of the 20th century."[25] "Barney" Kilgore came to DePauw from South Bend, Ind., as a Rector Scholar, edited the school newspaper and yearbook, graduated Phi Beta Kappa, and fresh out of college joined the *Wall Street Journal* as a 20-year-old cub reporter. The *Journal* at the time was a relatively small and parochial business paper.

Kilgore rose quickly from copy editor to San Francisco

Bernard Kilgore

editor by 1931, to editorial page columnist the following year, to Washington bureau chief in 1935 at age 27. As a writer, he became widely read by business and government leaders. President Franklin Roosevelt, often criticized by Kilgore editorially, nonetheless cited his writing on the National Labor Relations Board as definitive.[26] Kilgore entered the *Journal*'s top administrative ranks at New York headquarters in 1941 with his appointment as general manager. In 1945 he became president of the *Journal*'s parent, Dow Jones & Co.

During his tenure Kilgore was credited with raising the *Journal* to the status of the first national newspaper of its time. He revolutionized the paper's news reporting with broader and more timely coverage, redesigned its front page with a format successful for decades to come and exploited new technology to expand circulation.[27] Between the time he became Dow Jones president and his election to the board chairmanship 21 years later, the paper's readership rose from 33,000 to more than one million and the company's annual profits had risen from $211,000 to more than $13 million. Kilgore served twice as president of DePauw's Board of Trustees and an endowment in his memory supports journalistic activities at DePauw.

Performing Arts

Joseph Flummerfelt was an organist for three churches in Vincennes, Ind., along with being an honors student in high school when at age 17 he received a Rector scholarship enabling him to enroll at DePauw's School of Music. By the time he graduated in 1958 he had directed many of the major campus musical productions, served twice as director of the Collegians singing group, been elected to Gold Key for distinction in college activities and received the Van Denman Thompson Award as the outstanding senior in the School of Music.

Joseph Flummerfelt

After graduation, Flummerfelt pursued his love of music with study in France, then returned to the United States with specialization in choral direction. In 1964-68 he was again at DePauw, as director of choral activities. As his reputation for excellence in choral conducting grew, so did demand for his collaboration in orchestral performances in the United States and internationally.

After a term at Florida State University, Flummerfelt began 22 years of association with the renowned Spoleto Festival in Italy, conducting more than 50 performances. He moved to the New York area where he worked with many of the great names in classical music. As of the turn of the century he was Chorus Master of the New York Philharmonic and Artistic Director of the Westminster Choir College. His many honors include Grammies for works in which he participated, doctoral degrees, *Le Prix du President de la Republique* from L'Academice du Disque Francais, and praise from the legendary composer and conductor Leonard Bernstein as "the world's greatest choral conductor."[28]

U.S. Military Service

When **David M. Shoup**, hometown Covington, Ind., came to DePauw as a Rector Scholar in 1922, the Reserve Officers Training Corps was on campus and compulsory for men in their freshmen and sophomore years and optional for upperclassmen.[29] Shoup continued in ROTC through his senior year and after graduating in 1926 joined the Marine Corps.

Shoup went on the first of many overseas assignments as a U.S. Marine starting with an expeditionary Marine force in Tientsin, China, in 1927. On Dec. 7, 1941, he was in Iceland with the 1st Marine Brigade. Soon thereafter he went to Wellington, New Zealand, as a lieutenant colonel planning the U.S. assault on Tarawa. He commanded the 2nd Marines ashore during the assault and was awarded the nation's highest military decoration – the Medal of Honor – for his action Nov. 20-22, 1943, in the bitter contest for Betio, a Tarawa atoll.

David M. Shoup

Though wounded, the citation said, "by his brilliant leadership, daring tactics and selfless devotion to duty, Col. Shoup was largely responsible for the final decisive defeat of the enemy."

Shoup continued to receive promotions and decorations through the end of World War II and thereafter. President Eisenhower appointed Shoup as Marine Corps commandant, a four-star post that he assumed on Jan. 1, 1960. He was known as President Kennedy's "favorite general"[30] and continued as the Marine Corps' leader under President Johnson until his retirement at the end of 1963 after 37 years in the service, receiving a Distinguished Service Medal from Johnson in January 1964 for exceptionally meritorious service as Commandant.[31]

Space Science

Joseph P. Allen IV, son of a distinguished DePauw economics professor who was a Rector Scholar, also decided to attend DePauw after being awarded a Rector Scholarship.[32] He studied mathematics and physics, graduating Phi Beta Kappa in 1959. He went to Germany as a Fulbright scholar, and then returned to the United States to earn a master's degree in science from Yale in 1961 and a Ph.D. in physics four years later.

Joseph P. Allen IV

His subsequent career literally soared into outer space: in 1967, while a researcher at Washington University's Nuclear Physics Laboratory, the National Aeronautics and Space Administration picked him to be a scientist-astronaut.

Allen combined senior NASA political assignments in Washington with record-breaking space missions before leaving the agency in 1985 to head Space Industries International, Inc. He had logged more than 3,000 hours flying jet aircraft and a total 314 hours in space. He was a mission specialist aboard the *Columbia* in a 1982 flight that demonstrated successful operational capability of the space shuttle. He was on the *Discovery* flight in 1984 that deployed two satellites and achieved the first successful space salvage mission in history. His numerous honors included induction into the Astronaut Hall of Fame, and into DePauw's Athletic Hall of Fame for his collegiate prowess in the 123-pound class wrestling.[33]

Medical Science

Ferid Murad, son of a poor Albanian immigrant family in Whiting, Ind., wanted to be a physician and considered enrolling at the University of Chicago, but was lured instead to

Ferid Murad

DePauw with its Rector stipend. As a Phi Beta Kappa student at Greencastle 1954-58 he majored in pre-medicine and became intrigued with biology. At college he met Carol Leopold '58, his future wife.

After graduation from DePauw, Murad studied for seven years at Western Reserve University in Cleveland, Ohio, earning twin M.D. and Ph.D. (pharmacology) degrees in 1965. Murad then went into academic medicine, teaching and researching at several institutions, followed by a period in private industry as a vice president and corporate officer at

Abbott Laboratories in Chicago. He joined the University of Texas-Houston in 1977 as director of its Institute of Molecular Medicine. His specialty was molecular research in nitric oxide with its multi-faceted potential for medical benefits.

In 1996 Murad was honored with the Albert Lasker Basic Medical Research Award. In 1998 he won a Nobel Prize for Medicine or Physiology.[34]

Public Service – U.S.

Lee H. Hamilton

Lee H. Hamilton came to DePauw in 1948 from Evansville, Ind., as a Rector Scholar and soon established himself as a student leader, scholar and athlete. By the time he graduated *cum laude* in 1952 he had been awarded the Walker Cup as the senior who had contributed most to the University, had been president of his fraternity, and was a basketball star later honored by selection for the DePauw and Indiana Athletic Halls of Fame.

Hamilton studied at Goethe University in Germany for a year after DePauw and then returned to Indiana to earn a law degree from Indiana University in 1956. After practicing law for nearly a decade, he ran for the U.S. House of Representatives from his home district and began a Congressional career lasting a third of a century. Gaining a seat on the House Foreign Affairs Committee, he rose to a subcommittee chairmanship and eventually headed the full committee. He also chaired or co-chaired numerous other committees, including the Permanent Select Committee on Intelligence, the Joint Committee on the Organization of Congress and the Joint Economic Committee.

Reflecting what the *New York Times* once described as the "wide respect among his colleagues for his personal integrity and judicial temperament," Hamilton was a popular choice for leadership in investigating security issues at Los Alamos and co-chair of the commission looking into the 9/11 terrorist attacks. In 1999 he left Congress to head the Woodrow Wilson International Center for Scholars in Washington, D.C.

Earl W. Kintner, born on a farm near Corydon, Ind., attended DePauw under a Rector Scholarship, graduating in 1936. After earning a law degree from Indiana University Law School in 1938 he began a law practice in Princeton, Ind. where he became a prosecuting attorney. During World War II he served in the U.S. Navy, which in 1946 appointed him as Deputy Commissioner for the U.N. War Crimes Commission. After discharge from the Navy in 1948, he joined the Federal Trade Commission staff in Washington, D.C., as a trial lawyer. He had risen to the position of general counsel when President Eisenhower appointed him as FTC chairman in 1959.

As FTC chairman 1959-61 Kintner urged industry to regulate itself but he also quickly gained national recognition for vigorous enforcement of antitrust regulations. In fiscal year 1960 his agency issued a record number of complaints and orders against false advertising and other deceptive trade practices and monopolistic activities. Upon leaving the FTC in 1961 he joined a major Washington law firm where he directed its antitrust practice and was a prolific antitrust writer. He authored or coauthored seven antitrust and trade regulation primers, 11 volumes on federal antitrust legislative history and nine volumes of a treatise on international law. Other activities included teaching at the New York University School of Law and presidencies of the Federal Bar Association and the National Lawyers Club. Among his honors was a doctorate from DePauw in 1970.[35]

Joseph W. Barr reached the pinnacle of his distinguished public service career with appointment as U.S. Secretary of the Treasury during the closing weeks of the Johnson administration in 1968-1969. Barr, a Vincennes, Ind., native, was a Rector

Scholar graduating from DePauw
with Phi Beta Kappa honors in 1939.
His outstanding collegiate record
included president of the senior class,
captain of the football team and
election to the Gold Key activities
honorary. After attending Harvard
for a master's degree in economics
which he received in 1941, he joined
the Navy for World War II duty. He
commanded a subchaser credited
with sinking a submarine off Anzio
Beach, for which he received a bronze star.

Joseph W. Barr

After the war Barr returned to his family business in Indiana
which included grain elevators, farm equipment financing and
banking. In 1958 he ran successfully for a seat in the U.S. House
of Representatives as a Democrat. Defeated for reelection in 1960,
he joined the new Kennedy administration as Assistant Secretary
of the Treasury for Congressional Relations. From 1963 to 1965
he was chairman of the Federal Deposit Insurance Corporation.
Then he returned to Treasury as Undersecretary, the Department's
second ranking position. Among his accomplishments were
helping to build the Asian Development Bank and the Inter-
American Development Bank. After the Nixon administration
took office in 1969, Barr returned to senior banking positions in
the private sector.[36]

Public Service - International

Charles Hirotsugu (Chuck) Iikubo, a Rector Scholar and
son of a 1927 DePauw graduate, returned to his native Japan after
receiving a music degree from DePauw in 1957. In Tokyo Iikubo
entered into international business consulting, founding several
consulting companies. He published books on management,
decision-making, and international relations. In time he became
chairman and CEO of Decision Systems, Inc.

In the 1990s Iikubo founded and brought to fruition the A-50 project, an expression of gratitude for American assistance and friendship for Japan over the past 50 years since the end of World War II. Financed entirely by Japanese  business contributions, the project enlisted support from leading Japanese industrialists, politicians and diplomats. After an opening ceremony in Tokyo attended by senior officials (including then Prime Minister Junichiro Koizumi and former U.S. Vice President Dan Quayle, a DePauw graduate), the Japanese group sent representatives to the U.S. where they presented the A-50 Japanese expression of appreciation in 32 American cities.

Charles Hirotsugu (Chuck) Iikubo

Among Iikubo's many honors were an honorary ambassadorship to the state of Indiana and an honorary doctorate from DePauw. His generosity to his *alma mater* included housing on campus for an Asian and World Community art collection and devoted service as a trustee, notwithstanding he had to travel 8,000 miles from Tokyo twice a year for Board meetings.

RECTOR CONTRIBUTIONS –
A BROADER VIEW

While the contributions to society of those listed above have merited top awards, Edward Rector, were he able to examine results in the year 2000, might well be equally pleased with the cumulative benefit to humankind of the work of the many other Scholar graduates even if they were of less contemporary fame. He was solicitous of all of his "boys," not just the stars.

Rector alumni successful in their fields are not just one here and one there, but number literally in the thousands.

Evidence of this pattern is easily available, for instance, in a reading of obituary notes on Rector Scholars. Following are typical examples from the DePauw alumni magazines over the years, without identifying specific individuals:

After pre-med at DePauw, this Scholar earned a medical degree and practiced medicine for 50 years. He founded a Mental Health Center, which served 11 counties in Appalachia. He dedicated most of his career to helping patients who would not otherwise have proper mental health care. He treated traumatized servicemen during the Vietnam conflict. He served as president of his state psychiatric association, was chief of medical staff at a mental health institute, and held professorships at two major universities. He was a lifetime member of the DePauw Society, an organization of the larger donors to DePauw.[37]

Another Rector alumnus had careers both in the armed services and in civilian life. In the army and as a reservist, he served in both World War II and the Korean War, rising to the rank of colonel. He attended the General Staff and Command College and at the time of his retirement commanded an infantry reserve division. His civilian career began as a newspaperman with the *Wall Street Journal*. Subsequently he founded and became editor and publisher of a magazine for a major national trade organization. His civic service included presidency of a local civic association, membership on national boards of his Greek fraternity and the national journalist society and presidency of the DePauw alumni club of a large American city.[38]

A Rector alumnus entered the ministry, carried out his calling with distinction during his active service and retired as senior pastor of a large

Methodist Church in his state's capital city. He was well known for his television ministry in the state and had received an honorary doctorate of divinity degree. After retirement he served as a chaplain and Sunday School organizer at a local ecumenical retirement center, on the state code of ethics study commission, on its employment security advisory council and on an education study task force.[39]

A Rector graduate interested in education earned a doctorate at a major California university and after active World War II duty spent two years in occupied Germany as a director of teacher training. Returning to a western college where he had taught history, he was appointed founding dean of the College of Liberal Arts and Sciences there. After 10 years in that position, during which the parent college became a university, he returned to teaching full time, authored scholarly books and articles and was recipient of the College of Liberal Arts Distinguished Achievement Award.[40]

A woman student who enrolled at DePauw without a Rector Scholarship, which was then restricted to men at the entry level, won a Rector award by achieving the highest grades in her class. After graduation she was a wife, mother and homemaker, raising three children, one of whom chose DePauw for his college education. Professionally, she earned a master's degree in education and served as an investment adviser at two banks. Subsequently she became a teacher in the public school system. She helped establish a project for gifted children, later becoming director of programs for gifted children; and of a community library, where she volunteered until her death.[41]

A talented Rector alumnus became a university

professor with in-depth knowledge of biology, anatomy and world history. He was versed in 12 foreign languages. Known for his research and lectures, he was listed in *Who's Who in the World, Who's Who in America,* and other compilations of persons of distinction nationally and internationally.[42]

A journalist who owed his college education to Rector credited his benefactor indirectly with the influence of the journalist's 40 years of editorials and columns on the lives of his readers. He said his writings resulted in improving treatment of the mentally ill – "a difference that was really made possible by Edward Rector." Also he said it was "thanks to Edward Rector" that he was able to write columns on official misconduct and pursue a career that included meetings with Presidents Truman, Eisenhower, Nixon, Ford and Reagan.[43]

These anonymous but real samplings of Rector alumni achievements obviously list only a tiny fraction of the Scholars who have been and are continuing to contribute to society in so many ways. There will be many more in the years ahead. It is hard to imagine Edward Rector as being other than hugely pleased with the results of his investment were he to see them today.

***

A SUMMARY CONCLUSION

Edward Rector possessed a rare combination of grand vision and the means, talent and will to achieve it. Fortunately for society, his goal was to benefit humankind.

Fortunately for DePauw, this small Midwest school came to Rector's attention at a time in his life when he was interested in devoting more of his time and of his wealth to charitable causes. He valued education in particular as a means of improving the lives of the young and through them, society thereafter. DePauw would be his institutional instrument.

Several aspects of DePauw attracted Rector to "invest" in the school. The University was small enough that his donations, especially the historically grand scholarship program, would raise the whole school academically to an entirely new level. It was in Rector's home state of Indiana. It was close enough to Chicago to allow Rector, whose style was ever hands-on, to visit frequently and associate with those he lovingly called "my boys" – the Rector Scholars – and the school leadership. DePauw's managers were amenable to Rector's ideas and Rector himself in time became part of the University's leadership.

While Rector's brilliance and personal involvement keyed the success of the scholarship program's success in its early years, several others made contributions of inestimable value. Henry B. Longden, legendary with his 73 years at DePauw, devoted his wisdom and administrative skill to the program unstintingly from its start in 1919 until his retirement in 1935. Roy O. West, a DePauw alumnus and Rector friend, stoked Rector's interest in DePauw, served as Board Chairman for an unprecedented 26 years and likewise strongly supported the scholarship program throughout. And of course, Lucy Rowland Rector stood by her husband's side lovingly throughout their marriage and after Edward's death, continued as a beacon for his program until her death 24 years later.

During his lifetime Rector was highly pleased with the results of his scholarship program. Over the next 75 years following his death, as reported in this volume, the school had a mixed record in handling the program, both financially and administratively.

In reviewing the financial management of the Rector endowment, it can be contended – with 20-20 hindsight – that the University and its trustees should have acted sooner to protect its assets in the face of the impending Great Depression. Certainly, as was recognized at the time, its holdings should have been more diversified. Arguably the Rector funds were vital or at least of great importance to DePauw's survival during this period, though the methods of utilizing the moneys could not satisfy an accounting purist. On the plus side there was never a suspicion of dishonorable conduct by trustees or University management, who clearly worked diligently and conscientiously in doing what they thought at the time was best for DePauw.

The endowment was finally put on a sound growth pattern by the early 1980's, though in any event no investing technique could have overcome a huge decline in the endowment's scholarship award capabilities in the face of DePauw's 267-fold tuition cost increase (along with other college tuition increases) from 1919 to 2000. What was notable by the end of the century was that the Rector fund was still the second largest scholarship endowment at the University and was still able to attract many academically gifted youths.

On the administrative side the scholarship program in its first years after Rector's death blossomed beyond its founder's expectations. Some early serious problems were addressed ably by management. In later years difficulties arose beyond control of even the best administrators. Not only was the Rector endowment income shrinking in real-life terms, but also the student atmosphere was changing and competition from other schools and scholarship programs was rising. Though the administrators made valiant efforts in the face of these circumstances to keep the Rector program and its spirit as vibrant as in earlier years, they had at best only temporary modest success. With the passage of time, the former priority given the program faded. The once-prominent Edward Rector Scholarship Foundation disappeared from view.

One notable characteristic of the Foundation's administration was the high quality of its directors. Longden was the first, followed by others among the school's most capable managers – G. Herbert Smith, Robert H. Farber, John J. Wittich and Louis J. Fontaine. Most importantly, the University leadership by the end of the century rediscovered the value of the Rector legacy; it reinstated the program as the school's preeminent academic scholarship. To maintain this value in the future it will be incumbent on the leadership to continue active attention to the program without letup.

Overall, the results of Rector's "investment in humanity" could fairly be described as magnificent. A number of his Scholars to date have reached the pinnacle of achievement in their fields. Thousands of others have made worthy and lasting contributions to society, if less spectacularly, and more will be doing so in the future

Rector if he were alive today would have been proud of them all and pleased that his investment will be continuing to yield indefinitely in the years to come.

***

EPILOGUE

Nearly 90 years ago Edward Rector had a vision in which the best students of Indiana could attend college regardless of their financial means. This dream was motivated by his own financial inability to attend college despite his genius. Through his hard work, driving will, and biting intellect, he was able to forge a career for himself regardless of his lack of formal education, becoming one of the most successful corporate lawyers of his time. With success comes fortune, and with this fortune Rector was able to realize his dream by endowing DePauw University with a scholarship program that would not only attract gifted students to the University but also ensure that these gifted students could attend. For Rector, establishing the endowment was not enough. He knew that if he wanted to create true scholarship he must not only provide money, but also offer encouragement and create fellowship to ensure that "his boys" could become the men he knew could change the world – this was Rector's investment in humanity.

Today the Rector Scholarship Program continues to provide talented students with the privilege of a DePauw education. As tuition and boarding costs soar, prospective students, especially the best and brightest of the applicant pool, increasingly base their college choice on the merit scholarships offered to them. By extending the Rector Scholarship to these applicants, DePauw is able to compete with (and sometimes even lure applicants away from) other prestigious universities across the country. The scholarship also makes quality undergraduate study possible for many who could not otherwise afford it, a privilege that was denied Edward Rector.

Current Rector Scholars continue to add to the campus

community through their involvement in athletics, philanthropy, student organizations, Greek life, and the arts. They study various disciplines, ranging from psychology to music, and computer science to English literature. They excel in DePauw's honors programs and also participate in many national honor societies. Many scholars also contribute to the world community by utilizing the opportunity the Rector scholarship and DePauw's outstanding Off-Campus Study Program provides to work or study off-campus both domestically and internationally in places such as France, Chile, Japan and everywhere in between.

We are proud and grateful to attend DePauw University as Rector Scholars and to work on this book in our benefactor's honor. We know that as Rector Scholars, we join a prestigious group of men and women who have honed their natural talent at DePauw and used it to make top achievements in their respective fields. After graduation, we hope to extend the Rector tradition of excellence in our own unique ways, contributing to society both by following in the paths of the Rector Scholars who preceded us and also by striking out on our own paths on which we will strive to attain new levels of distinction. Wherever those paths may take us, we will always appreciate the generosity of the man who made our education possible.

Though the scholarship continues to attract superb students and offer them a quality of education many could not otherwise afford, the program in later times lost much of the originality and character that Rector worked so hard to build. Historically, the bonding of the Scholars has been an important and unique aspect of the Rector scholarship program. Rector himself worked diligently to build camaraderie among the scholarship recipients by personally associating with "his boys" during his lifetime. In contrast, during our first years on campus the Rector Scholars rarely, if ever, met as a group. The five of us would have been strangers to each other if it had not been for this project, and as of this writing we are still strangers to many of our Rector peers currently studying at DePauw. Some of us have had close friendships with Scholars for years before finding out that they too hold this extraordinary scholarship. We are pleased to see that DePauw University has taken steps to remedy this situation and hope for more in the future.

In general, it should be remembered that the Rector award was originally both an academic honor and a monetary gift. Over the years, as this book's account shows, there have been periods of flagging interest in the program by administrators causing the once-distinctive award to blend in with DePauw's numerous other scholarships. To maintain and enhance the program's value to both DePauw and humanity, it must be kept in mind that funding is not the only virtue of a Rector scholarship. Along with keeping the scholarships high in monetary value, DePauw University should emphasize the scholarship as its top merit award, treat recruits accordingly, and nurture the "Rector spirit" on both an individual and a group basis as did the founder of the program. Only then will the true intentions of Edward Rector be upheld for future generations of Rector Scholars.

***

The Epilogue is authored by five 21st Century Rector Scholars who volunteered, while students at DePauw, to assist in preparation of this book as a way of honoring their benefactor. The Rector team is shown above with President Robert G. Bottoms (left to right): Melissa R. Bock '10, Juliana P. Keller '09, Kasey M. Aderhold '10, Bottoms, Hannah L. Harp '10 and team leader Joanna J. Kieschnick '09.

Appendix

"MY INVESTMENT IN DEPAUW"

DePauw's Archives record only one major speech by Edward Rector. It was an overview of his philanthropies to the school. He delivered it to a DePauw University Dinner at the Claypool Hotel in Indianapolis, Ind., Jan. 30, 1923. Following is the text:[1]

Mr. Chairman and Ladies and Gentlemen:

If I had had time to prepare a speech for this occasion I think I should have selected as my topic "My Investment in DePauw," for it is altogether the most satisfactory and profitable investment I have ever made, and it is the thing of greatest interest in my life today.

As an avocation I practice law, and one reason I have not had time to collect my thoughts into the form of a speech for tonight is that I have been engaged all day in trying a law suit in the federal court here in Indianapolis, and those of you present who are lawyers and practice in that court know that it is sometimes strenuous work.

Mr. West[2] (interrupting): But he won his case today, so he is feeling very good tonight.

Mr. Rector: Yes, by some accident or good fortune justice did prevail today - at least my client thought so.

As I was saying, I practice law as an avocation, but my vocation is DePauw University - and there is material in my investment in that Institution and in my experience in connection with it for a real good speech, and I am very sorry that I have not had time to prepare it, and that even if I had had the time I have not the eloquent tongue of the Bishop and the statesmen who have preceded me to express it to you as I should like to do.

But if you will just consider yourselves in an old-fashioned Methodist class meeting and permit me to relate my experiences, I will give you some account of my investment in DePauw and some concrete illustrations which may perhaps explain why the investment has proved so pleasing and so profitable.

It would have been more correct, perhaps, to have referred to my investment in the plural because they have been successive ones, and each has proved more

---

1   DC 69 Folder 4. Rector delivered the speech without a prepared text. What appears here is a transcription of his oral remarks. Editing has included capitalizations, paragraphing and punctuation, but no changing of words.

2   Roy O. West, a prominent DePauw trustee and close friend of Rector.

satisfactory than its predecessor ones. They began in a very small way some seven or eight years ago with a modest subscription to the Building Fund for the Bowman Memorial Building at the instigation or solicitation of my friend Mr. West, who was at that time deeply interested in athletics - chiefly athletics of a political nature. He has not been nearly so much interested in such things in recent years, owing to some changed conditions in Chicago and in the State of Illinois, but his interest is now beginning to revive since "Big Bill"[3] has announced his intention of retiring from the office of Mayor of Chicago, so that my friend's hopes and prospects are rising.

As I was saying, my first investment in DePauw was a very modest one in the Bowman Memorial Building Fund. This was followed not long afterward by another small one in the way of a Loan Fund for the assistance of worthy and needy students who required some financial help to enable them to remain at the University and get through their college course.

In conversation with Doctor Grose I inquired whether there was any fund at the University available for such students. He said there was a fund provided by the Methodist Church, or possibly its board of education, but that there were restrictions upon its use which prevented it from being available to a good many students. It was a condition of that fund that loans from it should be made only to students who were members of the Methodist Church, and inasmuch as there were then, as now, hundreds of students at the University who were neither members of the Methodist Church or even of Methodist families – Catholics and Jews and Protestants of many other denominations, including students from all parts of the world – there were many instances in which this fund did not supply the pressing needs of the student body.

I told Doctor Grose I should like to provide a fund that should have no restrictions attached to it, that should be available for every worthy student whatever his "race, color, or previous condition of servitude," to say nothing of his religious beliefs and connections or lack of them. I found Doctor Grose immediately interested and appreciative of what I desired to do, and he enhanced my own interest and desire ten-fold by telling me of some appealing instances in his then recent experiences in which the restrictions upon the Loan Fund previously available had deprived some of the finest and most worthy students of its benefits.

As nothing appeals to one, or at least to me, so strongly as concrete illustrations, I will tell you of one instance which Doctor Grose related to me at that time. He said one of the finest students in the Senior Class of the year before had come to him a few months before commencement and said that she would be obliged to leave the University because her means were exhausted – that she had had a hard struggle throughout the years she had been there but had hoped and expected to be able to get through, but finally found that she had exhausted every resource and would simply have to give up and go home.

The President said to her, "Why, you belong to a Methodist family, why don't you avail yourself of the Loan Fund?" She replied that while that was true, she herself had never actually joined the Church - that she had always intended to do so, and still did, but had put it off from time to time, and that now she could not think of

---

3   William Hale "Big Bill" Thomson was a Republican mayor of Chicago 1915-23. West, a Republican from Chicago, was active in Illinois politics.

doing it at this time and in this emergency because it would appear that her action was prompted by her necessity.

Well, I naturally felt, as you would, that if there were any more girls like that at DePauw, and there doubtless were, they could have my last dollar, if need be, rather than to be obliged to go home and abandon their efforts to secure an education for the lack of such a pitiful sum of money as would enable them to continue and complete it. Doctor Grose said, of course, that a way was found to enable the young woman to continue on for the few remaining months and graduate with her class, but he said that such appealing cases were continually recurring and often caused embarrassment and actual distress of heart and mind on the part of the officers of the University who had to deal with them.

I will not take your time to multiply instances and illustrations, showing how the investment of a very small amount of money in work such as this may accomplish a world of good and be of the most far-reaching effect, and will mention only one other case of which Doctor Grose spoke to me at the time I first took the matter up with him, and that was a fine young fellow of a Catholic family who arrived on the DePauw Campus with just two dollars and a half in his pocket – his sole possessions – and announced that he had come to stay four years and get an education; and he did, working his way through and completing his course with high honors.

Now, what I started out to say, before my thought was diverted by memory of these individual cases of which Doctor Grose told me, was that in a few years this Students' Aid Fund, as it came to be called, had reached a point where it had become a revolving and self-perpetuating fund, and required no replenishment or addition. The students to whom the loans are made are allowed to fix their own time for repayment. They give their notes or receipts for the loans, calling for a small rate of interest, and both principal and interest have been repaid so regularly and completely that the small amount of income from interest has made up such trifling losses of principal as have occurred, so that the Fund is going round and round, year after year, furnishing the necessary assistance to a multitude of students.

So that was my second investment in DePauw, and I think you can realize, without my saying more, how exceedingly gratifying the results of it have been. Indeed, I do not know of any investment of a small or a large sum of money, that is likely to bring more direct returns and greater ones, of more far-reaching effect, than just such assistance to young men and young women who are eager for higher education in an institution such as DePauw, and have the capacity for it, but who in the absence of such assistance would be deprived of it.

My third investment in DePauw was in the building of the dormitory for the girls, now known as Rector Hall. Pardon me (I see some of them present here tonight), I should have said for the "young women," for we don't call them "girls" at DePauw.

Senator Beveridge[4] (interrupting): Why don't you call them "girls?"

Mr. Rector: Because, Senator, as the English would say, "it just isn't done," under the existing administration.

Senator Beveridge: They were called girls when I was there, and that's what I call them.

---

4   Albert J. Beveridge, an 1885 DePauw graduate, served in the U.S. Senate from Indiana for 12 years, 1899-1911.

Mr. Rector: Well, as I was saying, my third investment in DePauw was in the building and equipment of Rector Hall, the home of a hundred and thirty or forty young women, with dining room accommodations for three hundred, so that three times a day, as well as on other occasions, it is the gathering place of about that number. I am sure that to those of you who have visited it and seen those lovely young girls – pardon me, "young women" – no more need be said to assure you of the pleasure and satisfaction that I have derived, and continue to derive in increasing degree on each successive visit to Greencastle, from this third investment in DePauw University. If you could only bring home to those with whom you come in contact in the coming Endowment Campaign a realization of the satisfaction of such an investment I feel sure you would have no difficulty in raising twice the amount of money we have set as our goal – although, I fear, a great many of the contributors would want to build dormitories, and we might have an oversupply.

Following the building of the dormitory came our Endowment Campaign of five years ago, and a year or two later the raising of $100,000, now known as the Retiring Allowance Fund, the income from which makes provision in degree for the old age or incapacity of members of the faculty who have served the University long and well.

No one who is acquainted with that splendid body of men and women who constitute the faculty of DePauw University can fail to understand and appreciate, I think, the satisfaction derived from an investment in these two funds. The first one, the Endowment Fund, enabled the University, by the additional income derived from it, to increase in some measure the utterly inadequate salaries theretofore paid to the members of the faculty, while the latter made the first provision in the history of the University for the needs and comfort of retiring members of the faculty who have given their lives to its service.

There is no finer body of men and women in the world than those composing the faculty of such institutions as DePauw University, and none rendering greater or more inadequately paid service for humanity and the future of our country, and in contributing to an Endowment Fund whose income goes exclusively to their support one is making an investment of the very highest and finest character.

Now I come to my last, or perhaps I should say latest, investment in DePauw - the Scholarship Foundation. My previous investments had been so exceedingly satisfactory that I thought I would risk another one. So this Scholarship Foundation was established.

When I graduated from the Bedford High School forty-odd years ago, nearly all of my class went off to college, at least we called it that, and considered it so, although the institution was not a college but the school then being conducted by Mr. Brown and Mr. Kinzie at Valparaiso, later known as Valparaiso University. I felt very much abused that I did not have the means to accompany my classmates, and I always afterwards had a notion that if I were ever able I would like to help some fellows to go to college who were in the fix I was in at that time.

Finally the opportunity seemed to present itself, and this Scholarship Foundation at DePauw was established. It began four years ago and will graduate its first class next June. It began with about 50 students, selected from the various High Schools of the State on their scholarship records, and the recommendations of their

High School principals. Since then we have taken in something more than a hundred each year, until we now have on the Campus more than 300 of the finest young men in the State of Indiana, and a number from outside the State, in this group of Scholarship students, and the Scholarship Fund is yielding for their support $40,000 a year.

These Scholarship boys have not disappointed us. The experiment has proved satisfactory and successful beyond our highest anticipations. They have demonstrated the fact that there is nothing inconsistent between high scholarship and all manner of college activities, and it has come to be a common remark that they have made scholarship fashionable on the DePauw campus.

They are taking leading parts in every college activity, and have entirely dispelled the idea that a fine athlete cannot at the same time be a good scholar and make a creditable record. They are tending, I am told by the faculty and administration, to raise the standard of scholarship throughout the student body, and are also exciting interest in many of the high schools of the state and inducing the students there to strive for the honor and privileges of these scholarships.

We not only offer scholarships to the high school students making creditable records, but there are additional scholarships offered to the non-scholarship young men of the freshman class to the University, so that the number of Scholarship students coming from the high schools each year is augmented by a certain number of additional students who win their scholarships during their freshman year. The offering of these Scholarships to the members of the freshman class has naturally tended to increase interest in the Scholarship Foundation in the student body and led to increased intellectual efforts upon the part of all the members of the Freshman Class.

At the time the Scholarship Foundation was established, about the close of the war, the number of young women in attendance at DePauw was largely in excess of that of young men, for which reason, among others, the offer of scholarships was limited to young men, so far as the students coming from high schools were concerned, with the result that the relative numbers have been reversed and the young men are now in the majority - as they of course should be to enable them to better hold their own in competition with the young women! There was this exception made to the general plan, however, that a scholarship was offered without restriction as to sex to the student taking the highest honors in each of the four classes at the University, with the result that in the succeeding years many of these honors and these scholarships have been won by the young women.

We have already graduated four of them, among whom were some of the most brilliant students who have ever attended the University, and in the senior class of the present year we have a brilliant and charming young woman who won her scholarship in her sophomore year and bids fair to take the honors of her class in this, her senior year. So you see the scholarship loaf has been duly leavened and made more attractive and interesting.

The Scholarship Foundation is not only a thing of absorbing interest and intense satisfaction, but it affords abundant entertainment and diversion to those who are in touch with it, and if you will indulge me I will tell you of a few personal incidents which serve as illustrations:

Four or five years ago a young woman graduated from the University and went down into the southern part of the state to teach in a high school. There was an attractive young fellow in the senior class there, and what happened has so frequently happened upon the DePauw campus, even under the watchful eye of Doctor Gobin.

The high school teacher and the student were attracted to each other and became engaged and after the close of the school year were married. He had never expected to be able to attend college, but she was determined that he should have as good an education as she had, and so she remained at the high school and taught another year and earned money enough to enable him to come to DePauw with the assistance of one of these scholarships.

That young man made a very wonderful record at the University. He led his class in scholarship from the very beginning, and although he would have been in the senior class this year, he completed the four years course in three and was graduated with high honors last June. He is now teaching in the Greencastle High School at a good salary and earning money with which to go forward still further in his work of higher education as soon as he can prepare for it. I am immensely proud of the record he made as one of the first of our Scholarship students, and I shall be greatly mistaken if Coen Pierson is not heard from in a large way in the future.

But lest you may think that all of the Scholarship students are book-worms or "grinds," as you may have assumed Pierson to have been from what I have said, although in that you would be greatly mistaken, I will tell you something of another Scholarship student of a different stamp but of equal interest. His name is Scales, Rufus Scales.

I am very fond of telling about Rufus. He is what, as a lawyer, I would call my Exhibit "A." I fear I may have at times caused him some embarrassment by the freedom with which I have used his name and the publicity I have given him, but if so I hope he will forgive me, for I certainly consider him one of our prize students and shall watch his future career with great interest.

He came from Tennessee, down in the southwestern part of the state. He had been raising bees down there, and as he was obliged to do something to earn some money while going through college he brought half a dozen stands of bees with him when he came to Greencastle two years ago last fall. His bees thrived and prospered and multiplied, and at the same time worked hard and made a lot of honey for him, so that when June and the close of the college term came around Rufus had about a dozen stands of bees, well stocked with honey, instead of the original number.

But he did not quite know what to do with his bees during the summer vacation. He could not very well take them home and bring them back in the fall, and he could not leave them in Greencastle without someone to look after them. So he concluded he would have to stay there himself through the summer vacation and watch his bees and get something else to do to fill in the balance of his time.

He had been doing odd jobs of work around the campus throughout the year, and among other things had been working early mornings, during the spring, in Professor Longden's garden. One morning he came around a little bit late - I suppose it must have been about five o'clock instead of half past four, as you know Greencastle people get up with the sun in both summer and winter - but however that may have been, he was late and most profuse in his apologies and explanations. He said he had overslept himself and explained that he had been very tired when he went to bed the night before, which accounted for it.

When Professor Longden inquired what he had been doing that made him so tired, he said: "Well, last evening some of the fellows and I went downtown where they were holding a sort of a street fair or carnival and there was a professional wrestler there, up on a platform, who was challenging anybody to come up and wrestle with him, and said he would give five dollars to anybody who could throw him. I needed the five so I thought I would take him on. I went up on the platform and it took me 16 minutes to throw him, and I was pretty tired when I got through, but I got the five."

A few weeks later Professor Longden was looking around to see if he could find something for Rufus to do during the summer, to occupy his time while not looking after his bees, and enable him to earn some money in addition to that which he would receive from the honey which the bees were making for him. Among other places which Professor Longden visited with Rufus, in search of a job, was the cement mill at the edge of Greencastle. The manager said he was sorry that he had no job to offer Rufus, but business was dull and they were turning off men almost every day, and he couldn't do anything for him.

But as they were leaving Professor Longden had the happy thought – a real inspiration, I think – of telling the manager the wrestling story I have just related. The manager was interested, of course, and scratched his head and thought a minute or so and then finally said he thought he'd find something for Rufus to do, so he took him on and gave him a job at $25 or $30 a week for the remainder of the summer - and Rufus still had time enough left to look after his bees. When fall came and the college term opened and Rufus had to give up his job he had a considerable sum saved from his earnings at the cement plant, and a still larger sum which he had received from the sale of a thousand pounds of honey that his bees had had been making for him, so that, like his bees, he was in clover, and ready for another year in college.

Another incident of a student, of another character:

Inquiry is often made as to whether the Scholarship Foundation is intended primarily for the benefit of young men without means to secure a college education. The answer is "No, the scholarships are awarded upon the basis of scholarship and character, and nothing else." No inquiry is made respecting the financial status of the applicant. That is not taken into consideration, and ordinarily nothing is known about it, and yet, incidentally and inevitably perhaps, the Scholarships do enable many students to come to the University who would otherwise not be able to do so, or in any event would not undertake it.

Upon a showing of hands on one occasion, at the instance of Doctor Grose, it appeared that one-half of the Scholarship students were at DePauw because of the Scholarships, and a single instance will show that in some cases the students have great difficulty in maintaining themselves even with the aid of the Scholarships, and but for the further assistance of the Loan Fund would not be able to remain at the University.

A year ago, just before the Christmas vacation, when the students were all preparing to go home, one of the Scholarship boys came to Professor Longden and, with an expression of great anxiety on his face, said he wished to ask Professor Longden's advice regarding a matter which was troubling him. He seemed so concerned and distressed that the Professor thought perhaps the boy had become discouraged and was about to give up and go home to stay, but he told him to tell him what his trouble was and he would give him the best advice he could.

He said: "Well, I wanted to know whether you thought I would be justified in borrowing enough money from the Loan Fund to buy an overcoat. I have never had an overcoat in my life. I got through high school all right without one, and maybe I can get through here, but nearly all the fellows seem to have them, and I thought maybe I ought to have one."

Of course Professor Longden told him he thought he should have an overcoat, and told him to go downtown and visit the clothing stores and see whether he could find one that suited him at a reasonable price. He came back an hour later and said he had found one that would be exactly right for twenty-four dollars, Professor Longden gave him an order on the Treasurer for that sum, and he went off and got the coat and came back proudly wearing it, to show it to the Professor, and then started off home for the holidays, the happiest student that left the campus.

Now, I might go on indefinitely telling you about individual students and groups of students among these Scholarship boys over at DePauw. Indeed, it is hardly fair to single out two or three and tell you of them, while saying nothing of a hundred others who are leaders on the DePauw campus now, and they will be leaders in after life wherever they go. They are making history on the campus today, and adding to the inspiring traditions of the Old School.

And you know, DePauw has traditions, found on facts, that are as interesting and inspiring as those of which any other institution can boast. There is one of them that I am very fond of relating, because it so well illustrates the democracy of the institution, which to my mind is one of its greatest attractions and assets.

Almost one-half of the young men at DePauw, both Scholarship and non-scholarship students, are doing more or less work, outside of their studies and college activities, to earn money with which to help pay their expenses through the institution, and a very considerable percentage of young women are doing the same. Indeed, one of the most difficult things Professor Longden has encountered, in his oversight of the Scholarship students, has been to restrain many of them from undertaking too much outside work in their determination to earn money enough to pay their own way and not call on the Scholarship Loan Fund for assistance.

I have forgotten to mention that Fund, which was established with the Foundation and provides for loans in reasonable sums, not exceeding a hundred dollars a year, to Scholarship students who are in need of more assistance than their Scholarship affords. Now, notwithstanding the existence and availability of this Fund, there have been scores and scores of these Scholarship boys who have undertaken and carried on many hours a day of outside work, much of it the hardest kind of manual labor, rather than assistance from the Loan Fund.

I might give you dozens of concrete illustrations. Let me just tell you of one:

During the early part of his freshman year one of the finest and most promising young men of the present senior class was working six or seven hours a day in a lumber yard, and at the same time making a determined effort to keep up with his Scholarship work. Professor Longden warned him that he was undertaking too much and that he would either fall behind in his studies or injure his health. Instead of heeding the warning, however, the young man soon afterward had an offer from the local representative of one of the oil companies to drive a delivery wagon for the concern at $90 a month, but requiring practically all of his time during the day.

The temptation was too great, and he yielded to it, but still kept on with his college work. The result was that he failed to make his grades and lost his Scholarship at the end of the first year. He then realized his mistake, but returned the following year without any Scholarship, but with a determination to make up his deficiency. He succeeded in such a remarkable degree that his Scholarship was restored to him, and he has made a splendid record in his sophomore and junior years and will be graduated next June among the leaders of the senior class.

I could tell you of scores of instances in which such students have had to be almost physically restrained from overdoing and undertaking the impossible, in their efforts to make their own way through the University, and this is in the face of the fact that they might pursue a path of less resistance by availing themselves of the provisions which have been made for them.

Surely these young men are made of the right sort of stuff - the stuff which we expected to find in the successful men of the future. And among the young men who are doing these things, and the young women who are doing similar work, are men of the leading and most popular students upon the campus, illustrating that democracy which I have mentioned as one of the greatest attractions of DePauw.

You cannot imagine anything like snobbishness or undue deference to wealth or social position on the DePauw Campus. As I said before, in another connection, it simply "isn't done" – there is no place for it there.

But I am digressing too far – as you see I never know where to stop when I get to talking about those young people over at DePauw. But what I have just said will illustrate the democratic spirit of the Institution which has prevailed from its earliest days.

In the freshman class of 1839 there was a young man named Harlan who had tramped to Greencastle with his pack on his back, no money in his pocket, but with a determination to get an education. He had not been there long, however, before the difficulties confronting him appeared insurmountable, and he became discouraged and gave up, putting his pack on his back again and tramping off toward home.

Some of his friends and acquaintances who had been trying to persuade him to remain told President Simpson (afterward Bishop Simpson) about him shortly after he had started home, and the President set out after him and overtook him and persuaded him to return. He found him a job as the college janitor, which he held for four years and with the money earned from that and other work he managed to get through.

There were no young women in the institution at that time - they were not admitted until a quarter of a century later - and at commencement time the young men were always put to it to find enough girls to make it interesting. Young Harlan had a college chum named Gooding, who came from Greenfield, over east of Indianapolis. Gooding had a sister, whom he sent for to come over and help celebrate commencement week, and she brought with her a chum who had a millinery store in Greenfield and was popularly and affectionately known among her friends as the "Little Milliner."

And then there happened on the DePauw campus what has happened a thousand times since - the college janitor and the little milliner met and fell in love with each other at first sight, and it was all over but tying the knot and providing for the future. They were married in due course, and the remainder of the class became scattered about the country.

Young Gooding went to California, where he remained and made his home. He did not come east again, or at any rate did not see his old chum, the college janitor, for thirty years. When he next saw him Gooding was on his way to Europe, and stopped in Washington.

The college janitor was then United States Senator from Iowa, and he gave Gooding a note of introduction to his son-in-law – the husband of the daughter of the college janitor and the little milliner – who was then the Ambassador of the United States at the Court of St. James – the son of our great President, Robert T. Lincoln.

One more incident and I am done. Some time in the seventies a young man graduated at DePauw and went to Japan as a Missionary. In the course of a few years he sent back to DePauw four young Japs – Chinda, Sato, and two others.

None of them had any money, but the Missionary managed to get them to Greencastle and some provision was made for taking care of them. They rented a shack or a shanty somewhere in town, and kept batch for themselves during the four years they were there, making fine scholarship records and graduating with honors in the class of '81.

Two of the four died within the course of a few years, but thirty years later Chinda returned to America as the Ambassador of his country at Washington, and after remaining there several years was transferred to London as the Ambassador of his country to the Court of St. James, and was succeeded at Washington by his old classmate Sato. Chinda remained at London for a number of years, and finally headed the Peace Delegation of Japan at the Conference of Versailles at the close of the Great War, and is now the personal adviser of his Emperor in Tokyo.

I have been talking about my investments in DePauw, but they are not investments in DePauw University, they are investments in humanity, in the men and women who are to carry on the work of our country and the world when you and I are gone - the Harlans, and Beveridges, and Chindas of the future. DePauw is merely the medium through which we may make such an investment for the future, and offers us the opportunity and the privilege, and a real opportunity and real privilege it is.

DePauw is a peculiar institution – the more you do for her the more she does for you, and the greater your indebtedness and obligation to her become. My indebtedness and my obligation to her were never so great as they are today, and I hope they may continue to increase as time goes on. Tell your friends in the coming campaign that if they want to live long and happily and remain young, to invest in DePauw.

I thank you.

(The then-president of DePauw, George R. Grose, had only a brief entry in his diary on the date of this address and no mention of this speech. Grose wrote: DePauw dinner at Claypool opened campaign for 1 million for endowment and new buildings. Dinner was very successful with about 125 guests including Rector.)[5]

***

---

5   DPU Vol #1206 Grose 1923 Diary

Appendix

THE RECTOR SCHOLARSHIP PROPOSAL*
June 6, 1919

To the President and Board of Trustees of DePauw University:

Gentlemen:

I propose, with the approval of the Board of Trustees and their acceptance of the terms on which they are offered, to establish and endow one hundred free scholarships in DePauw University, to be distributed among the High Schools of the State of Indiana, and to be awarded year by year to the best students in the graduating classes of the respective schools.

I have several objects in view in making this offer. One is to afford an opportunity to some of the young people of the State to secure a college education, of the kind that can be had at DePauw, who might not otherwise be able to do so. Another is to bring into the University, in each Freshman class, a hundred of the brightest High School students of the State, with a consequent raising of the standard of scholarship in the University. Another is to link up and connect the High Schools of the State with the University as closely and permanently as possible, for it is upon the High Schools of the State that we must primarily rely for the future students of the University. Another is, by a wide distribution of the scholarships in all parts of the State, to create an interest in and active support of the University in some localities where it does not now exist.

If the plan proposed is accepted, and works out as successfully as hoped for, it will result in bringing into the University approximately one hundred of these scholarship students each year, so that with the beginning of the fourth year of the plan, and continuously thereafter, we would have in the University four hundred of these scholarship students, minus whatever number might have dropped out during the preceding years – perhaps, on a reasonable estimate, somewhere between three hundred and four hundred of such students. In view of this large number of scholarships to be taken care of, I ask that they be granted by the Board of Trustees at a cost of $75.00 each. This is the present regular charge for tuition or so-called "incidental fees", but in addition there are some special fees which many students, and perhaps most of them, are called upon to pay. I ask that these special fees, whatever they may amount to, be included in the cost of $75.00 for each of the scholarships proposed.

I plan to provide a fund, the income from which will furnish $100.00 for each scholarship, but I desire to reserve $25.00 of each $100.00 for the purpose of establishing a fund from which a moderate amount of financial assistance, in the form of loans, may be given to scholarship students who need it, and who might not otherwise be able to avail themselves of the scholarships awarded to them. I should hope that, with the provision of this fund, and with such assistance as may be available from other funds for the purpose, no student who might be awarded a scholarship would be unable to take advantage of it for lack of financial means to do so.

In view of the fact that the young women at DePauw largely outnumber the young men, and the further fact that our accommodations for young women are already overtaxed, these scholarships will have to be limited, for the present and perhaps permanently, to young men. It is with some reluctance that I have reached this conclusion, for I should have been glad to have had them awarded on the basis of scholarship alone, in free competition between the boys and girls of the various High Schools, but for the reasons mentioned this does not seem feasible, and I am satisfied that the conclusion which has been reached is a sound one. It will tend to reestablish an approximate equality in the number of men and women students at the University, while at the same time raising the standard of scholarship.

It may be possible, if the plan now proposed for the one hundred scholarships per year shall work out as successfully and satisfactorily as it is hoped it will, to increase the number later; and in that event I shall wish the privilege of adding to the number on the same basis as those now granted.

Very Respectfully,
Edward Rector

***

---

*DC 414 Folder 14. *A letter from Rector to President Grose indicates Rector gave a copy of the proposal to Grose for his review before Rector submitted it to the Board.*

Appendix

MINUTES OF THE FIRST MEETING OF THE EDWARD RECTOR SCHOLARSHIP FOUNDATION COMMITTEE

*Following is the verbatim text of the July 25, 1919, meeting as contained typewritten on five small loose-leaf notebook pages in the DePauw Archives.**

The first meeting of the Committee of the Edward Rector Scholarship Foundation was held in the President's office July 25, 1919. All of the members were present, namely: President George R. Grose, Edward Rector, H.H. Hornbrook, and Henry B. Longden. It was decided that President Grose should be President of the Committee and that H.B. Longden should be Secretary.

A statement was made in the beginning by Mr. Rector, the founder, as to his chief motive in making the Foundation. He indicated that it was his desire, first of all, to encourage high grade scholarship, especially in the state of Indiana, and that he hoped in this way to encourage young men all over the state to compete for this Scholarship. His chief motive was not charity, nor helping indigent students, nor the increased attendance of young men at DePauw, but that he desired always the chief requisite to be scholarship.

It was at first his idea that only the young men taking first or second honors in their class should be eligible, but on further consideration it was finally decided that the following sliding scale might be used, at any rate for the present:

In a class numbering from 100 to 150, the highest young man out of the high 12; from 70 to 100, 10; from 40 to 70, 8; from 20 to 40, 5; from 8 to 20, 3; 8 or below, 2 – or, in a general way, the highest young man in the high ten percent. It was not thought advisable to go below the high ten percent in the election of Scholars.

LOCALITY

It was further agreed that after this year, as far as possible, one student should be taken from each of the ninety-two counties of the state, it being the intention to select the best male student from all the high schools of the county.

The remaining Scholarships were to be apportioned to different high schools outside of the state, but those schools were not fixed upon at this meeting.

---

*DC 444 Folder 1

These Scholarships are to continue throughout the college course, provided the student continues to make a grade of _____ [1] while in college and shows himself by his conduct and general demeanor in every way worthy of the honor.

AMOUNT OF SCHOLARSHIP

The holder of a Scholarship is granted tuition and all regular fees in the College of Liberal Arts, which on the average, it was found, amounted to about $100.

At the suggestion of Mr. Rector it was agreed that a Scholarship be given to that student, man or woman, of the Freshman, Sophomore and Junior years who made the highest grade. What should be done if a young man already holding a Rector Scholarship should be the honor man of his class was not determined.

LOANS

A loan of not more than $100.00 could be made to those Rector Scholars who gave evidence that they actually needed the help. This was to be regarded as a loan on which a low rate of interest was to be charged with the expectation that it should be paid back into the fund just as soon after graduation as the Scholar was able to do so. The loans were to be made by the President upon the recommendation of the Secretary of the Committee.

***

---

1 Grade left blank in the original.

[Attached to the typewritten minutes are 17 pages of printed material describing scholarships at other institutions. See also DC 414 Folder 14.]

Appendix

RECTOR WILL[1]

I, Edward Rector, of Chicago, Illinois, being of sound and disposing mind and memory, do make and publish this my last will and testament, hereby revoking all others heretofore made by me.

I give and devise all of my estate, both real and personal and wheresoever situated, as follows:

1. To my wife, Lucy Rowland Rector, and her heirs, our homestead premises No. 4917 Greenwood Avenue, Chicago, and all of the personal property of whatsoever nature therein.
2. To my cousins, Louis B. and Caroline D. Erwin, the sum of Ten Thousand Dollars each.
3. To my cousins, Daniel R. Dunihue and Rector Lyon, the sum of Five Thousand Dollars each.
4. To each of the five children, Mary, Richard, Stanton, Lucy and Edward, all of my wife's nephews, Richard E. Rowland, of Salt Lake City, Utah, Five Thousand Dollars, making a total of Twenty Five Thousand Dollars.
5. To my wife's said nephew, Richard E. Rowland, the mortgage notes, amounting to Six Thousand Dollars and interest, which I hold, secured on his residence in Salt Lake City.
6. To each of the two children, Wilbur and David, of my wife's deceased nephew, Wilbur L. Rowland, of Salt Lake City, Utah, Five Thousand Dollars.
7. To my law partners, Samuel L. Hibben, Frank P. Davis, John B. Macauley, George T. May, Jr., Louis B. Erwin, Harry W. Lindsey, Jr. and Glen N. Smith, my interest in the assets, excepting accounts and bills receivable, of the law firm of Rector, Hibben, Davis & Macauley.
8. I give and devise all of the remainder of my estate, both real and personal and wheresoever situation, to DePauw University, at Greencastle, Indiana, for the following purposes and upon the following terms and conditions:
   (a) There shall first be paid from the income therefrom to my wife, Lucy Rowland Rector, during the remainder of her life, an annuity of Ten Thousand Dollars per year, such annuity to be paid in quarterly installments each year.

---

1 DC 1068 Folder 10 and DC69 Folder 6

(b) One Hundred Thousand Dollars of said bequest shall be added to the Retiring Allowance Fund of the University, for the benefit of retiring members of the Faculty and Administration.

(c) Two Hundred and Fifty Thousand Dollars of said bequest shall be devoted to the building and equipment of an additional hall of residence for the young women students of the University, to be known as Lucy Rowland Hall, in honor and memory of my wife.

(d) Two Hundred and Fifty Thousand Dollars of said bequest shall be devoted to the building and equipment of an additional hall of residence for young men students of the University, to be known as Longden Hall, in honor of Professor Henry B. Longden and in appreciation both of his long and valued services to the University and of his special services to the Edward Rector Scholarship Foundation, to which the success of that Foundation is so largely due.

(e) The remainder of my estate bequeathed to the University under this item shall be devoted to the purposes of the Edward Rector Scholarship Foundation, it being my desire that a sufficient number of scholarships shall be provided from the income of said fund to enable a scholarship to be offered each year to each high school in the State of Indiana upon such terms and conditions as the authorities having charge of the administration of the scholarship fund may determine, and also to enable such additional scholarships to be offered, either within or without the State, as those authorities may deem advisable.

9. In event DePauw University shall fail or decline to accept the bequest made to it in the preceding item, upon the terms and conditions and for the purposes therein provided, or in event such bequest fails for any other reason, then and in that event, I give and devise all of my estate covered by item 8 to my wife, Lucy Rowland Rector, and her heirs, to use and dispose of as she may see fit.

10. I appoint the Chicago Title & Trust Company, of Chicago, Illinois, Executor of this my last will and testament.

In testimony whereof I have hereunto set my hand seal this 26th day of June, 1925.

(Signed) Edward Rector (SEAL)

The foregoing instrument was on the date thereof signed and sealed by the said testator, Edward Rector, and by him declared to be his last will and testament, in our presence, who at his request and in his presence and in the presence of each other, have hereunto set our hands as subscribing witnesses this 26th day of June, 1925.

(Signed) Robert Dobbeman

(Signed) Fidelis Maichen

***

Appendix

TYPICAL RECTOR LETTER TO INCOMING
RECTOR SCHOLARS*

EDWARD RECTOR
SAMUEL E. HIBBEN
FRANK PARKER DAVIS
JOHN B. MACAULEY
GEORGE T. MAY, JR.
LOUIS B. ERWIN
HARRY W. LINDSEY, JR.
GLEN E. SMITH

LAW OFFICES OF

RECTOR, HIBBEN, DAVIS & MACAULEY

1958 McCORMICK BUILDING

332 S. MICHIGAN AVENUE

CHICAGO

TELEPHONE
8716 HARRISON

CABLE ADDRESS
RECTOR, CHICAGO

August 14, 1925.

Mr. Maurice Krahl,

Columbia City, Indiana.

My dear Mr. Krahl:

I am advised by Professor Longden that you have been awarded a Scholarship at DePauw University for the coming year, and am addressing you this note to congratulate you upon the good work which you have evidently done in your High School, and to extend to you a cordial welcome to the University and to the fellowship of the Scholarship students already there. Those who have preceded you, numbering more than seven hundred, have done splendid work at the University and established a high standard of scholarship, which will assure for you and your associates coming in this fall a cordial welcome from both the faculty and the student-body.

If you have been in touch with any of the Scholarship students you will doubtless have learned from them how extremely fortunate they are in having at their service the advice and assistance and devoted interest of Professor Longden, the Secretary of the Scholarship Foundation, who regards every one of them as his very own. He is a graduate of DePauw, has been a member of the faculty for more than forty years, and is familiar with all of the activities of college life, and qualified to view them with a sympathetic interest from the standpoint of the student as well as that of the college administration and faculty. You will find

---

*DC 1068 Folder 1 (Rector Scholarship miscellaneous letters)

-2   RECTOR, HIBBEN, DAVIS & MACAULEY

him and the President of the University wise counselors and sincere
friends, and you should consult them freely when you need advice
and assistance in the solution of any problem or difficulties
with which you may be confronted.   I cannot conceive of any finer
training or more delightful experience for a young man than to
spend four years on the DePauw Campus, under the influence and
among the traditions of the old school, and heartily congratulate
you upon the opportunity that lies before you.

      I have had sent to each of the Scholarship students who
has preceded you a little book entitled "Should Students Study?",
and am having a like copy mailed to you, which I hope you will read
with interest and profit.   It expresses so forcibly and so accur-
ately the views which I personally hold regarding both the value
of a college education (having been denied one myself) and the
attitude which a college student should maintain on the Campus,
that I wish a copy of the little book could be placed in the hands
of every young man entering college anywhere in the United States.
I am old-fashioned enough still to believe that the main purpose
for which a young man should go to college should be to get an
education, and that an education of the right sort cannot be had
without hard work and diligent and conscientious study.   I am
aware that there is a popular impression that many things are more
important at college than study, but I hope and believe that the
little book which I am sending you will satisfy you beyond question
that people who entertain such views are entirely mistaken, and
that the securing of an education should be the real and serious

-3   RECTOR, HIBBEN, DAVIS & MACAULEY

part of college life, to which all other interests and activities should be subordinated without being eliminated.   The Edward Rector Scholarship Foundation is intended to be exactly what its name implies, a Foundation for Scholarship, and its success and usefulness will be measured by the degree to which that end is attained.   I earnestly hope, therefore, that you will come to the University with a firm resolve to make the highest and best use of your scholarship of which you are capable.

With sincere regards and best wishes, I am,

Yours very truly,

EDWARD RECTOR

R/B

P.S.:   One of the last things arranged for by Mr. Rector was the preparation of this letter.   I am therefore sending it out in accordance with his wish.

Sincerely,

HENRY B. LONGDEN

Appendix

RECTOR VILLAGE[1]

Edward Rector's first large donation to DePauw came in 1916. It was $100,000 for a women's dormitory. Typically for Rector with his DePauw "investments", he followed through on his vision with energetic personal involvement in the design and construction of the building, putting "himself into every brick and mortar" and giving another $100,000 to cover additional costs. The dormitory was named for Rector's father, Isaac Rector, who once was a DePauw trustee and who had supported admission of women to the university. (See Chapter 3)

The result was a stately, well-appointed landmark regarded at the time as one of the best women's dormitories in the Midwest. It adjoined the campus center in a U-shape with a frontage of 193 feet and a north wing of 115 feet. Two pillared entrances led into a central drawing room 56 x 60 feet. Adjacent was a paneled banquet hall which could seat 275. Above were three residential floors with comfortable rooms for students. There were also some quarters for guests.

Rector Hall proved immediately to be a popular residence for the women. Its dining facilities served not only students but also many banquet gatherings. Distinguished visitors eating and sometimes overnighting there in subsequent years included, among others, Edward Rector and his wife, Lucy Rowland Rector.

Rector Hall continued in active use through the remainder of the 20th century. It anchored the central, east end of a quadrangle. On the quad's south side was Lucy Rowland Hall, another Rector gift, completed in 1928 after his death, and on the north side in 1940 was built a third elegant student residence, Mason Hall, named after an alumnus donor, A. L. Mason.

On Sunday April 7, 2002, disaster struck Rector Hall. Shortly after 7:30 a.m. an electrical malfunction on the top residential floor set off a blaze. Firemen arrived quickly but were unable to put out the fire before the roof and much of the top (fourth) floor were destroyed. None of the 116 student residents were injured, though four firefighters suffered minor injuries. The other three floors incurred significant water and smoke damage.

The initial reaction by trustees was to restore and renovate the much-admired hall which had been home to so many generations of students. But after further damage to the roofless structure from heavy rains and concerns about its reconstruction

---

1   The material in Appendix F is drawn from Chapter 3 and from the *DePauw Magazine:* 2002 Spring, Vol. 65, Issue 3, p. 4; 2003 Spring Vol. 66, Issue 3, p. 2; 2003 Summer, Vol. 67, Issue 1, p. 4; 2003 Fall, Vol. 67, Issue 2, p. 2; 2004 Spring, Vol. 67, Issue 3, pp. 4-5; and 2004 Summer, Vol. 68, Issue 1, pp. 6-7.

Rector Hall ablaze

expense and long-term condition, the University leadership opted to raze the historic building and erect instead a series of townhomes with accommodations popular with 21st century students.

The new residential quarters would be a cluster of seven smaller, three-story brick buildings sited in the area of the old hall. The exteriors would be designed tastefully to fit with the décor of the original and remaining adjoining dormitories. The complex would comprise a "Rector Village" able to house up to 136 students.

The interiors of the new town houses would feature suite-style layouts. On each floor would be single or double occupancy rooms adjoined by shared living, kitchen and eating spaces.

All seven of the replacement halls were constructed by 2004, thanks to the generosity of DePauw alumni and friends. Again, as with the original Rector Hall in 1917, the facilities proved to be immediately popular and there was a waiting list to get in.

The center building in the new Rector Village was **Reese Hall**, set at the quad's east end where Rector Hall once reigned. Reese Hall featured a commons area on the ground level to serve the entire Village complex. It included a student lounge, game room, laundry facilities and offices for student services. On each of the upper two floors were study/bedrooms for eight students, kitchen, gathering room and two bathrooms.

Funding for Reese Hall came from the *J. Gilbert* and *Louella Reese* family. All five of the Reese children had attended DePauw. Reese, a banker and lawyer in Newark, Ohio, with a strong interest in education, said the gift was "to express our appreciation to DePauw and invest in its future."

To the sides and rear of Reese Hall were the other six Village townhouses. Two of the units had 12 beds in suite-style arrangements, four on each floor, and four had 24, eight per floor.

The names and donors for the other Rector Village halls were:

Holmberg Hall: *Ronald K. Holmberg*, '54, retired executive vice president of Aon Corp., and his wife *Cynthia Brooks Holmberg*, '56, of Wilmette, Illinois. Holmberg said student residential life had changed greatly from their days in college a half century earlier and they liked the idea of replacing one large building (Rector Hall) with living units that are smaller, more intimate, and with individual rooms.

Warne Hall: *Richard A.* and *Jane Leahy Warne*, of Indianapolis. Both graduated from DePauw 50 years earlier. Warne was a retired vice president for finance from Eli Lilly and Co. Both were active in alumni and community affairs. A long Warne family history of connections with DePauw included their son and daughter who also graduated from there.

Leis Hall: *Chuck* and *Marilyn Newpart Leis,* class of '52. Chuck was chief executive officer of A. F. Leis Co., Vandalia, Ohio. They had previously established a merit scholarship award to help deserving students attend DePauw. Two daughters graduated from DePauw.

Strasma Hall: *Norman E. Strasma* and his wife, *Janice,* of Kankakee, Illinois. Strasma, a civic and business leader, graduated from DePauw in 1955. His family also had longtime connections with the school. His parents were DePauw alumni as were a daughter and son-in-law.

Montgomery Hall: *Darlene Montgomery Ryan,* class of '76, who had lived in Mason Hall next door to Rector Hall as a freshman and worked in the Rector Hall cafeteria. Ryan, founder of PharmaFab, a Grand Prairie, Texas, pharmaceutical company, said of the new Hall (named in honor of her father Ken and brother Bruce): "I love the private rooms with the shared living and kitchen areas, like apartments, but right in the middle of campus."

Chabraja Hall: *Nick* and *Eleanor Chabraja* never attended DePauw but all three of their children did, all three had lived in the residence quadrangle which included Rector Hall and all three married DePauw graduates.

Nick Chabraja, chairman of General Dynamics Corp., Falls Church, Virginia, had been a trustee and generous donor to DePauw. He recalled that as chair of a trustee committee overseeing living arrangements he had walked through many residential units. "The concept of replacing a large dormitory with a cluster of smaller, attractive buildings is a good one for students," he said. "It's a more modern concept."

***

Reese Hall

ACKNOWLEDGMENTS

One of my most important, and pleasant, learning experiences in researching for this book was with the Archives and Special Collections in the Roy O. West Library at DePauw University. Almost by definition, these Archives would be a prime source of information about Edward Rector and his scholarship program. Furthermore, I found assistance by the Archives director, Wesley W. Wilson, and staff including Linda Y. Butler, Linda C. Sebree and Jennifer J. Taylor, to be outstanding.

I was an on-and-off camper in the Archives reading room literally for years. Wilson not only made materials from the stacks available to me, but he was generous in sharing his valuable knowledge and experience on the countless occasions when I came to him for advice. Equally devoted to service in their tasks were the other staff members. I cannot say "thanks" enough.

The Office of the President, Robert G. Bottoms, provided access to otherwise restricted material when I so requested for my research. Dr. Bottoms himself was among those whom I interviewed, but he did not see my draft manuscript until it was essentially completed. I am immensely grateful not only for his supportive policy but also for the absence of any effort by the University leadership to direct the course of my research.

A great stroke of fortune for me was the availability of Dr. John J. Baughman, DePauw's distinguished historian *emeritus* who continues to live in Greencastle in retirement and who happens also to be an old friend from our undergraduate days

From left, Lewis Gulick, Wesley W. Wilson and John J. Baughman

at DePauw. His many writings include co-authorship of *DePauw: A Pictorial History*, published by the University in 1987. Both his intimate knowledge of DePauw and of Indiana history and his insistence on an historian's scholarly discipline were invaluable for my project from beginning to end.

Likewise fortunate for me was the willingness of J. Michael Lillich, a former DePauw editor, to apply his professional skill to the manuscript in moments he could spare from his current demanding position at the University of Illinois. Lillich's firsthand knowledge of DePauw added an important dimension to his sound editing.

Also serendipitous was the availability for interviews of so many of the persons named in the book, particularly in the field of admissions that covers administration of the Rector scholarship program. Most of them still reside in Greencastle. An outstanding source was longtime dean Robert H. Farber, whose firsthand experience with the scholarships dates back to the early 1930s. Dr. John J. Wittich supplemented the researcher's paper trail with his oral recollections and review. Louis J. Fontaine responded patiently and knowledgeably on various occasions to questions about events during his lengthy tenure as head of the Rector Scholarship Foundation. Madeleine R. Eagon both shared her experiences as admissions director and aided strongly in the book publication process.

In trying to fathom the mystique of university finances, I was helped graciously by officers both incumbent and retired. Bonnie A. Norton as Director of Finance was able to identify Rector account material relevant to my research, and before her, Edward (Nick) Pearson. Thomas E. Dixon as a retired DePauw vice president for finance was excellent in explaining both the principles and the history of the school's financing system. I am indebted too to Norman J. Knights, a former executive vice president, and Margaret E. Catanese, a former vice president for finance, for their reviews.

Off-campus institutions whose assistance was much appreciated include the Lawrence County Museum of History, Bedford, Ind., and the Chicago History Museum.

The final stage of transforming the draft manuscript into a published book had many helping hands starting with the leadership in the president's cabinet. Those involved included Eagon, then Vice President for Strategic Communication and Financial Aid, Lisa Hollander, Vice President for Development and Alumni Relations, and Stefanie Niles, Vice President for Admission and Financial Aid.

Dian Der Ohanian Phillips, Director of Publications, designed the dustjacket and text pages of the book, and assisted with image selections. Her graphic design expertise was essential to publication. Annette Woolsey, Special Projects and Events Coordinator in the President's Office, provided indispensable basic services, as did her successor, Erin Confer-Staggers.

Dian D. Phillips

The contributions of the student Rector research team are strewn throughout the book. They range from editings in the chapters to picture selections and copyreading and to the Epilogue which bears their names. Their input was essential for a 21st century view, and Edward Rector surely would be pleased by their effort to honor him were he alive today.

Many others have helped me along the way, directly or indirectly, who are not given individual mention here, but I am grateful to all.

***

SOURCES AND NOTES

Nearly all of the written source material for this book was or is now available at the Archives and Special Collections in the Roy O. West Library at DePauw University. "DC" in the notes stands for Document Case in the Archives.

Other library files drawn from were in the Lawrence County Museum of History at Bedford, Ind., and the Chicago History Museum.

Interviews and bibliographical sources are as indicated in the chapter endnotes. Pictures are from the Archives and the Publications Office files at DePauw, plus several contributed by individuals.

***

ENDNOTES

Chapter 1

1 Except where otherwise indicated, material for this chapter was drawn largely from Manhart, George B. *DePauw Through the Years*. Vols. I & II. Chicago, Ill: The Lakeside Press, 1962; Sweet, William Warren. *Indiana Asbury-DePauw University, 1837-1937*. New York: The Abingdon Press, 1937; Phillips, Clifton J., and Baughman, John J. *DePauw: A Pictorial History*. Greencastle, Ind.: DePauw University, 1987; and Brown, Irving Frederic. *Indiana Asbury University. DePauw University. A History*. Greencastle, Ind.: DePauw University, 1914.

2 David E. Lilienthal. "Making Scholarship Popular - The Story of the Rector Scholarship Foundation." *The American Review* May-June 1926. DC 1069 Folder 3

3 Sweet. 11

4 The Methodist Episcopal Church was the official name of the denomination. In the United States, many Church laymen, non-Church members, and even some clergy usually use the generic term Methodist, which is used in this book. Indiana Asbury and DePauw University were related to the Methodist Episcopal Church (1784-1939), which then became the Methodist Church (1939-1968), and then the United Methodist Church (1968-present). (Courtesy of Dr. John J. Baughman, DePauw historian *emeritus*)

5 Sweet. 87

6 From a description by Indiana Asbury's first president, Matthew Simpson, in 1839. Phillips and Baughman. 7

7 Sweet. 46

8 Sweet. 255

9   As of the year 2000 tuition at DePauw was $20,200 a year. Student fees included a $250 non-refundable enrollment deposit, $80 per semester for health services and $75 a semester for student activities. Room and board at resident halls was $3,162 a semester. *DePauw University Catalog 2000-2002.* 164

10   Sweet. 87

11   Brown. 40

12   Manhart. 93

13   Manhart. 142 When football came into vogue, the athletic rivalry between DePauw and Wabash focused on their annual gridiron contest, which in time became nationally televised. After the Monon Railroad donated one of its old locomotive bells in 1932, the Monon Bell became a prize trophy for the winner. Manhart. 466

14   Manhart. 136

15   Sweet. 121

16   Manhart. 109

17   Sweet. 126

18   Sweet. 127

19   Sweet. 132

20   Phillips and Baughman. 66

21   Sweet. 137

22   Sweet. 157

23   Manhart. 225

24   Philips and Baughman. 74

25   DC 1068 Folder 15

26   Manhart. 247

Chapter 2

1   Much of the material in this chapter is drawn from an unpublished autobiography by Edward Rector, a 107-page typewritten manuscript in the DePauw University Archives (DC 414 Folder 6) and from a small book (95 pp.), Grose, George Richmond, *Edward Rector. A Story of the Middle West.* New York: The Abington Press, 1928, also available in the Archives.

The Rector autobiography, hereinafter cited as "Autobiography," was probably not handwritten but dictated by Rector as was his custom in many instances. It is undated as it appears in the files but its internal content indicates it was composed about 1920. The narrative basically ends with the start of Rector's law practice in Chicago in the early 1890s and does not include his subsequent association with DePauw University.   Grose, a Methodist minister, was president of DePauw

(1912-24) during Rector's association with the school. He left the position upon being elected a bishop of the Church in 1924. The Edward Rector Scholarship Foundation paid Grose $150 for secretarial help in writing the short book, with intentions of giving a copy to each incoming Rector scholar. (DC 57, Longden Correspondence A-G, Folder 10) The Grose volume, hereinafter cited as "Gross, *Rector*", also draws substantially from the unpublished Autobiography.

When the Gross book was published in 1928 the Foundation offered it to Rector Scholars not for free but for $1 a copy. ($1 then was the equivalent of $37 in 2000, according to the Composite Price Index.) Until 1928 each new Scholar had been given a copy of a short book by Foster, William Trufant, LL.D. President of Reed College: *Should Students Study?* New York and London: Harper & Brothers Publishers, March, 1917. While Rector was alive the Foster book accompanied the personal greetings letter he sent each incoming Scholar. (DC 1068 Folder 6)

2   Family tree chart in Rector file at Lawrence County Historical Museum of History, Bedford, Ind.

3   Letter by Mrs. Joe L. Rector, Shawnee Mission, Kansas, to James A. Martindale, Librarian, DePauw University, dated Sept. 10, 1973. DC 69 Folder 7

4   Lawrence County Museum of History Rector file.

5   Autobiography. 7

6   Autobiography. 9

7   Autobiography. 8

8   Roll, Charles. *Colonel Dick Thompson*. Indianapolis: Indiana Historical Bureau, 1948. 28

9   Roll, *Colonel Dick Thompson*. 199 Roll says Thompson served on a committee to organize a department of law for Asbury and was tendered a position of professor of law there in 1846. He also states that both Thompson and Isaac Rector were believers in higher education for women. 131`

10   That Edward Rector stayed in touch with Win is evidenced by a letter in which he urged his brother to join him in a trip to Europe with his family. Win died in Wichita in November 1920. (letter to editor from J. A. Maxwell, DC 69 Folder 1)

11   Guthrie, James M. *Thirty Three Years in the History of Lawrence County, Indiana, 1884-1917.* Greenfield, Ind: Mitchell-Fleming Printing, Inc., 1958. 181

12   Autobiography. 13

13   Guthrie, *Thirty Three Years*. 181

14   Guthrie, James M. *A Quarter Century in Lawrence County, 1917-1941.* Bedford, Ind: The Stone City Press, 1984. 49

15   Guthrie, *Quarter Century*. 401 A photograph taken in 1900 with a frontal view shows a dignified large two-story residence with five windows across the second floor, and four chimneys. (See Lawrence County Museum Rector archives

Rector file)

16   Guthrie, *Quarter Century*. 274

17   Autobiography. 21

18   Autobiography. 19

19   Autobiography. 27-30

20   Guthrie, *Thirty Three Years*. 147

21   A poem written by a classmate, Carrie M. Webb, in 1911 described Rector as a "prodigy" whose initially childish appearance on stage - "not five feet tall - & with very white hair" - was superseded by a masterful presence as soon as he "thundered forth" his speech. DC 69 Folder 1

22   Autobiography. 31

23   Autobiography. 31-2 Rector later said that always after that, he had in mind that if he could he "would like to help some fellows go to college who were in the fix I was in at the time." See Appendix A

24   Autobiography. 39

25   Autobiography. 36

26   Obituary in the Bedford *Tri-Weekly Magnet*, Dec.6, 1879. (courtesy of Lawrence County Museum of History)

27   Autobiography. 55

28   Guthrie, *Thirty Three Years*. 181

29   Autobiography. 62 According to the Bedford *Times-Mail*, June 30, 1988, p. A-5, "He had thought in earlier years he might become a printer or a shoemaker, but his uncle Richard W. Thompson (prominent in Indiana Law circles), and others close to him had a lot to do with getting Rector interested in law as a profession." DC 69 folder 5

30   Autobiography. 71-3

31   Autobiography. 83

32   Autobiography. 89-90

33   Autobiography. 102

34   Autobiography. 107

35   Grose, *Rector*. 37

36   Grose, *Rector*. 47-8

37   Rector letter to Longden, Feb. 2, 1925. DC237 Folder 5

38   Longden talk at Rector Hall Oct. 18, 1939. DC 69 Folder 9 Tributes. Longden's files suggest that the locale was Little Traverse Bay, where the Methodist Church had a resort and retreat community. DC 237

39   Grose, Diary. DPU Vol. 1205 April 2-5, 1921

40   Grose, *Rector.* 61

41   Longden talk at Rector Hall Oct. 18, 1939. DC 69 Folder 9 Tributes

42   Chicago History Museum research assistant Annie Chase said in a Feb. 2, 2007, telephone conversation that Rector's home address in the city directory in the late 1890s was 4411 Berkeley Ave., and that he apparently moved to the Greenwood Ave. home in the early 1900s.

43   Chicago *Daily Tribune*, Oct. 5, 1907. 18 (photocopy courtesy of Chicago Historical Society) Based on the historical Composite Price Index compiled by the U. S. Office for National Statistics, the purchasing power of $35,000 in 1907 would be worth about $2.5 million in 2000.

44   Grose, Rector. 69

45   History of Rector Hall, by Hazel Longden (Mrs. Grafton Longden, Sr.) May 23, 1957 Audio CD #80 at DePauw Archives (dubbed from Audiotape Reel #41), hereinafter referred to as Hazel Longden recording.

46   Grose, Rector. 59

47   Longden at Rector's memorial service. Longden said his last letter from Rector was in longhand dated June 22, which Longden said was five days before Rector made his will and seven days before he was stricken in Cleveland. Rector Vertical File DPU photos. There is no evidence that Rector's timing on the will was related to a premonition of imminent or early death. In his Autobiography, authored while he was in his late 50's, Rector noted the longevity of some of his father's siblings and said that his father's vigorous health "up to the day of his sudden death, at the age of eighty-three, indicated that he might live well on toward a hundred." 9

48   DC 237 Folder 6

49   Greencastle *Daily Banner*, Aug. 3, 1925. DC 69 Folder 5

50   Greencastle *Daily Banner.* DC 69 Folder 5

51   *DePauw Magazine* fall 1994 21. DC 69 Folder 5.

52   Greencastle *Daily Banner*, Aug. 4, 1925. DC 69 Folder 5

Chapter 3

1   Edward Rector's unpublished memoirs do not mention his brother "Win's" schooling, although he came to know Win better in later years during family visits. A letter to the editor from a "J.A. (John) Maxwell" in the Rector files at DePauw's Archives describes Jesse Winfield Rector as a leading attorney in Wichita and an authority on Civil War history. Maxwell said he had read a letter from Edward Rector enclosing a letter from a family friend written a year or so before the Civil War, and also proposing that Win join Edward in a trip to Europe." Jesse W. Rector was an alumnus of DePauw University, coming directly from there to

swing his shingle to the breezes of Kansas as a lawyer in a day when Washington [Kansas] and the state were young," Maxwell said. DC 69 Folder 5

2   Grose, *Rector* 79. Rector's unpublished memoirs do not mention his father's association with Indiana Asbury.

3   Edward Rector Memorial Edition of *The DePauw*, Oct. 16, 1925. (DC 69 Folder 5) Murlin, who had been president of Boston University, was picked for the DePauw presidency by a trustee committee headed by Rector.

4   DePauw historian George Manhart's brief mention of Rector's Methodist Church trusteeship, in an article in the December 1969 *DePauw Alumnus*, and that by Grose in his Rector biography, 59, are among the few available references to Rector's church affiliation and activity.

5   Greencastle *Daily Banner* Aug. 3, 1925. DC 69 Folder 5

6   Grose, *Rector.* 79

7   Greencastle *Daily Banner*, Aug. 8, 1925. DC 69 Folder 5

8   Rector Hall dedication program, Oct. 16, 1917. DC 69 Folder 2

9   See Rector's account in Appendix A. Neither Rector nor Grose mention the amount of Rector's gift for the student loan fund in their descriptions of it, and Salem Town, DePauw's financial secretary, did not include it in his listing of Rector's donations to the University published following Rector's death (see Greencastle *Daily Banner*, Aug. 8, 1925. DC 69 Folder 5)

10   See Appendix A.

11   The Indiana Asbury *Catalogues* of that time list an "I. Rector, M.D." of Bedford among the trustees in the 1865-6 *Catalogue*, but not in other years.

12   Grose, *Rector.* 80-81

13   Manhart. 225

14   Grose, *Rector.* 82-5

15   Manhart. 229 Manhart said Mrs. Rector and Katharine S. Alvord, dean of women, "were equally interested in every detail of furnishings and decorations."

16   Manhart. 229

17   Rector Hall dedication program.

18   See Appendix F on Rector Hall's destruction by fire in 2002 and its replacement by Rector Village.

19   Grose' diaries contain references to staying and dining at the Hall. For instance, an entry for April 16, 1926, says "Had a delightful stay at Rector Hall. I am so much at home there." DPU Vol. 1202

20   See Appendix D.

21   DePauw Archives reference materials indicate a sharp drop in the civilian student

body in the 1918-19 war years, with enrollment down to 466 of whom 431 were women. The S.A.T.C. on campus inducted 500 men. The previous year enrollment had been 736, of whom 290 were men and 446 women.

22 Eulogy of Rector. Funeral Memorial Book, Oct. 16, 1925. DC 414 folder 13

23 Manhart. 307

24 Manhart. 225

25 Greencastle *Daily Banner*, Aug. 3, 1925. DC 69 Folder 5

26 Indianapolis *News*, Aug. 11, 1925.

27 See Appendix D.

28 See figures in Greencastle *Daily Banner*, Aug. 8, 1925. However this story suggested there might be some adjustments in the estimated amounts after further review, and there would have to be appraisals of the actual market value of the assets in Rector's estate. The valuation of the scholarship endowment was carried on DePauw's books at around $2 million for many years. In May 1930 the University's acting treasurer, Harold E. Robbins, reported the value of the Rector Foundation endowment at $2,207,307.63. In November 1937 G. Herbert Smith, then Foundation director, gave the same figure (DC 577 Folder 1). In 1940 a master's thesis concerning the scholarship program presented by Robert H. Farber, a Rector Scholar involved in the program at DePauw (see Chapter VII), said that "in all," Rector endowed the program with $2,206,641.71.

29 Rector historical balance sheet.

30 Greencastle *Daily Banner*, Aug. 8, 1925.

Chapter 4

1 *DePauw Alumnus* December 1949. 1

2 Biographical sketch of Edward Rector in *Who's Who in America 1924-25*. DC 69

3 Lucy Rowland Rector letter to Longden Apr. 29, 1926. DC 1068 Folder 2

4 *DePauw Alumnus* December 1949. 1

5 The exact date given here is derived from a birthday telegram Longden sent to Lucy Rector on this day in 1926. The Western Union message was addressed to Mrs. Edward Rector at 646 East 17th South St., Salt Lake City, Utah, c/o Richard E. Rowland, a nephew. DC 237 Folder 6

6 DC 69 Folder 7

7 Bedford historian James M. Guthrie wrote that "W.A. (Billie) Webb married Carrie Messick in the early eighties and people said that Carrie's other suitor, Edward Rector, left town in disgust, never to return." (Guthrie, "Thirty Three Years". 178) While Rector might have had romantic interests as a Bedford teenager, Guthrie's gossipy report is dubious when compared with Rector's own stated reason for leaving Bedford in 1882, which was to get a law degree in

Cincinnati. It is flatly incorrect to say Rector never returned to Bedford, which he did on occasions such as high school reunions. In another volume (Guthrie, "Quarter Century". 274) Guthrie says Rector made one of his last visits home in June 1921, accompanied by his wife.

8   pp. 85 and 104.

9   Hazel Longden recording.

10 Lucy Rowland Rector letter to Longden Feb. 20, 1930. DC 1068 Folder 2

11 *DePauw Magazine* Spring 1995. 53

12 A report in the *DePauw Magazine* Spring 1995 53, that Edward gave Lucy a yellow rose daily throughout their marriage is probably an exaggeration. Hazel Longden said he gave Lucy a yellow rose every Saturday during their seven-year courtship. A definitive account from Lucy herself came in a thank you letter to Rector Scholars for a gift of flowers, written June 2, 1926. "Your roses are the same as Mr. Rector sent me every Sunday morning for years, before we were married," she said. "I took them to Oakwood's (cemetery) on Sunday morning and I placed them near Mr. Rector." In a P.S., she added "A letter from Dr. Longden tells me that a wreath from you, was taken to the place which awaits our coming at Forest Hill." DC 414 unnumbered folder

13 Winona Welch on "The Rectors." DC 69 Folder 8

14 Welch DC 69 Folder 8

15 George Richmond Grose 1915, 1926 Diary /Journal. The Grose diaries present some ambiguity on their dates. In this case it appears that Grose had a diary book printed for 1915, but he used it for 1926, a year in which the days of the month fell on the same days as in 1915. This particular reference spans Tuesday March 30 through Thursday April l. DPU Vol. 1203

16 See previous reference to Grose, *Edward Rector. A Story of the Middle West,* published in 1928.

17 Grose Diary entry for May 25, 1926. DPU Vol. 1203

18 Grose Diary entries June 19 and 30, 1926. DPU Vol. 1203

19 Grose 1920 Diary May 30. DPU Vol. #1204

20 Hazel Longden recording.

21 Catherine Tillotson McCord, interview with author in February 2000.

22 Board meeting notes of Sep. 7, 1925.

23 Lucy Rowland Rector letter to Longden April 29, 1926. DC 1058 Folder 2

24 Board meeting notes of Murlin annual report, June 7, 1926.

25 Lucy Rowland Rector letter to Longden, Oct. 18, 1929. DC 1068 Folder 2

26 DC 1068 Folder 2

27 West letter to Oxnam April 24, 1933. DC 444 Folder 14

28 4917 Greenwood Ave., Hyde Park Station. Chicago History Museum research assistant Annie Chase said in a Feb. 2, 2007, telephone conversation that Rector's home address in the city directory in the late 1890s was 4411 Berkeley Ave., and that he apparently moved to the Greenwood Ave. home in the early 1900s.

29 Lucy Rowland letter to Longden Feb. 5, 1930. DC 1068 Folder 2

30 *DePauw Magazine* Summer 1995. 53

31 Some published accounts incorrectly place the location of the map as being in Rector's law office. Longden's authoritative history of the program stated that it was a map of Indiana "in the Rector home." "Inspiration, Origin and Purpose of the Edward Rector Scholarship Foundation," by Henry B. Longden, Director, 1934. 28 DC 1711 Folders 2 and 4

32 *DePauw Magazine* Summer 1995. 53

33 Lucy Rowland Rector letter to Longden Dec. 19, 1927. DC 1068 Folder 2

34 Lucy Rowland Rector letter to Longden March 27, 1930. DC 1068 Folder 2

35 Lucy Rowland Rector letter to Longden Dec. Sept. 1, 1929. DC 1068 Folder 2

36 Lucy Rowland Rector letter to Longden. DC 1068 Folder 2

37 Lucy Rowland Rector letters to Longden Oct. 29, 1928, and July 5, 1931. DC 1068 Folder 2

38 Lucy Rowland Rector letter to Salzer, Oct. 19, 1942. DC 69 Folder 7

39 One letter dated April 28, 1942, was signed by Mrs. Lucy Rowland Jenson, a niece. Another was signed by Marie M. Norton, who was "spending the day" with Lucy Rector. DC 69 Folder 7

40 *DePauw Magazine* Summer 1995. 14

41 The Edward Rector Scholarship Foundation directory dated November 1948 listed the "Committee," largely honorary at the time, as composed of Wildman, Mrs. Edward Rector, and West; and an "Administrative Committee" composed of Wildman, Cummings (Dean), H.H. Brooks (Comptroller), and Robert Farber (Foundation Director). Archive shelves.

42 *DePauw Magazine* December 1949. 1

Chapter 5

1 Most of the biographical material on Longden comes from his voluminous papers at the DePauw Archives. These include biographical sketches in the *DePauw Alumnus* December 1948 and other publications at the time of his death on Nov. 7, 1948, and a short autobiographical account of his earlier years. The Archives files show that in 1953 Mrs. A. Percival Wyman, of Waterville, Maine, was gathering information for a biography of Longden but there is no indication that the biography was ever published.

2 Correspondence to Mrs. Wyman from J. M. Walker. DC 36 Folder 2

3   Longden said he once wore a new Prince Albert coat to the dedication of Rector Hall in 1917, thinking that to be the proper attire of the occasion. "During the evening a visitor came to me and said, 'aren't you Bishop Nicholson?'," Longden related in a speech at Rector Hall 22 years later. "I went home and took off that Prince Albert coat, and from that day to this I have never worn a Prince Albert coat. I gave it to a colored preacher the next week." DC 56 Folder 6

4   Letter Dec. 11, 1955 to Mrs. Wyman from U.S. Army Lt. Col. Carl E. Brose, then stationed in Germany. DC 36 Folder 2

5   Olcott letter to Mrs. Wyman, Nov. 9, 1953. DC 36 Folder 2

6   Brose letter to Mrs. Wyman Dec. 11, 1955. DC 36 Folder 2

7   Olcott letter to Mrs. Wyman Nov. 9, 1953. DC 36 Folder 2

8   The discomfited waiter was E. G. Stanley Baker who himself went on to a distinguished teaching career. Baker was head of the Zoology Department at Drew University at the time he recalled the incident for Mrs. Wyman in 1953. DC 36 Folder 2

9   Tribute to Longden by DePauw President Clyde E. Wildman, *DePauw Alumnus* December 1948. 2

10   Olcott letter to Mrs. Wyman Nov. 9, 1953.

11   See DC 56 Folder 7, Tributes.

12   Longden letter to Lucy Rector Jan. 7, 1936. DC 237 Folder 6

13   See DC 56 Folder 7, Tributes.

14   1947-8 *DePauw University Bulletin*.

Chapter 6

1   DC 414 Folder 14

2   See Appendix C.

3   May 1, 1919, letter to President Grose. DC 414 Folder 14

4   See Appendix B.

5   Longden subsequently said of the Foundation: "It has no charter and its management is under the direction of the Trustees of the University … " June 12, 1928, letter to John Weaver. DC 444 Folder 1. Rector in his will bequeathing the bulk of his estate to the scholarship program did not allot it directly to the Foundation, but rather to DePauw to be "devoted to the purposes of the Edward Rector Scholarship Foundation."

6   "Inspiration, Origin and Purpose of the Edward Rector Scholarship Foundation" by Henry B. Longden, Director. 4 This summary history of the scholarship program was presented by Longden to University President Oxnam Nov. 13, 1934, as Longden was retiring from his long stewardship of the program. The 31-page typewritten document apparently has never been published but is available in

the Archives DC 1711 Folders 2 and 4. It is cited hereinafter as Longden, Rector program history.

7   Longden, Rector program history. 4

8   See Appendix C.

9   Manhart. 308

10   Trustees minutes, June 7, 1926 annual report to Trustees.

11   See Appendix D.

12   Longden, Rector program history. 28

13   Rector letter to Longden, Feb. 2, 1925. DC 237 Folder 5

14   Longden, Rector program history. 28

15   Manhart. 308

16   Indianapolis *Star*, Aug. 7, 1925. DC 69 folder 5

17   Longden, Rector program history. 22

18   Longden, Rector program history. 22

19   *DePauw Magazine* Fall 1994. 17

20   See Appendix A.

21   Foundation Secretary's annual report for 1924-25, *DePauw University Bulletin*. 29 According to Sweet, 227, by the end of 1926, $43,572.50 had been loaned and $15,932.86 repaid. There were two funds – one short term, up to $100/year, not requiring security, and a long-term fund for loans up to $300 per year, to be secured by a bankable note with approved security. As of 1932, loans were $30,00 from both funds.

22   DC 69 Folder 13

23   DC 1069 unnumbered folder

24   *DePauw Magazine* Fall 1994. 22

25   See Edward Rector Scholarship Fund of DePauw University 1919-1934. Archives shelves

26   Letter to Longden quoted in Longden, Rector program history. 3

27   See Appendix D.

28   DC 1068 Folder 6

29   See Appendix A.

30   President's annual report to trustees. Board minutes June 7, 1926

31   See Appendix A.

32   Lilienthal, "Making Scholarship Popular." DC 1069 Folder 3

Chapter 7

1   Annual Edward Rector Scholarship Foundation (hereinafter referred to as ERSF) report for 1925-26. DC 1068 Folder 6

2   *Indianapolis Star*, Aug. 10, 1928.

3   Longden annual ERSF report for 1928-29. DC 414 Folder 10

4   Longden annual ERSF report for 1928-9. DC 414 Folder 10

5   *The Rector Record*. DC 1068 Folder 9

6   Manhart II. 308

7   *The Rector Record*, Nov. 4, 1929. DC 1069 Folder 9

8   Pearl Irene Brown, "A Unique Investment in Humanity," *Zion's Herald*, Sept. 11, 1929. DC 1069 unnumbered folder

9   Longden 11th annual ERSF report, 1929-30.

10 Annual ERSF report, 1929-30.

11 DC 444 Folder 12

12 12 President's report to Joint Board Jan. 12, 1932. DC 1771

13 DePauw University *Bulletin* Vol. XX No.2, April 1933.

14 Methodist 1930-31 Survey. 302

15 Methodist 1930-31 Survey. 300

16 "Study of the Rector Scholarship Foundation, 1919-1932." DC 1068

17 Longden summary presented in 1933. DC 1060 Folder 14

18 Letter from West to Oxnam, April 24, 1933. DC 444 Folder 14

19 Robert Holton Farber, "An Evaluation of the Award of Scholarships in a Liberal Arts College." Dissertation submitted in candidacy for the degree of Master of Arts, Department of Education, University of Chicago, Chicago, Ill., December 1940.

20 DC 414 Folder 16

21 DC 1711 Folder 2

Chapter 8

1   Except where otherwise indicated, the principal sources of financial information in this Chapter come from minutes of DePauw trustee meetings during this period.

2   Rector letter to Longden, Jan. 24, 1925. DC 237 Folder 5

3   Semi-annual Report of the President to the Board of Trustees and Visitors, February 25, 1925. DC 1711 Longden Folder 5

4   Rector letter to Longden, Dec. 10, 1924. DC 237 Folder 5

5   Rector letter to Longden Jan. 24, 1925. DC237 Folder 5

6   Manhart. 344

7   Investing Committee minutes, Nov. 24, 1925.

8   Robbins reports to trustees dated June 7 and June 30, 1930.

9   Board minutes January 17 and June 8, 1928.

10 Board minutes of June 8, 1929.

11 Methodist 1930-31 Survey. See also Manhart. 349

12 Officer's reports Jan. 17, 1933; President's report. DC 1771

13 Officer's reports June 6, 1931. DC 1771

14 Manhart 314 and 350. See also Miller, Robert Moats. *Bishop G. Bromley Oxnam. Paladin of Liberal Protestantism.* Nashville: Abingdon Press, 1990. 122

15 Officer's notes. DC 1771

16 Manhart. 350

17 Financial statement presented at a Dec. 6, 1932, meeting of the Executive Committee of the trustees.

18 Minutes of joint meeting of Executive Committee and Committee on Investments and Real Estate, April 18, 1932.

19 Manhart. 351

20 DC 444 Folder 17

21 *DePauw Alumnus,* May 1937. DC 577 Folder 1

22 *New York Times,* Aug. 22, 1942. DC 557 Folder 5 1942/3

23 Evans report at joint Board meeting June 24,1944. See reference to Foundation, University debt pay-offs in following chapter.

Chapter 9

1   The principal sources for this Chapter fell into three groups: the Board files containing minutes of meetings and reports of University officers, a detailed balance sheet for the Rector endowment showing all receipts and expenditures 1936-1998 (hereinafter referred to as "Rector historical balance sheet"), and numerous interviews by the author with present and past University officials familiar with aspects of DePauw's financial system.

2   Minutes of Joint Board Oct. 24, 1936.

3   Manhart 351 and Minutes of Joint Board Oct. 24, 1936.

4   Minutes of Joint Board Oct. 24, 1936.

5   Minutes Jan. 24, 1942.

6   President's report to trustees meeting June 15, 1946.

7   Rector historical balance sheet.

8   Minutes of Board meeting June 8, 1940.

9   Report to Board meeting Oct. 18, 1940.

10   Minutes of Board meeting June 8, 1940.

11   President's report to Board meeting May 15, 1943.

12   President's report to Board meeting Nov. 5, 1943.

13   Comptroller's report for 6 months ending Dec. 31, 1938.

14   Minutes of June 11, 1937 meeting.

15   President's report to joint trustees May 15, 1943.

16   Minutes Nov. 5, 1943.

17   Joint Board minutes June 24, 1944.

18   Joint Board minutes June 24, 1944.

19   Rector historical balance sheet.

20   This section is drawn from the Rector historical balance sheet and from interviews with personnel knowledgeable about DePauw endowment management.

21   See "Managing Educational Finance. Report to the Ford Foundation." (Barker report). 1969. Ford Foundation, Office of Reports, NY, NY.

22   DePauw University Director of Finance to author.

Chapter 10

1   *A Word About Scholarship Numbers*

In this chapter and elsewhere in the book are given numbers of Rector Scholars. If the reader finds the different figures cited to be confusing, he/she is justified. Almost from the beginning of the program in 1919 varying numbers appear in different citations, often without precise definition of what is being counted.

Any cumulative total for Rector scholarships can vary widely depending on the criteria used. One method would be to count all awards whether the grantee enrolled at DePauw or not. Another would be to count only those who enrolled. Another would be to count only those who enrolled and graduated. There could be sub-categories covering those who enrolled and graduated but lost their scholarship for one semester or more, or those who won scholarships after matriculating. Still further distinctions could be made between those who received full tuition, partial tuition, tuition plus room and board, and honorary scholarships without remuneration.

The latest published exact count of "entering scholars" in the DePauw archives appears to be Smith's study cited in this chapter which covered the period 1919-37. It totals the number of "entering scholars" over this time at 3,033, but of this total fewer than half graduated. The May-June 1937 issue of the

DePauw Alumnus (p. 7) said Rector's "benefactions" had "seen more than 1,250 young men and women through college." An unpublished 1940 master's thesis by Robert Farber (p. 7) gave a precise total for entering scholars in 1919-1940 of 3,245, but said that of that number 1,166 lost their scholarships due to low grades.

Further published totals thereafter obviously were mostly higher but still ranged widely without precise definition. The Rector alumni directory in 1948 spoke of the scholarship program as "helping more than 1,500 young men" secure college degrees. The 1952 Rector alumni directory gave the same figure. The directory in 1986 said there had been "more than five thousand" scholarships granted and 4,500 graduated. An article by DePauw historian George Manhart in the December 1969 *DePauw Alumnus* said that "More than 5,000 men and a few women have shared to the extent of $4,063,358 in the Rector 'investment in humanity.'" (p. 9)

Some later estimates were lower. The *DePauw Magazine* Fall 1994 spoke of "more than 3,500" Rector Scholars since 1919. Bottom's 1999 reference to "some 4,000 Rector scholars" (see Chapter 12) was probably as good a cumulative round number of Rector graduates by then as possible given the lack of more precise data.

A complete accounting of Rector scholarships numerically since their beginning is probably impossible now given the passage of time and the difficulty of access to some aging documents – if they still exist. Today's more modern digital record keeping at DePauw enhances the prospects for more accurate scholarship counting in the future, but from a data base narrower than would be the case if the University had had computer capability since 1919. In 2008 a computerized list compiled by DePauw's development office for mail-outs carried a total of 3,776 Rector Scholars whether graduated or not, of whom 2,615 were living and 1,161 had died. (courtesy Denise L. Gentry and Stephen K. Gauly) DC 1069 Folder 12

2   DC 1711 Folder 2. See Chapter 3.

3   See *A Word About Scholarship Numbers* above.

4   The Methodist 1930-31 Survey saw the Rector Scholar organizational activities as posing "grave danger." It said "they are likely to exalt the scholarships and the scholars out of all proportion to their worth and there is a serious possibility that they will become a divisive influence in the University." It questioned why there should be Rector alumni associations separate from the general DePauw alumni groups. (p. 301) There is no evidence that University officials paid much heed to this Survey recommendation, and Rector organizational activities in fact declined in later years for other reasons.

5   DC 1068 Folder 9

6   DePauw *Alumnus* May-June 1937 10. DC 69 Folder 5

7   DePauw *Alumnus* May-June, 1937 2.

8   Solicitation letter from Julian Forbes, President, Rector Scholar Alumni, May 24,

1937. Vertical file Rector Scholar Classes DPU vf

9   Interviews in October 2005 with DePauw finance director, Roy O. West Library acquisitions manager, and the library's gift planning director.

10 Feb. 20, 1947 letter to Rector Scholar alumni from Terence A. Kleckner, President, Rector Scholar Association. Casualty list in DC 414 folder.

11 *The New York Times* Aug. 22, 1942.

12 *DePauw University Bulletin* 1945-46. By the 1946 winter term, enrollment was back up to 2,022 of whom 1048 were men.

13 Greencastle *Banner* Sept. 2, 1942.

14 Notice to Rector Scholars Jan. 7, 1943. DC 577 Folder 7

15 ERSF Director annual report, 1946/47. DC 557 Folder 11

16 ERSF Director letter to scholars, Oct. 1, 1947. DC 414 Folder 2

17 Longden, Rector program history.

18 Board minutes June 8, 1940.

19 Farber interview May 11, 2005.

20 See Appendix A.

21 Joint Board minutes Feb. 28, 1948.

22 See Appendix B.

23 Manhart. 308

24 Joint Board minutes June 11, 1948.

25 Manhart. 382

26 Board minutes June 5, 1953.

27 DePauw Reports 1953-4.

28 DePauw Reports 1954-5.

29 DePauw Reports 1958-9.

30 Interview with author in 2005.

31 Norman J. Knights, interview with author, March 29, 2000.

32 Interviews with author in 2005.

33 Interview with author Oct 28., 2005.

34 See *Edward Rector Scholarship Fund of DePauw University 1919-1934*. Archives shelves

35 Longden replied to an inquirer, Miss Isabelle Whitcomb, in an April 10, 1933, letter: "Unfortunately, DePauw University has no scholarships for young women except a few loan scholarships whereby the student can borrow enough money for her tuition and repay it in installments after graduation." DC 1068 Folder 6

The *DePauw University Bulletin* for 1933-34 listed a number of scholarships specifically for women or for which women would be eligible, but they were small and/or narrowly defined. For example, the Howes Scholarship Fund provided tuition and fees annually for only one student of either gender. An Association of Women Students' Scholarship was for women students based on scholarship and service to the University, but provided only $125.

36   Interview with author in 2005 and also *DePauw Magazine* Fall 1994. 22

37   Board minutes April 22-23, 1982.

38   Interviews with author in 2005.

39   *DePauw Magazine* Winter 2000. 16

40   Board minutes Oct. 22, 1999.

41   See Appendix A.

42   Wildman report to Board June 9, 1939.

43   Eagon interview.

Chapter 11

1   Information on the Holtons and their donation in this chapter includes material from files kept by the office of the University president.

2   Watson profile in NNDB Web site.

3   *DePauw Magazine* winter 2000. 25

4   DePauw University press release May 16, 1997.

5   John Holton also had a distinguished career with Inland Container, rising to vice president.

6   Author's interview with Robert G. Bottoms, Sept. 7, 2001.

7   DePauw University background paper prepared as Attachment I in connection with the August, 1999, Holton gift announcement, but not published.

8   DePauw University press release, May 16, 1997.

9   See *Wall Street Journal,* "College Green," March 8, 2001. 1

Chapter 12

1   Chapter 12. See Appendix A.

2   See Appendix A.

3   Report to Board June 9, 1939.

4   DePauw press release Aug. 19, 1999.

5   Author's conversation with Lisa Hollander, DePauw Vice President for Development and Alumni Relations, Oct. 29, 2005.

6   *DePauw Magazine* Fall 1994. 20 See also "The DePauw Sesquecentennial Campaign Story," a 33-page booklet in the Archives. It reported that in surveying 3,000 Rector Scholars about fund-raising feasibility, "an astonishing 71 percent" returned lengthy questionnaires compared with 47 percent of all other alumni.

7   DePauw University press release Aug. 19, 1999.

8   Author's conversations in December 2005 with Edwards friends and with son Jonathan.

9   *DePauw Alumnus* Spring 1984. 10

10   Sept. 25, 2001, letter from attorney James W. Denhardt. Vertical File – Edward Rector Scholarship Winners vj

11   Conversations with author.

12   See Appendix A.

13   *DePauw Magazine* Fall 1994. 19 See also Cady obituary in DePauw magazine fall 1996. 67

14   *DePauw Magazine* Fall 1994. 17

15   DePauw Archives web site, vertical file, and George W. Gore Jr. biographical information at www.tnstate.edu/library/digital/gorebio.htm.

16   Manhart in an April 10, 1970, article in the *Indianapolis Star* reported 10 Rector alumni college presidents by then.

17   See Appendix A.

18   *DePauw Magazine* July 1972 vol. 36. 32

19   Manhart. 383

20   Rector Silver Anniversary Edition, 1924-49. See also obituary in *The DePauw* newspaper April 24, 1970 8 and DC 1433.

21   Following are the Rector Scholar winners of the Old Gold Goblet: Joseph P. Allen IV, Edwin C. Boswell, James T. Brown , John W. Burkhart, John W. Christensen, Lawrence W. Clarkson , Robert E. Crouch, Eugene L. Delves, Robert H. Farber, John H. Filer, Joseph R. Flummerfelt, C. Norman Frees, Lee H. Hamilton, Sam T. Hanna, Hirotsugu Iikubo, Bernard Kilgore, Earl W. Kintner, Michael R. Maine, John David Millett, David J. Morehead, Alvin J. Rockwell, David M. Shoup, J. Stanford Smith, Norval B. Stephens Jr., David B. Stevens, Timothy H. Ubben and William F. Welch. Sources DePauw University Development Office and Archives

22   Summary of Farber biography in Farber papers at DePauw Archives. DC 1084

23   DePauw Archives vertical file on Filer and New York *Times* obituary Sept. 20, 1994.

24   *New York Times*, July 19, 1987.

25 *DePauw Magazine* Winter 2001 11. *DePauw Magazine* Summer-fall 2000 56. See also reference to TJFR group on DePauw site edu/news/index.

26 DePauw University Journalism Hall of Fame citation.

27 *DePauw Magazine* Winter 1993-4. 12

28 *Indianapolis News*, Jan. 11, 1989. DePauw Archives vertical file. See also Flummerfelt website.

29 Manhart. 341

30 *DePauw Magazine* Spring 1998.

31 U. S. Marine Corps MC History and Museums Division, Historical Who's Who.

32 *DePauw Magazine* Fall 1994. 29

33 Biography on www.jsc.nasa.gov/bios, DePauw edu/news/index. Also see *DePauw Magazine* Winter 1994 for "Perk" Allen.

34 *DePauw Magazine* Spring 1999.

35 Archives Vertical File and *New York Times* obituary Jan. 1, 1992.

36 *New York Times* obituary Feb. 29, 1996; Wikipedia; articles in *The DePauw* newspaper in 1939.

37 *DePauw Magazine* Fall 1994. 54

38 *DePauw Magazine* Winter 1994-5. 44

39 *DePauw Magazine* Winter 1994-5. 46

40 *DePauw Magazine* Spring 1995. 48

41 *DePauw Magazine* Fall 1995. 54

42 *DePauw Magazine* Summer 1996. 62

43 *DePauw Magazine* Summer-Fall 2000. 17

***

INDEX